MW00787350

Threads in the Tapestry:
Conflict and Resolution in the Middle East

Is the Two-State Solution the Only Viable Option for Middle East Peace?

by

Cherub Angela Nicholls

Foreword by

Moshe Aumann retired Israeli Diplomat

To: Shalom TV
From: Cherub Angela
Tues Nov 25, 2014

DORRANCE PUBLISHING CO., INC.
PITTSBURGH, PENNSYLVANIA 15222

The contents of this work including, but not limited to, the accuracy of events, people, and places depicted; opinions expressed; permission to use previously published materials included; and any advice given or actions advocated are solely the responsibility of the author, who assumes all liability for said work and indemnifies the publisher against any claims stemming from publication of the work.

Scripture quotations are from:
The *Prophecy Study Bible*, New King James Version (NKJV), John C. Hagee, General Editor (Nashville: Used by permission of Thomas Nelson, Inc., © 1997). Good News Bible, Good News Translation (New York: The American Bible Society, © 1992).
Spirit Filled Life Bible, New King James Version (NKJV), Jack W. Hayford, Litt. D., General Editor (Nashville: Thomas Nelson, Inc., © 1991).

Note:
Special permission has been granted by the following authors for citations of their work:

i). Moshe Aumann. <u>Conflict & Connection</u>. The Jewish-Christian-Israel Triangle (Jerusalem: Gefen Publishing House, 2003).

ii). Aryeh Rottenberg. The Etzion Bloc in the Hills of Judea (Jerusalem, 2003).

iii). Israel Eldad & Arieh Eldad. The Challenge of Jerusalem. Betwixt Thicket and Altar (Israel: Alex Klevitsky, 1998). Dr Arieh Eldad, MK, gave the author his permission for citations.

iv). Minister for Social Affairs & Services of Israel & Member of the Knesset, Isaac Herzog, granted to the author permission to use citations from the book written by his father, Chaim Herzog.

Chaim Herzog. The War of Atonement. The Inside Story of the Yom Kippur War. New Introduction by Brigadier General Michael Herzog (London: Greenhill Books, 2003).

Other approvals with requests for special notice:

i). The Jerusalem Post articles —www.jpost.com— first appeared in the Jerusalem Post and are reprinted here by permission. Likewise, the articles from The Jerusalem Post/Christian Edition in collaboration with the Christian Embassy in Jerusalem are also reprinted by permission.

ii). Map illustrated on page 181© United Bible Societies, 1976.

iii). © The Nobel Foundation 1906.

iv). David Brog, Standing With Israel (Lake Mary, FL: Frontline, 2006), Used by permission.

Special credit for photographs:
International Zionist Center, Jerusalem
The International Christian Embassy, Jerusalem
Christian Friends of Israel, Jerusalem
Yad Vashem, The Auschwitz Album
Abigail Klein

Cary Jarrett
Chaim Mandel
Cherub Nicholls
Jennifer Harvey
Yulia Kutishev
Ariel Jerozolimski

Following my seven months intensive research in 2009 and writing of the manuscript which was completed by the end of June 2010. A number of geopolitical events of great proportions have taken place. There has been a phenomenon called the Arab Spring which has resulted in the removal of two leaders with more than three decades, each, in office, namely: President Hosni Mubarak of Egypt who is currently facing retrial, and President Mummar al-Qadhafi who was killed in the aftermath of an armed conflict with rebel forces in Libya. Both countries have new political leadership.

Meanwhile, Syria's President Bashar al-Assad is engaged in a civil war for the past two years. The US has called for Assad's departure. Since the fighting started in March 2011 more than 100,000 Syrians have been killed and more than a million persons are refugees to neighbouring States, and, or are internally displaced.

Moreover, US President Barack Obama and Israeli Prime Minister Binyamin Netanyahu were reelected to office and were both sworn in to their second consecutive terms in early 2013.

Work by Cherub Angela Nicholls
Book: The Legitimacy of the Holy Bible as a Legal Instrument
Copyright 2006, Published by Xulon Press
Blog. To read blog, visit: www.cherubnichols.com

All Rights Reserved
Copyright © 2013 by Cherub Angela Nicholls

No part of this book may be reproduced or transmitted, downloaded, distributed, reverse engineered, or stored in or introduced into any information storage and retrieval system, in any form or by any means, including photocopying and recording, whether electronic or mechanical, now known or hereinafter invented without permission in writing from the publisher.

Dorrance Publishing Co., Inc.
701 Smithfield Street
Pittsburgh, PA 15222
Visit our website at *www.dorrancebookstore.com*

ISBN: 978-1-4349-1531-3
eISBN: 978-1-4349-1543-6

Threads in the Tapestry: Conflict and Resolution in the Middle East

Is the Two-State Solution the only Viable Option for Middle East Peace?

Cherub Angela Nicholls

Brentnol Nicholls, husband of Cherub Nicholls

This work is dedicated
To the memory of my friend and brother in Christ,
Dwayne J. Hanna, a Bahamian Attorney. He loved his God, he loved
his family and his politics passionately.

He departed from this world at the early age of 46, in March 2010.
Dwayne stood up firmly for his beliefs and so His death serves as a re-
minder that:

We too, must hold true to what we believe and press on with our vision,
urgently. We do not know when we'll be 'recalled' from this world, so we
must take a stance and maximise every opportunity that comes our way
so that life would be worth living.

Dwayne's sudden death gives me the impetus to: live life to the full, not
waste time, or it would be life wasted and glorious opportunities missed.

It is also dedicated
To my absolutely supportive family, my husband Eleazer, our sons
Gabriel & Michael;

and it is dedicated finally
To all the brave soldiers of the Israeli Defence Force (IDF), who will
continue to defend the State of Israel, militarily; the Israeli Diplomatic
Corps who defend the Jewish State politically, and the Zionists for their
love for the State of Israel and their willingness to stand with the Jewish
people in the face of danger.

Cherub Angela Nicholls

"Jerusalem is held sacred by half of mankind [but] it has been and always will be Israel's capital. We never had another and it has never been the capital of any other people."
Prime Minister Binyamin Netanyahu
Jerusalem Day, celebrations marking 42 years of Jerusalem's reunification
2009

The Lord:
The Lord Almighty, the God of Israel says, "When I restore the
people to their land, they will once again say in the land of
Judah and in its towns, 'May the Lord bless the sacred
hills of Jerusalem, the holy place where He lives.'..."
"And just as I took care to uproot, to pull down, to overthrow,
to destroy, and to demolish them, so I will take care to
plant them and to build them up."
(*Good News Trans. Jeremiah 31: 23, 28*).

Contents

Section Three: The Region

Section Four: The Case for Israel

Section Five: An Analysis – The Two-State Solution...
Assessment of Questions put to Interlocutors in the
Conflict: In Jerusalem, London, Washington DC
and New York

Section Six: The Ulterior Motive

Appendices

Foreword

This book is a labour of love – a heartfelt and abiding love and respect, on the part of its author, for the State of Israel and its purpose as a nation.

Cherub Angela Nicholls is no "armchair strategist." She is personally and deeply involved in the subject that forms the substance of this book. Cherub approached the task of writing *Threads in the Tapestry* with the rich background of her personal experience as a student of international law and as a diplomat in the service of her country and of the United Nations. In addition, she spent three months in Israel, speaking with Israeli statesmen, lawmakers, academics and ordinary Israelis – and with Arabs in the areas of the land now administered by the Palestinian Authority – and researching her subject at Israel's National Library in Jerusalem.

On her way back to her home, Cherub met with a variety of foreign (including Arab and Israeli) diplomats in London, Washington and New York, to augment the knowledge she had gained during her sojourn in Israel. For me, personally, it was a delight to observe the earnestness and devotion with which the author applied herself to her task while in Israel.

The results of her painstaking research are blended, in this book, with Cherub's intimate knowledge of the Bible, to challenge the "conventional wisdom" notion that the only way out of the Arab-Israeli impasse in the Middle East is the so-called two-state solution.

The reader is invited to follow the "Threads in the Tapestry" in what promises to be a fascinating intellectual and spiritual journey.

Bon Voyage!
Moshe Aumann
Minister (Ret.)
Israel Ministry of Foreign Affairs
June 2011

Acknowledgements

The splendour and majesty of Israel resonate with me even to this day. I am absolutely grateful for the warmth, friendship and loving care I experienced during my three month period of enquiry in Israel.

Special thanks to my mentor retired diplomat Moshe Aumann for his years of invaluable counsel and his youthful disposition, albeit he is in his eighties. Thanks for facilitating a number of privately arranged tours, meetings and advice. Thanks also to his brother, the winner of the Noble Prize in Economics (in 2005), Prof. Robert Aumann who instructed me on the principles of Game Theory. I'd like to also express my heartfelt appreciation to my mentor's son, whose name is Benny Aumann, who wore many hats as he provided assistance to me, and to Miri who is also an Aumann, who took me on the guided tour through the Yad Vashem, the Holocaust Memorial.

It was an honour for me to have met with some esteemed Members of the Knesset who participated in the interviews: MK & Minister for Social Affairs and Services Isaac Herzog, MK Prof. Arieh Eldad, MK Cabinet Member Benjamin "Benny" Begin and MK Danny Danon.

Gratitude is also extended to Dr Mordechai Kedar, a highly regarded Israeli Scholar and Expert on Arabic Literature and Culture. Dr Kedar provided me with valuable insight into the Arab people's culture. Thanks also to Maj.-General Robert Mood,

Chief of Staff and Head of Mission of the United Nations Truce Supervision Organisation (UNTSO). Thanks also to Mr Moshe Benzioni, Political Advisor to the Mayor of Jerusalem. Mr Benzioni, a career diplomat, can be described as Ambassador extraordinaire. He took me on my first tour to the Old City of Jerusalem and also participated in sitting an interview with me. Appreciation goes out to the Mayor of Jerusalem Nir Barkat, for also participating in the interview process. Thanks as well to the Jerusalem Post. In order to get a media perspective in coverage of the conflict Mr Gershom Gale of the Jerusalem Post dedicated a generous amount of time to answering my questions.

Special thanks to the leadership and their staff of the various Christian communities in Israel: The International Christian Embassy, Christian Friends of Israel, The International Christian Zionist Center, The Ecumenical Theological Research Fraternity, Bridges for Peace and The Latin Patriarchate of Jerusalem. Thanks for their participation in interviews, tours and subsequent friendships. Thanks also to Cary Jarrett, CFI's Chairman of Communities Under Attack, and the resource members of the Sderot Community in Israel, which lies 15 seconds from a Hamas rocket launch. A heartfelt thank you to the pastor of the Jerusalem Baptist Church Dr Albert Nucciarone III and his lovely wife Billie, they and their congregation made me feel at home and they personally took me on tour of Bethlehem and the Arab side of Hebron.

Gratitude to my *Israeli parents*: Norman and Lola Cohen for the great times of interaction and their many friends they availed for my contacts, especially Chaim Mandel and his wife Frieda. Norman & Lola also took me on a number of guided tours. I recall on one occasion we sought refuge in Noah's Ark at the Biblical Zoo in Jerusalem, it was on the day the Israeli government was carrying out a security exercise and everyone was mandated to be indoors. Their friend Chaim took me on tour to Gush Etzion, the Herodium and to meet the many people, including renowned Jewish Historian Aryeh Routtenberg.

Who can forget the energetic David Wilder of Hebron? David is an astute and articulate man who loves the city where the

Patriarch Abraham settled sometime around 1735 BCE. He vigorously defends the Jews right to live in Hebron.

In Mt Carmel, I met an Arab Christian family who loves Israel. Instead of cursing the Jewish people, they speak of the blessings the Jews are to the world and they bless them as well. We toured the mountain on which the prophet Elijah called down God's fire to burn up the evening sacrifices in the ultimate showdown of ancient times as to who is God.

High regard and appreciation are expressed to the Ambassadors of Missions to the United Nations in New York, as well as the Observer Mission of Palestine to the UN, Embassies in London and Washington DC. I would like to also express special thanks to the US Department of State, to US Representative Doug Lamborn and aides to Senators on Capitol Hill. Gratitude is also extended to the very petite Sarah Stern, a Washington Lobbyist for whom there is no "giant" that can stand in her way. She is a dedicated advocate for Israel.

I am indebted to the staffs of the libraries at Israel's National Library in Jerusalem, which is located in the Hebrew University compound in Jerusalem, the multiple libraries in London and the one I used at Oxford, the New York Public Library and the Library of Congress in Washington. The staffs at these locations are all highly professional! Thanks also to the proof reader Constance Chambers, also very strong advocate for Israel.

Special thanks to all those persons who contributed in every way to helping make this project a success; they include pastors in New York and elsewhere, friends also in New York, New Jersey and Maryland, friends in London, in Nassau Bahamas, Bermuda, Canada and Guyana. The well-wishers and renewal of acquaintances were added benefits to this exercise. Special thanks to my relatives everywhere; also appreciation is expressed to my mother and siblings.

Heartfelt gratitude goes to my husband Eleazer. He has taught our two sons by example, lessons such as: how to be strong and tenacious. My husband does not believe in taking the short-cut because there, it might be easier, or the opposition might be absent; no, he is forthright and strong, godly and humble. He loves his wife and gives his support to her unwaveringly. Thank you husband!

Finally, thanks to the Lord God who thru' Israel shows me constantly that He is good. I thank Him for availing to me the glorious opportunity in 2009 to travel to Israel, the United Kingdom and elsewhere, during the time of my gathering of data for this work. I thank the Lord for His protection, provision and access...

Thanks to everyone!

Section 1
The History

Chapter 1

A Jewish State: The Long-Held Aspirations of a Dispersed People

Embrace the Jews for Historical Precedence

For more than nineteen hundred years the Jewish people have lived as a distinct *community* among the peoples or inhabitants in lands where they found refuge. Such places include a number of European States and Russia, the United States of America and Canada, Brazil and Latin America, North Africa and the Middle East, the Caribbean and Southern Africa. The Jews have been held together by the unseen bond of a covenant. This covenant was not established by their initiative but it is one that dates back more than 4,000 years, "well in advance of any of them being born."

The Jewish people are to the rest of humanity what the sun and moon serve to our planet. Yes! It's quite true. The sun gives our heavily populated planet the energy and light we need for our existence; added benefits include food production and so forth. Whereas, the moon reflects the light of the sun and helps scientists determine the manner of the tides and oceanic currents. Ostensibly, the Jewish people were placed in our midst to serve as a nation of priests and guide the nations to the true and living God.

The underpinning fact is that human beings have never doubted the value and critical importance of the sun or the moon to human existence. No one has ever campaigned to rid the world of these two elements. Yet, there has been a concerted effort *from time immemorial* to remove the Jews from the midst of humanity. Why remove the witness that tells us God is real? Why remove the witness that keeps showing up "like cream in milk which floats to the top of a glass?" Why try to destroy the evidence because they were chosen for this very purpose? Why deny them the right to enjoy their full territory like all other nations? Why the concerted effort to repress them over and over again? Why is there the strident denial that they were and still remain God's chosen people?

It's a paradox, isn't it? When we see the rainbow in the sky we are somehow reminded that a promise was given by God to mankind and that the rainbow serves as a reminder of that covenant. In Genesis we have an account of the moral decadence of the human race. The depravity of man left very little to the imagination. And God saw it all.

Then the Lord saw that the wickedness of man was great in the earth, and that every intent of the thoughts of his heart was only evil continually.
And the Lord was sorry that He had made man on the earth, and He was grieved in His heart.
So the Lord said, I will destroy man whom I have created from the face of the earth, both man and beast, creeping thing and birds of the air, for I am sorry that I have made them. (Genesis 6: 5-7) [1]

God did as He had spoken to Himself.

Except for Noah, a man of whom it is said "walked with God," his wife, their three sons and their wives, and all kinds of animals, which found refuge in the Ark that Noah built, everyone else was killed in the flood. However, this unprecedented event led to a remarkable sign being placed in the heavens; the rainbow covenant. Yes, the rainbow has been around for a very long time and it is still with us today.

Then God spoke to Noah and to his sons with him, saying:... Thus I establish My covenant with you: Never again shall all flesh be cut off by the waters of the flood; never again shall there be a flood to destroy the earth.

And God said: This is the sign of the covenant which I make between Me and you, and every living creature that is with you, for perpetual generations:

I set My rainbow in the cloud, and it shall be for the sign of the covenant between Me and the earth.[2]

Similarly, the Jews are God's gift to us as a testimony of His efforts to engage mankind in a relationship with Him. Why the Jews you'll ask? Well, they are the heirs to the covenant God made with their forefather Abraham. God specifically identified Abraham and his son Isaac and his grandson Jacob and their descendants for this special relationship. God spoke to Abraham and said:

"Get out of your country,
From your kindred and from your father's house,
To a land that I will show you.
I will make you a great nation; I will bless you and make your name great;
And you shall be a blessing."[3]

Included in the blessing is the promise that the descendants of Abraham will be a great nation. Consequently, the Jews, the heirs of this blessing, are indeed a great nation. One must recognise that their greatness is evidenced in their achievements and successes and leadership in law, science, medicine, engineering, research, education, music, governance, military tactics, agriculture and other areas of human endeavours.

It must be specifically emphasised that the heirs of the covenant which Abraham received from God are Isaac, Jacob and their descendants. This argument is supported by the very actions of Abraham. In his latter days he separates his son Isaac from the other sons born to him. *"But Abraham gave gifts to the sons of the concubines which Abraham had; and while he was still living he sent them eastward, away from Isaac his son, to the country of the east.*"[4]

To validate His approval of Abraham's selection of Isaac, God appears to Isaac and speaks with him. God was pleased with Abraham's choice of Isaac as the sole heir to all of Abraham's possessions. God had given to Abraham great possessions including all the land of Canaan. Inclusive, today's State of Israel, Jordan and lots more territory. It was not God's intent that there should be conflict or controversy over the inheritance for His people. The inheritance included the entire territory of Canaan as an everlasting possession as it was a blood covenant between God and Abraham.

When God appeared to Isaac, He was making it clear to all that He intended to bestow upon Isaac the said covenant He had given to his father Abraham. God's actions therefore should have caused all others to concede that His plans are perfect and that His choice is final. In fact, God's personal involvement should render all claims by others to this very covenant null and void. But, no, there now wages a perennial conflict over this very covenant. A large number of people today call themselves "descendants of Abraham" and have stridently pressed to be recognised as heirs to this covenant. One must recall that the covenant did not stop with Abraham, but the giver, God Himself, streamed it thru' Isaac, from Isaac to Jacob and from Jacob to his descendants. Not the other way around... Not Abraham and all his sons. Those outside of the Jacob family tree who *now* lay claim to Israel's inheritance are thieves.

During the time of God's visit with Isaac there was a terrible challenge to the inhabitants of the land. There was a famine in the land. Since Isaac had inherited all of his father's huge flock of animals and cattle, the pragmatic thing to do was to leave the place where the famine was, so as to save the livestock and the members of the household. However, the Lord discourages Isaac from doing any such thing. Instead, He tells him to do the unthinkable: *Sojourn in this land, and I will be with you and bless you; for to you and your descendants I give all these lands, and I will perform the oath which I swore to Abraham your father. Further, I will make your descendants multiply as the stars of heaven; I will give to your descen-*

dants all these lands; and in your seed all the nations of the earth shall be blessed [5]

Jacob becomes the heir of his father's covenant, for this was the way God would have it. The sons born to Isaac were Esau who later became known as Edom and Jacob also became known as Israel. God is good and His ways are perfect! Conversely, however, many people attempt to judge God's actions from their own sense of justice, from their biases, and from their limited knowledge of God. The Scripture answers God's critics even at the beginning, so that everyone could appreciate the sovereignty of God.

God is not man and this salient truth is often forgotten, hence the continuation of the Arab-Israeli conflict for which most people ridicule Israel and give support to the Arab grouping now known as Palestinians. Is there a man who is in his right mind who can say categorically that there is evil in God's actions? Really, there is no man, included the self-proclaimed atheists. Why then the judgement on God's character?

For in the case of Esau and Jacob, while they were still unborn to parents: Isaac and Rebecca, something dramatic took place. Rebecca felt a struggle taking place in her womb and so she asked the Lord the meaning of what was going on inside of her. Imagine how difficult it must have been for her during her pregnancy. Paul the apostle surmises the situation in this fashion:

Nor are all of Abraham's descendants the children of God. God said to Abraham, "It is through Isaac that you will have the descendants I promised you." This means that the children born in the usual way are not the children of God; instead, the children born as a result of God's promise are regarded as the true descendants. For God's promise was made in these words: "At the right time I will come back, and Sarah will have a son."

And this is not all. For Rebecca's two sons had the same father, our ancestor Isaac. But in order that the choice of one son might be completely the result of God's own purpose, God said to her, "The older will serve the younger." He said this before they were born, before they had done anything either good or bad; so God's choice was based on His call, and not on anything they had done. As the Scripture says, "I loved Jacob, but hated Esau."[6]

Jacob's name was subsequently changed to Israel following a supernatural experience. His name-change followed his encounter with God... *But he said, I will not let You go unless You bless me! So He said to him, "What is your name?" And he said, Jacob. And He said, "Your name shall no longer be called Jacob, but Israel; for you have struggled with God and with men, and have prevailed."* (Genesis 32: 26-28).[7] The Jewish people are also known by the name Israel, from their father Israel. Since then, their ancestors that followed were actually known among the Gentiles as Israelites.

The question is often asked: What's in a name? There is much significance in names. Names often point to one's destiny or provide descriptions of the bearer's character. The name Israel is very telling. It will serve the descendants of Jacob well. It will reveal the tenacity of these people. It will separate them from other nations and tribes. The name will give them impetus as they wander through the plains among the multitudes of men, it will encourage them to freely express their faith in God and enable them to preserve their identity. Their name has empowered them to aspire for their homeland for the present and future generations. And this name, Israel, will motivate them to keep the covenant land, now that they have come into possession of it once again.

Israel! What a legacy. Israel has struggled with God and man and has prevailed! Even today, Israel continues their struggles and they continue to prevail. It is clear that this power to prevail comes from God Himself. Listen to this:

For you are a holy people to the Lord your God; the Lord your God has chosen you to be a people for Himself, a special treasure above all the peoples on the face of the earth... Therefore know that the Lord your God, He is God, the faithful God who keeps covenant and mercy for a thousand generations with those who love Him and keep His commandments.[8]

When I was in the Middle East in the spring of 2009, an Arab man contemptuously declared that when the State of Israel is divided (he hopes, based on the international community's covenant to the Arabs), then all will see what will happen to the Israelis as God's chosen people. This is the spirit that Israel has struggled against historically. This spirit is imbued in many nations: the spirit of hatred toward the people of Israel. The struggle thus continues and Israel will yet again prevail!

The Dispersion and the Return: Israel's Struggles with Men

When a people are so privileged to hear the voice of God as a population and live, then it is natural for that nation to speak of this encounter and the many others, which have undoubtedly altered the course of their lives. Not only has there been the oral tradition of the Jewish experience but there are also written accounts in books namely, the Torah and the Holy Bible. Written are the miraculous accounts of the great exodus of this nation from the territory of Egypt to the land of Canaan.

Canaan, Palestine and Israel are the names used to identify the same Jewish homeland. The land is also known as the Holy Land. When the Romans invaded the Holy Land, they renamed it Palestine as they attempted to remove Jewish identity from the land. They also passed laws ordering the punishment of any Jew who dared to enter Jerusalem and burnt the Temple, the focal point of Jewish identity, culture and place of worship. Subsequent powers including the Crusaders (1099-1291) and more recently the Jordanians (1949-1967), also sought to remove the Jewish identity from the city Jerusalem as well as the rest of the land.

The name Palestine is Roman and not Arabic. Over the centuries the geographical location of the territory has remained the same and so those who deny the Jews historical ties to the land are doing so out of contempt for the truth. They are really saying that God is *a liar* and that the Jewish people are also liars. This is not so! For example, there is only one Red Sea, one Jordan River, one Jerusalem, one Judea and one Samaria, one Hebron, one Galilee, one Bethlehem, one Egypt, one Lebanon, one Damascus, and so forth. Those who are students of the Holy Bible should never be confused with the rhetoric and posturing of the Arabs and the mass media. These places are mentioned in the Torah and the Bible. Mentioned are also accounts of relations between Israel and neighbouring States; those which were Israel's allies and those who were her enemies. One thing is certain, nothing has changed from ancient times to the present in Middle East politics.

There are numerous accounts of invasions of the Holy Land in Biblical times. Modern history books are also laced with accounts of invasion of the Holy Land in the last two centuries. On numerous occasions these invasions led to the Dispersions of the children of Israel, the descendants of Abraham, Isaac and Jacob. For example, one such removal of Jews from the Holy Land was undertaken by the Babylonian army led by king Nebuchadnezzar. The people were taken to Babylon. Included in the lot were Daniel and Ezekiel. Seventy years later the first return of the Dispersed Tribes of Judah took place when Cyrus king of Persia so ordered their return in the first year of his reign.

In as much as there are numerous accounts of Israel's Dispersions, there are also a proliferation of prophecies telling of God's plans to return the Israelites to their homeland from which they were taken into captivity. One ought to accept that just as the Dispersion of the Israelites was an historic fact, then, similarly, it should not come as a surprise to us that the very just God who kept His word and scattered, must by dint of His virtue, keep His word to return. The Prophet Jeremiah foretold of the first return and it was corroborated in the Book of Ezra.

For thus says the Lord: After seventy years are completed at Babylon, I will visit you and perform My good word toward you, and cause you to return to this place... I will be found by you, says the Lord, and I will bring you back from your captivity; I will gather you from all the nations and from all the places where I have driven you, says the Lord, and I will bring you to the place from which I caused you to be carried away captive.[9]

Now in the first year of Cyrus king of Persia (renamed Iran), that the word of the Lord spoken by the mouth of Jeremiah might be fulfilled, the Lord stirred up the spirit of Cyrus king of Persia, so that he made a proclamation throughout all his kingdom, and also put it in writing, saying,

Thus says Cyrus king of Persia: All the kingdoms of the earth the Lord God of heaven has given me. And He has commanded me to build Him a house at Jerusalem which is in Judah. Who there among you of all His people? May his God be with him! Now let him go up to Jerusalem, which is in Judah, and build the house of the

Lord God of Israel (He is God), which is in Jerusalem. And whoever remains in any place where he sojourn, let the men of his place help him with silver and gold, with goods and livestock, besides the freewill offerings for the house of God which is in Jerusalem.[10]

Today, the return of the Jews to their homeland in Judah and Samaria is a reality, albeit one treated with trepidation by Israel's neighbours as well as the broader international community. A little more than a hundred years ago the return of Jews *en masse* (also known as aliyah) was nearly impossible. During this period there was no Jewish State. There were many barriers to the Jew, established by Empires: The Ottoman and the British Empires which occupied the Holy Land in recent history. They governed the area under the same prohibitions against Jews as were created by rulers prior to their times. Rules designed to restrict and or prevent the Jews from returning to their homeland (especially to Jerusalem), even with the threat of death, and in some instances enforcing those threats.

Despite the terrible things done against the Jews, there were always the one or two individuals who were willing to step-up to the plate to help them. Therefore, long before the Jews received their State, there were men calling for a State for the people. Two men who lived in the 1800s, one a Gentile and the other a Jew: William E. Blackstone, an American evangelist and Theodor Herzl, a Jewish journalist from Switzerland, believed that the Jews had an inalienable right to return to the land given by the True and Living God to their forefathers and by the law of inheritance to those of the present generations. The Jews faced horrendous persecutions such as the pogroms, the inquisition, the crusades, the expulsions and the Holocaust. Now however, despite the fact they are in their own homeland and sovereign State they do live with the ever present threats of intifadas and terrorism which place the State in a perennial state of war. The State of Israel has actually survived two intifadas and numerous wars with their neighbours. Their survival speaks to the endurance of the sons and daughters of Israel and of the faithfulness of their God who honours His covenant to His people. What's in the name Israel?

The Jewish Experience

Wherever the Jews have lived, for however long their generations may have resided in that particular territory, they were hardly allowed to feel at home in that jurisdiction. The bile known as antisemitism or hatred flowed abundantly toward them in the centuries of their Dispersions, to a greater degree in places such Russia and Europe, the Middle East and North Africa. In many instances the Jews were forced to live in ghettos as a matter of the particular State's domestic policies. They were branded. They were told that they must wear the Star of David on their clothing. They were deprived of the right to own property, deprived of the right to education and to transact business freely and they were forbidden to travel extensively within the territory without permits. This was in reality, the Jewish experience. It was not only their experience in Germany. In fact the Germans adopted this policy after many other European States and Russia.

Imagine the ardent advocate of free thought François – Marie Arouet (Voltaire) of France in 1756, appealing for the Jews not to be burnt, but in his arguments he spews of some of the most contemptible words vilifying the Jewish community.

Voltaire submits that the Guebers, the Banyans and the Jews are the only nations which exist dispersed, having no alliance with any people, are perpetuated among foreign nations, and continue apart from the rest of the world... He contends, their stay in Babylon and in Alexandria during which individuals might acquire wisdom and knowledge trained the (Jewish) people as a whole in no art save that of usury... Voltaire further argues, "In short, find in them only an ignorant and barbarous people, who have long united the most sordid avarice with the most detestable superstition and the most invincible hatred for every people by whom they are tolerated and enriched. Still, we ought not to burn them."[11]

Isaac de Pinto, a philosopher and economist of Portuguese-Jewish origins who also lived in the 1700s, challenged Voltaire's dossier and questioned his intent. The Jewish gentleman argues that they (the Jews) do not, then, deserve those epithets which M. Voltaire lavishes on them. The Jews of Holland brought thither great riches at the end of the fifteenth century; and with manners irreproachable, greatly improved the trade of that commonwealth. Their Synagogue was like an assembly of senators, and, when German noblemen went into it, they could not be persuaded that those there present were of the same nation with those of Germany. They have been of greater use to Holland, at the beginning of the seventeenth century, than the French refugees were at the end of it... Scarcely can one instance be given of a Portuguese Jew executed at Amsterdam or The Hague, during two centuries. It would be hard to find in the annals of mankind so numerous a body of people as that of the Portuguese and Spanish Jews settled in Holland and England, among whom so few crimes punished by law have been committed; and to this I call to witness all well informed Christians of those nations...[12]

De Pinto defiantly posits "It is not sufficient to abstain from burning people with faggots; they may be burned with the pen; and this fire is so much more to be dreaded, because it lasts to future generations."[13]

Meanwhile, John P. McTernan provides a further picture of how hostility in a State could result in antisemitism and crimes against the Jews. On March 1, 1881, Tsar Alexander II of Russia was assassinated. This incident set off a series of events that cascaded down through history to this day. The Russian government blamed the assassination on the Jews and violence broke out immediately. The terrible pogrom of 1881 resulted in the murder of hundreds of Jews with thousands injured, their homes and property destroyed.[14]

The Russian government did nothing to stop the pogroms and actually blamed the destruction of Jews on the Jews! Jewish life was terrible before the pogrom, but it was about to significantly worsen. On March 3, 1882, the Russian government enacted what became known as the May Laws. The May Law did not only confine the Jews to ghettos, but it included the provisions barring of Jews from purchasing land or houses and it also included the restrictions of Jewish education for the Jews themselves.[15]

Similarly, in Germany the Jews were singled out by Adolf Hitler and the Third Reich for persecution, also know today as the Holocaust. Hitler's actions against the Jews were committed in stages and so they did not raise the ire of the international community in the beginning. The eventual result of German hatred led to the mass seizure of the Jewish people possessions, then their freedoms and eventually the lives of Jewish boys and girls, women and men that totalled six million Jews, also included were some of the brave Christians who sought to provide refuge to the Israelites and were caught by the authorities so doing. Other minority ethnic groups and the disadvantaged were also killed by the Germans namely: the Gypsies, disabled people and others. These events occurred not so long ago, they took place in the Twentieth Century, some seventy-five years ago. Those who conducted this vicious campaign most likely thought of themselves as having been 'well cultured.' Nevertheless, barbarism still lurks in the heart of mankind, especially in the hearts of those who "hate" what God loves, and "loves" what God hates. It's a lesson the wise.

Meanwhile, there are three major religions in the world: Judaism, Christianity and Islam. In subsequent chapters we will examine the influence of Islam on Arabs and Muslims in their slandering of the Jews and their pernicious quest for the Holy Land. On the other hand, the Christian community has not always welcomed the Jews in their midst either, and have persecuted them for one reason or another.

Jules Isaacs, a Frenchman, a Jew and a member of France's intellectual society searched for answers in the time of the most severe test to the Jews in Europe. The Holocaust! Isaacs pointed the finger of ultimate blame not at the Nazis, but at the Christian church. He contended while the German responsibility for the Holocaust was "overwhelming," it was only a derivative responsibility." The real culprit, Isaacs asserted was the centuries-old tradition of Christian antisemitism.[16] The Christian attitude stemmed from the embrace of the teaching of contempt and a "replacement theology," which held that the church had superseded the Jews as God's chosen people.[17]

David Brog identifies the foremost spokesperson of early replacement theology. The man was Justin Martyr, one of the leading theologians and a Gentile convert to Christianity. The

Martyr lived in Christian communities around the Mediterranean, in the mid-second century. Before his death at the hands of the Romans, he wrote in his text: *Dialogue with Trypho*, claiming that Christians were now the spiritual Israel. Justin maintains that the Jews—physical Israel—will inherit none of the benefits of the Abrahamic covenants, *not even the physical benefits*. Everything once promised to the Jews, including the land of Israel itself, will now flow to the church.[18]

In this, the Twenty First Century, there is an awakening taking place in the Christian community. This awakening comes in the form of Christian Zionism and has been gaining momentum since its commencement way back in the Nineteenth Century. Today, much of Christendom acknowledges the right of the Jewish people to their homeland, i.e., the State of Israel. They also support the State's existence in its present location in the Holy Land. While, there may still be some Christians who believe otherwise, there is a growing number and a very vocal group of Christians who overtly support the Jewish people.

Retired Israeli diplomat Moshe Aumann, who served in the United States capital, Washington DC, as an envoy to the Christian Churches for three years from 1987-1990, gives a first-hand view on the emerging changes involving Christians toward the Jewish people. Aumann in his book: *Conflict & Connection; The Jewish–Christian–Israeli Triangle.*, argues there has been a dramatic positive change in the attitude of some of the major Christian Churches – Protestant, Catholic and, to a lesser extent, Orthodox – towards the Jewish religion. Many among the general public, Jews and Christians are unaware – or only dimly aware – of this change. But it is a matter of record, and it is pregnant with meaning and with the possibility of a thoroughgoing transformation, in the long term, of the entire Church-Synagogue relationship, with all that this would imply with regard to (a) relations between the Christian and the Jewish communities and (b) the attitude of the churches towards the modern rebirth and regeneration of Israel and toward the State of Israel as such.[19]

Aumann further reveals that: One of the most important and effective tools in the ongoing promotion of greater understanding and respect between the Christian and Jewish communities has been the dialogue between the two. Without it, it is doubtful that the bold initial steps taken by the Church in the 1960s, in generating the re-thinking of Church doctrines and dogmas concerning Judaism and the Jewish people, could have been sustained and, indeed, advanced to the point where we are now.[20]

In the final analysis, the journey of the people of Israel has been fraught with laughter, tears, sufferings, rejections, imprisonment, Dispersion, explosions and longing for their homeland. Indeed, the Jews are a people of survival! They have learnt to overcome adversities, they know how to stick together, they love to dance and they strive to maintain their faith and confidence in the God of their forefathers. The Jew, like Israel, his forefather has struggled with God and man and has survived. Inherent in the Jewish experience is the lesson for life.

Chapter 2

Jews Persistent Survival: The Establishment of the State of Israel

The Declaration of Independence

When David Ben-Gurion issued the Declaration of Independence of the State of Israel on May 14, 1948, he unwittingly invited a global struggle with men. For the name Israel reveals that Israel shall inadvertently maintain their struggle with men, but they will nevertheless ultimately prevail against them. Consequently, the five Arab armed forces unaware of the fact that despite their huge numbers and military prowess they would still be unable to defeat the ill-equipped Israelis.

Ben-Gurion in the Declaration of the Establishment of the State of Israel submits:

After being forcibly exiled from their land, the people kept faith with it throughout their Dispersion and never ceased to pray and hope for their return to it and for the restoration in it of their political freedom.

Impelled by this historic and traditional attachment, Jews strove in every successive generation to re-establish themselves in the ancient homeland. In recent decades they returned in their masses. Pioneers, defiant returnees, and defenders, they made deserts bloom, revived the

Hebrew language, built villages and towns, and created a thriving community controlling its own economy and culture, loving peace but knowing how to defend itself, bringing the blessings of progress to all the country's inhabitants, and aspiring towards independent nationhood.[1]

Ben-Gurion continues: Accordingly we, members of the People's Council, representatives of the Jewish Community of Eretz-Israel and of the Zionist Movement, are here assembled on the day of the termination of the British Mandate over Eretz-Israel and, by virtue of our natural and historic right and on the strength of the resolution of the United Nations General Assembly, hereby declare the establishment of a Jewish State in Eretz-Israel, to be known as the State of Israel.[2]

Centuries ago when the Israelites first obtained their independence from Egypt, their God, who visibly orchestrated the entire event by His mighty right hand vis-à-vis His opening up the Red Sea for their crossing, their journey through the wilderness and His supernatural presence and His feeding them manna from heaven for 40 years are engrained in the Jewish psyche. For God is their deliverer, provider and helper then, and now.

In 1948, though the recreation of the State of Israel was based on different circumstances, Israel recognised the opportunity and the unfolding of their destiny in century's old promises God gave to the prophets saying that He will re-gather his people to their land from which they were scattered. The expiration of the British Mandate availed to the descendants of Abraham, Isaac and Jacob the opportunity to take hold of their inheritance. It brought to an end direct control or rule of the covenant land by Gentiles, which had gone on for centuries.

Prior to this current era of return in our times, there was another historic return of the exiles to the land. The initial return of the children of Israel to their land took place seventy years after their first captivity at the hands of the king of Babylon, King Nebuchadnezzar. Following this era, Israel was again scattered and a similar covenant was given that they will return to the land albeit it took approximately 1900 years, yet, it has come to pass. Never again will the Israelites be annihilated from their homeland. The Gentiles will continually make war with the Jewish people of the land, but as it has already been established, Israel will prevail against her enemies.

Israel Wrestles for Possession of her Covenant

The twenty-one Arab States in the Middle East refused to accept or welcome the creation of the Jewish State. Seized with outrage five among them namely, Iraq, Egypt, Syria, Lebanon and Jordan decided to attack Israel. They did not anticipate that this new State with the name Israel was destined to conquer its enemies. In less than twenty-four hours upon the Declaration of the Jewish State, the Arab coalition attacked. They were armed with a plan to destroy this fledgling nation but they themselves were defeated. Although, Jordan did walk away with parts of Israel and then rename same as East Jerusalem and the West Bank, and, Egypt, took Gaza as well, the annihilation the Arabs envisioned never occurred.

The War of Independence and the defeat of the well armoured Arabs were reminiscent of an ancient War of Independence. The independence of the Israelite slaves from Egypt. This battle involved the Lord of hosts' overt involvement. He fought Israel's battles for her. He slaughtered the firstborn of the Egyptians and then ultimately destroyed the Pharaoh's army in the Red Sea. Forever, Israel celebrates this supernatural event during the Passover.

The 1948 War took the lives of many young men who had enlisted in the service to defend this country after they themselves fled persecutions in Russia and Europe. While in Jerusalem, I was taken to a Park with a Memorial and there told a story by an Israeli woman who recounted it as it was told to her. It concerns the victory a small Jewish neighbourhood experienced during the War of Independence... it may have very well been the hand of God fighting on the behalf of His covenanted people.

The San Simon Park is located on a high hill in the southern district of Jerusalem. There is a monument at the Park to remember the fallen soldiers who fought to defend the area from the Arab invaders. The Park was the site of a decisive battle for Katamon and the south of Jerusalem. Three Arab armies: Iraq,

Egypt and Jordan attacked the area simultaneously and the fighting was fierce.

In the midst of the intense battle both the Arab enemies and the Israelites had numerous causalities. Just when the Jewish defenders were considering withdrawal so that their wounded could obtain medical treatment, they received word that the Arabs had retreated. This sudden retreat did not only save the lives of the wounded soldiers, for whom it was uncertain as to how they could be taken away without them and other soldiers encountering a barrage of sniper fire, but, the withdrawal also saved an entire community from falling into the hands of their Arab enemies.

Meanwhile, in another Jewish community, the Mekor Chaim neighbourhood which is situated below the hills of Katamon they were watching the progress of the battle on the hills above at San Simon Park, they saw what amounts to a miracle. The Mekor Chaim fighters were quite low on ammunition and had resigned themselves to the possibility of surrendering. Suddenly however, they saw the Arabs fleeing through the valley from Baka, the German Colony, Katamon and other Arab neighbourhoods to Beit Safafa (which is still today an Arab community), the Jews down in Mekor Chaim then realised that the battle for Karamon had been won. This inspired them to hold out just a little longer and save the Mekor Chaim neighbourhood, as well. (*For more information on: The Battle for Katamon and the South of Jerusalem, kindly read, "Jerusalem, a walk through time", Volume II, (Jerusalem: Yad Ben-Zvi Press, 1999)*).

Another front in the War of Independence was the Etzion Bloc, a community located in the Judean Hills which I also visited. The Etzion Bloc, or Gush Etzion as it is called in Hebrew, is located on the "Path of the Patriarchs" in the heart of the historic homeland of the Jewish people. Nestling in the Judean Hills, the Etzion Bloc is situated on the ancient mountain route midway between Jerusalem – the city of David, and Hebron – the city of the Patriarchs.[3]

As of the autumn of 1947, Etzion Bloc was composed of four Jewish settlements in various stages of development. Its total population was slightly more than four hundred inhabitants.

There were approximately 2,500 acres of land in Jewish owner-ship in the Etzion Bloc region.[4] The thriving kibbutzim at Etzion Bloc would be the first to face Arab attacks. As soon as the United Nations Resolution of November 29, 1947 (*Resolution 181*) was passed which provided for the partition of the Holy Land (a violation of God's intent), the Arabs did not only reject the partition plan but they went on a rampage attacking Jews and their communities.

The young, strong and visionary pioneers that planted trees to reforest their land and to bring back life to deserted hills which were left barren for years as though in mourning for the departed sons and daughters – the heirs of the land; were now thrust into battle. Most of them had recently escaped the ghettos of Europe and the Holocaust. Now they were to defend the land of their forefathers given in sacred covenant by the God of Abraham, the God of Isaac and the God of Jacob, the same God, who is eternal.

The major events which transpired in the Etzion Bloc are worth recounting. Jewish historian Aryeh Routtenberg submits the transition period between the passing of the United Nations resolution and the founding of the State of Israel, were five trying months of siege and battle. They tested the endurance of the de-fenders daily. Knowledge that their efforts were helping to save a besieged Jerusalem provided additional strength to continue the struggle. Vastly outnumbered and possessing limited amounts of light arms and ammunition, hope was still maintained that aid would come. Instead, the well trained and superior equipped Jordanian Legion diverted its course from Jerusalem and directed its attack on the outposts of Gush Etzion. In the three day battle which ensued, the Etzion Bloc fell, and 151 of her defenders were killed. A great sacrifice was offered up on the altar of the State of Israel.[5]

The Gush Etzion story does not end with the sacrifice of the men who died defending their State. These men who were hus-bands, fathers, brothers and some sons had the foresight to pro-tect their families and they did not die in vain. For Israel they died and it was Israel who took care of their families. The men had taken the precaution to send away their women and children to a safe place while they themselves remained behind to defend

Etzion Bloc. Their women and children were first kept together but some years later some of them separated, however, the children were aware of their father's sacrifice. Consequently, when Jordan lost its eighteen year strangle-hold of Judea in another war in 1967, Etzion Bloc was rebuilt by Jews many of them survivors of Gush Etzion. Today some of the residents of Etzion Bloc include those who were children of Gush Etzion. Adults now, they tell the story of Israel's struggle and their father's fate and of how Israel was worth the struggle her men faced-off against their enemies.

Israel's First War for Possession in the Land of Canaan

Meet the new leader of Israel, Joshua. When Moses died east of the Jordan River, the children of Israel were still en route to their final destination, the land of Canaan. In order to avoid a leadership crisis, Moses before his death had anointed his personal assistant, Joshua to lead the people. During the act of transferring the leadership to the young man, Moses told Joshua and the people:

The Lord your God Himself crosses over before you; He will destroy these nations from before you, and you shall dispossess them. Joshua himself crosses over before you, just as the Lord has said... Then Moses called Joshua and said to him in the sight of all Israel, "Be strong and of good courage, for you must go with this people to the land which the Lord has sworn to their fathers to give them, and you shall cause them to inherit it. And the Lord, He is the one who goes before you. He will be with you, He will not leave you nor forsake you; do not fear nor be dismayed."[6]

Now, after the death of Moses the servant of the Lord, it came to pass that the Lord spoke to Joshua the son of Nun, Moses' assistant saying ... From the wilderness and this Lebanon as far as the great river, the River Euphrates, all the land of the Hittites, and to the Great Sea toward the going down of the sun, shall be your territory. No man shall be able to stand before you all the days of your life; as I was with Moses, so I will be with you. I will not leave you nor forsake you.[7]

Here we see the Lord, Himself, defines Israel's boundaries. This land was quite large, much, much larger than Israel has possession of today (see Appendix VI & VII). Yet, Israel is being told to give up even portions of what she possesses for the sake of quieting her enemies. This was not the way Joshua and his people obtained possession of the land in the first round. They fought for it and they took possession and afterward retained possession of the territory, the Lord, their God, had given them.

Joshua the ruler was fearless and God made him a mighty warrior in Israel. The task he had been entrusted was one for the possession of Israel and to preserve its domestic security. Israel could not afford to gamble with its security interests lest her enemies eventually form a coalition against her and come up and over take her suddenly as has happened in modern times. The accounts of Joshua's victories reveal a man who believed the word of God and was led by God to obtain possession of the land for the descendants of Abraham, Isaac and Israel.

Joshua's legacy as a warrior has indeed been the pattern for most of Israel's contemporary leadership. From the date of independence in 1948 to present, most of the State's Prime Ministers have had to do battle in the region. Battles to guarantee their continued possession of the land that Joshua and his men so ably fought for centuries ago. The land which however, continues to be contested by the enemies on Israel's borders and within. Enemies who use *peace* to make war against the Jews because Israel is *not one of them, the State of Israel is not an Islamic country.*

Is there any similarity between the group below and those of Egypt, Iraq, Jordan, Lebanon and Syria?

And it came to pass when all the kings who were on this side of the Jordan, in the hills and in the lowland and in all the coasts of the Great Sea toward Lebanon–the Hittite, the Amorite, the Canaanite, the Perizzite, the Hivite, and the Jebusite–heard of it, that they gathered together to fight with Joshua and Israel with one accord.[8]

In the final analysis: *Joshua took all this land: the mountain country, all the South, all the land of Goshen, the lowland, and the Jordan plain – the mountains of Israel and its lowlands... there was not a city that made peace with the children of Israel, except the Hivites, the inhabitants of Gibeon. All the others they took in battle. For it was of the Lord to harden their hearts, that they should come against Israel in battle, that He might utterly destroy them, and that they might have no mercy, but that He might destroy them, as the Lord had commanded Moses. So Joshua took the whole land, according to all that the Lord had said to Moses; and Joshua gave it as an inheritance to Israel according to their divisions by their tribes. Then the land rested from war.*[9]

The question is, is there a leader in Israel, in this generation, who would possess the fighting strength of Joshua to object to calls for cease-fires at the height of battle and who would once-and-for-all do battle with her enemies and not leave any opportunity for them to re-gather small arms and light weapons, neither missiles, or will avert the acquisition of weapons of mass destruction (WMDs), all of which could be used to fight Israel another day?

Prime Minister Netanyahu in his book: *A Durable Peace. Israel and Its Place among the Nations* posits: The State of Israel is not only the repository of the millennial Jewish hopes for redemption; it is also the one practical instrument for assuring Jewish survival.

Assuring that survival is not free of problems. Israel has yet to complete the circle of peace around its borders, a peace that must be based on security if it is to last...[10]

Then, during his three years as Prime Minister (1996-1999), Netanyahu pinpoints his strategies: I firmly pursued these principles for a realistic peace, despite a torrent of criticism and abuse from those who cavalierly refuse to understand that in the volatile Middle East, peace without security is a sham. Such shortsightedness ought not to deflect Israel from pursuing lasting peace that will endure not a flicker of time but for generations to come.[11]

The transformation of the Jewish condition from one of utter powerlessness to one of effective self-defence marks the great change that the founding of Israel introduced into Jewish life, in fact making that life possible. As Herzl and the founding fathers of Zionism foresaw, the founding of the Jewish State would not necessarily stop the attacks on the Jewish people, but would assuredly give the Jews the means to resist and repel those attacks.[12]

Struggles for Recognition of the Modern State of Israel

When the bells of independence of the modern Jewish State were chimed, they marked a new era in global politics; for no State in this generation had ever experienced the phenomenon of such importance as having the Jewish State as a member of the international community.

On 29 November 1947, the United Nations General Assembly (UNGA), after an exhaustive study of the Jewish-Arab conflict in Palestine, endorsed the majority recommendation of its Special Commission on Palestine and resolved to partition the country into two independent States–a Jewish State and an Arab State–linked in economic union.[13]

As matters turned out, that peaceful solution was not forthcoming–because the Arab States refused to accept the United Nations (UN) decision in which it was envisaged or to cooperate in implementing it. On the contrary, they did all in their power to prevent fulfilment.[14]

With gangs of Palestinian Arabs, reinforced by irregulars from neighbouring Arab countries, delivering attacks on Jewish villages and lines of communication within days of the UN vote, the gravity of Jerusalem's position was at once apparent. Except for a few small villages to the north and south, Jerusalem was cut off from other Jewish centres of population, its only link with them the winding Tel Aviv-Jerusalem highway that was exposed to Arab assault at more than one point...[15]

It must be emphasised that: the legal title of the Jewish people to the mandated territory of Palestine in all of its historical parts and dimensions was first acknowledged and recognised under modern international law on 24 April 1920. That is when the Supreme Council of the Principal Allied Powers, consisting of Great Britain, France, Italy and Japan, after a heated debate between the highest British and French representatives, decided to approve the Balfour Declaration of 2 November 1917, and thereby give international legal effect to its provisions...[16]

Consequently, the establishment of a Jewish National Home in Palestine simultaneously meant creating the State and country of Palestine which then did not officially exist as a legal entity under international law. That in turn meant Palestine in its entirety was reserved exclusively for the self-determination of the Jewish people. These two new entities in international law, the Jewish National Home and Palestine, were therefore synonymous since they were both created at the very same time and for the very same purpose. The Jewish National Home was to be housed in Palestine and Palestine was to be the Jewish National Home, i.e., the Jewish State...[17]

Furthermore, Jewish legal rights and title of sovereignty to Palestine, which were firmly and irrevocably established under international law by the global political and legal settlement worked out by the coalition of the Principal Allied Powers during and after World War I, were never altered afterwards by any other binding act or instrument of international law which met the test of legality.[18]

The UNGA Resolution 181 of 29 November 1947 was approved with 33 votes in favour, 13 against and 10 abstentions and one absent.[19]

Meanwhile, the geopolitical reality of the day saw the end of the British Empire and the gradual emergence of the United States as a global power. It will supersede Britain in influence and become the greatest nation on earth. This was not without cause. The British had moved from support for the establishment of a Jewish National Home in Palestine (The Balfour Declaration in 1917) to appeasing the Arabs with the issuance of a White Paper (in 1939). Thus signalling its intent to compromise Jewish sovereignty over the territory, hence her fall.

United States President Harry Truman was the first world leader to acknowledge the State of Israel upon its Declaration of Independence.

A mere eleven minutes after Israel declared her independence, President Truman recognised the new Jewish State by signing the following statement:

This government has been informed that a Jewish State has been proclaimed in Palestine, and recognition has been requested by the provisional government thereof.

The United States recognises the provisional government as the de facto authority of the State of Israel.[20]

Despite the fact it's now more than 60 years since the event of Jewish independence has passed, Israel continues to struggle for her survival to live in peace and security in the midst of a hostile community. Netanyahu as Prime Minister of Israel for a second time, stated, in March (2010):

I said that we face great challenges to our security, but we also face unprecedented challenges to our legitimacy. Now this assault on our legitimacy comes in many forms – it comes from the so-called human rights bodies in the UN which would deny Israel its legitimate rights to self-defence, it comes by falsely charging Israel's political and military leaders with imaginary war crimes, and it comes by the outrageous waging campaigns to boycott, divest and sanction Israel.

But I think that there is an even greater assault on our legitimacy. I think it is the attempt to perpetrate one of the greatest lies of history – to deny the connection between the people of Israel and the land of Israel; to cast the Jewish people as foreigners in this land is an attempt to deny our future in this land. That is why to defend our past is to defend our future...[21]

Netanyahu is absolutely right to affirm Israel's legitimacy in the land. How then would the Lord say certain things to Israel if it were untrue that they did have legitimacy to possess the land of Israel? The Lord says:

Then the Lord your God will bring you to the land which your fathers possessed, and you shall possess it. He will prosper you and multiply you more than your fathers.[22]

And I will bring them out from the peoples and gather them from the countries, and will bring them to their own land; I will feed them on the mountains of Israel, in the valleys and in all the inhabited places of the country.[23]

The people of Israel enduring trust in God will sustain them in the land He has given them. They are home!

Section 2

The International Factor

Chapter 3

The International Community's Intrusion into Israel's Internal Affairs

Jerusalem & the Settlement Controversy

> "Jerusalem is not a settlement. It is our capital."
> *(Israel Prime Minister Benjamin Netanyahu).*[1]

Jerusalem is the *jewel* of Israel's crown. It is the capital of Israel! As the nation of Israel's capital, Jerusalem has the infrastructure and institutions pertinent for the smooth functioning of the government, all of these serve to enhance the conduct of good governance and the rule of law. Jerusalem, as an ancient city is filled with wonder and beauty. It is described as a city that *is built, compact together, where the tribes go up, the tribes of the Lord, to the testimony of Israel, to give thanks to the name of the Lord...*[2] Jerusalem, will outlast all other cities and the descendants of Israel are assured of God's protection of them with Jerusalem being used as a symbol of strength and protection. The promise states: *As the mountains surround Jerusalem, so the Lord surrounds His people from this time forth and forever.*[3]

Jerusalem must remain undivided! Why should Jerusalem suffer destruction at the hands of foreign powers who demand of the guardians of this illustrious city they give up significant parts of their ancient capital and their history? There is no precedence or record of Jerusalem ever being divided prior to the War of Independence of 1948, when Jordan seized a portion of Jerusalem in 1949. Eighteen years later, in another War in 1967, Israel recaptured the portion it lost to Jordan and ever since Jerusalem has been naturally reunified. Hence today's dispute.

Prime Minister Netanyahu told a gathering of Israelis and other supporters at a conference in Washington DC on 22 March 2010 that: The connection between the Jewish people and the land of Israel cannot be denied. The connection between the Jewish people and Jerusalem cannot be denied. The Jewish people were building Jerusalem 3,000 years ago and the Jewish people are building Jerusalem today.[4] Jerusalem is not a settlement. It is our capital[5] emphasises the Prime Minister.

Netanyahu stresses: In Jerusalem, my government has maintained the policies of all Israeli governments since 1967, including those led by Golda Meir, Menachem Begin and Yitzhak Rabin. Today, nearly a quarter of a million Jews, almost half of the city's Jewish population, live in neighbourhoods that are just beyond the 1949 armistice lines. All these neighbourhoods are within a five minute drive from the Knesset. They are an integral and inextricable part of modern Jerusalem. Everyone knows that these neighbourhoods will be part of Israel in any peace settlement. Therefore, building in them in no way precludes the possibility of a two-state solution,[6] he concludes.

Meanwhile, the international community has ignored Israel's ownership of the city and her right to sole sovereignty over it, saying that its future will be determined by division (into East and West Jerusalem). The great powers in concert with the United Nations and the European Union insist that that portion for which Israel *struggled against men* and recaptured in 1967 does not belong to Israel. They instead, have decided that that portion of the *eternal city* belongs to another grouping of Arabs, who for the sustenance of the dispute calls themselves Palestinians, after the name Palestine, the Romans gave to the Holy Land, years prior to 70 AD, and by which Jews were also called prior to the independence of Israel. Then, Jews and also Arabs in the Holy Land were known as Palestinians!

In Moscow, also in March 2010, the body of significant global powers known as the Quartet, met and disseminated the following orders to Israel, a democratic and sovereign State.

The Quartet urges the government of Israel to freeze all settlement activities... and to refrain from demolitions and evictions.[7] The United Nations Secretary-General Ban Ki-moon condemned the decision by the government of Israel to advance planning for new housing units in Jerusalem. The Quartet demands that all parties should promote peace talks as part of moves toward establishing a Palestinian State in Gaza and in *Judea and Samaria* within twenty-four months.[8]

The Quartet comprises Member States as well as international bodies, namely the United States, and Russia, the United Nations and the European Union. Their criticism against Israel comes at a time when the government of Prime Minister Netanyahu announced plans to construct 1,600 new homes for Israelis in Jerusalem.

Conversely, the Wall Street Journal notes that: In recent weeks, the Obama Administration has endorsed "healthy relations" between Iran and Syria, mildly rebuked Syrian President Bashar Assad for accusing the US of "colonialism," and publicly apologised to Moammar Gadhafi for treating him with less than appropriate deference after the Libyan called for a "jihad" against Switzerland.[9]

When it comes to Israel, however, the administration has no trouble rising to a high pitch of public indignation. On a visit to Israel in March, Vice President Joe Biden condemned the announcement by a mid-level Israeli official that the government had approved a planning stage the fourth out of seven required for the construction of 1,600 housing units in north Jerusalem. Assuming final approval, no ground will be broken on the project for at least three years. [10]

After Secretary of State Hillary Clinton called the Israelis plan an "insult," Vice President Biden "thanked" the Israeli government for "putting in place a process to prevent the recurrence" of similar incidents.[11]

The Administration as well as the international community's hysteria against Israel's domestic policies has given impetus to a belligerent Arab community which presses for more and more preconditions on Israel, in the wake of calls by the Israeli government for the resumption of negotiations between the parties. The current "diplomatic" standoff between Washington and Jerusalem "puts" Israel under *siege* within and outside of the Middle East.

Consequently, the Journal posits that if the Obama Administration opts to transform itself, as the Europeans have, into another set of lawyers for the Palestinians, it will find Israeli concessions increasingly hard to come by. However, that may be the preferred outcome for Israel's enemies, both in the Arab world and the West, since it allows them to paint Israel as the intransigent party standing in the way of "peace." Why an Administration that repeatedly avers its friendship with Israel would want that is another question. Then again, this episode does fit Obama's foreign policy pattern to date: Our enemies get courted; our friends get the squeeze. It has happened to Poland, the Czech Republic, Honduras and Colombia. Now it's Israel's turn.[12]

Jerusalem: Today's Opposition Mirrors Ancient Rows

"Next year in Jerusalem" was the ardent cry for generations of Jews at the end of the Passover celebrations also known as Pesach, during the years of their exile from the land of Promise, Eretz-Israel. Well, the Jews have come home! Jerusalem is their capital and they now enjoy their inalienable right, access and freedom to the city; the freedom to assemble without permits and taxes, the freedom to live in and the freedom to celebrate their feasts to the Lord, their God.

Jerusalem or Yerushalayim in Hebrew, also known as the City of David or Zion and also the City of the Great King, is majestic; surrounded by mountains which stand as fortresses guarding the ancient peoples and their descendants, the Jews.

Israel's renowned and highly respected medical doctor Professor Arieh Eldad and his father Israel Eldad in their book *The Challenge of Jerusalem...* note King David conquered Jerusalem and made it the capital of land and people for the first time. His son Solomon completed the process and made God's Sanctuary.[13]

In the years following the building of Jerusalem, God's people committed acts of abominations and harlotry against Him. So He sent word to His people condemning their lifestyles through His various prophets. One of them He sent was, Ezekiel. God spoke to Ezekiel saying: *Son of man, when a land sins against Me by persistent unfaithfulness, I will stretch out My hand against it; I will cut off its supply of bread, send famine on it, and cut off man and beast from it.* [14]

Consequently, Israel and Jerusalem fell into the hands of their enemies. The Eldads have argued that: The message of peace went forth from Jerusalem, but peace itself was never its lot and many wars swept through Jerusalem. It was destroyed and was re-built, was destroyed a second time and its rebuilding was commenced in the days of Bar-Kochba, again it fell and again it was rebuilt. This time, however, a total effort was made to eradicate its ancient and holy name. Emperor Hadrian of Rome was obliged to deploy his best legions to suppress the revolt. It seems that he realised the power in the name Jerusalem and the spell which it cast upon the Jews both in Judea and the Diaspora. He therefore resolved to subdue the Jews by altering the two names, the name of the country and the city. No more "Judah" or "Judea" but Syria Palestina.[15] To Jerusalem, Hadrian, gave the name Aelia Capitolina. Aelia – Hadrian's own name, Capitol – in honour of Jupiter Capitolini, the Roman god.[16]

Hadrian and his legions ensured the total destruction the Temple in Jerusalem, slaying hundreds of Jews in the process. The Temple stood in its glory as it shone, gleaming in the sun-light as the gold on the building exuded its radiance. Henceforth, the Romans threw down every bit of the massive stones to loot the gold. What they could not get from the fallen stones, they burnt so as to collect the melted gold.

The destruction of the Temple brought an end to the sacrifices that atoned for Israel's sins and to the pilgrimages, and many categories of mitzvot connected with the Temple and its service fell into disuse, and so to some extent did numerous other mitzvot associated with festivals, such as the blowing of the Shofar on the

New Year and the waving of the lulav on Tabernacles, which were mainly observed in the Temple and only partially outside it. The Temple was also the political, juridical basis of the Jewish communal structure. Centering round it in the Persian and Hellenistic periods, Judea derived its constitutional power from the Temple, the nation's glory as far as the outside world was concerned and the focal point of the Jewish people both in Eretz-Israel and in the Diaspora. In the Second Temple period Jerusalem was not only the capital of the State but the theatre of every spiritual creativity and political occasion. Coalescing as it were with the Temple, the city was intertwined in the practical life of the people and in the complex of the basic values of the nation's thought. The destruction of the temple left a vacuum in the spiritual and practical life of the Jews.[17]

In order for the Jews to rebuild the Second Temple after King Solomon's First Temple was destroyed, the Jews encountered no less opposition in the ancient world than the Jews of the today's Twenty-First Century.

Jerusalem's Predicted Destruction; Mandate to Rebuild; Unified Opposition

The destruction of the First Temple occurred at a time the Lord was angry with His people in Judah because of their sin. He sent Jeremiah to warn the people of impending judgement. Even in His judgement, God proclaims His tender mercy to His people. Jeremiah tells them: *Nevertheless in those days, says the Lord, I will not make a complete end of you. And it will be when you say, 'Why does the Lord our God do all these things to us?' Then you shall answer them, 'Just as you have forsaken Me and served foreign gods in your land, so you shall serve aliens in a land that is not yours.'*[18]

It was important for the Jews to refrain from idolatry as this is the first command God gave to them. He demands of them that they: *Do not worship any other god, because I, the Lord, tolerate no rivals.*[19] God called for their allegiance because it is He: *the Lord who gives rain, both the former and the latter, in its season. He reserves for them the appointed weeks of the harvest.*[20] The Lord is faithful!

Prior to the destruction of Jerusalem, even as the king of Babylon's army besieged Jerusalem, Jeremiah the prophet was shut up in the court of the prison, which was in the king of Judah's house. The word of the Lord came to Jeremiah, saying: *Behold, Hanameel the son of Shallum your uncle will come to you, saying, "Buy my field which is in Anathoth, for the right of redemption is yours to buy it."*[21] *... And I signed the deed and sealed it, took witnesses, and weighed the money in the balances. So I took the purchase deed, both that which was sealed according to the law and custom, and that which was open; and I gave the purchase deed to Baruch the son of Neriah, son of Mahseiah, in the presence of Hanameel my uncle's son, and in the presence of the witnesses who signed the purchase deed, before all the Jews who sat in the court of the prison. Then I charged Baruch before them, saying, Thus says the Lord of hosts, the God of Israel: "Take these deeds, both the purchase deed which is sealed and this deed which is open, and put them in an earthen vessel, that they may last many days." For thus says the Lord of hosts, the God of Israel: "Houses and fields and vineyards shall be possessed again in this land."*[22]

The Lord reiterates His plans to Jeremiah. Plans concerning the destruction of Jerusalem. However, He did not leave it there He makes a promise of restoration for the very Jews He will send into captivity. He states that Jerusalem: shall be delivered into the hand of the king of Babylon by the sword, by the famine, and by the pestilence.[23] However, here is His promise:

Behold, I will gather them out of all countries where I have driven them in My anger, in My fury, and in great wrath; I will bring them back to this place, and I will cause them to dwell safely. They shall be My people, and I will be their God...[24]

It is imperative to retrace these events so as to pinpoint a certain flaw in the Arabs argument. The author interviewed quite a number of Arab diplomats, most of them held fast to the position that the God of Israel put the Jews out of the land because of their idolatry and as far as they, the Arabs, are concerned the Jews are to remain outside of the land. The Arab position is inherent in their beliefs and they seek to use it to legitimise their claim on the State of Israel. However, the word of the Lord does not support this view. On the contrary, on every occasion the Jews faced Dispersion, the Lord accompanied the impending captivity with a promise of return. This fact, the international community needs to take note of.

Therefore, as it is today, when the Jewish exiles returned to Jerusalem, at the command of Cyrus, king of the Persian Empire, those aliens who were put there to live in the land after the Jews were taken away, raised furious objections to the rebuilding programmes undertaken by the Jews. The Jews were taken to Babylon by King Nebuchadnezzar and after seventy years had passed, in accordance to the word of the Lord, spoken of by His prophets, the exiles were encouraged to return to their land and to rebuild their city Jerusalem, and villages.

Isaiah the prophet records these words from the Lord:

I am the One who made the earth and created human beings to live there. By My power I stretched out the heavens; I control the sun, the moon, and the stars. I Myself have stirred Cyrus to action to fulfil My purpose and put things right. I will straighten out every road he travels. He will rebuild My city, Jerusalem, and set My captive people free. No one has hired him or bribed him to do this. The Lord Almighty has spoken.[25]

Now although the word of the Lord ordered the rebuilding of Jerusalem at that time, the process was not without controversy. The enemies of Israel made the exercise of rebuilding, a very difficult process. This reminds us of Jerusalem today! Israel faces harsh criticism, boycotts, threats, sidelined by her allies, shifts in arm sales and other bilateral agreements, and the like because of her building plans for Jerusalem and the fact that these plans are out-of-sync with the mores of the global community.

The Scriptures note: The enemies of the people of Judah and Benjamin heard that those who had returned from exile were rebuilding the Temple of the Lord, the God of Israel... Then the people who had been living in the land tried to discourage and frighten the Jews and keep them from building. They also bribed Persian government officials to work against them (the Jews). They kept on doing this throughout the reign of Emperor Cyrus and into the reign of Emperor Darius.[26]

After years of disruptions and false reports against them, the Lord granted the Jews favour with King Darius. After the Jews were ordered by King Artazerxes of Persia to stop rebuilding the city, the people took courage under King Darius and recommenced building. Meanwhile, Israel's enemies were in opposition, yet again, to the continuation of the building of homes, the Temple and businesses in Jerusalem by the Jews... sounds familiar.

Darius subsequently orders Israel's enemies to leave them alone. He states: Stay away from the Temple and do not interfere with its construction. Let the governor of Judah and the Jewish leaders rebuild the Temple of God where it stood before. I hereby command you to help them rebuild it... May the God who chose Jerusalem as the place where He is to be worshipped overthrow any king (ruler) or nation that defied this command and tries to destroy the Temple there.[27]

One can see that Jerusalem is no ordinary city. It has been established before the great metropolises of Europe and North America. Therefore, Jerusalem should not be relegated to a village or settlement. It's the City of the Great King, the Lord of hosts.

The tremendous load which Jerusalem bears, or still better – the vast power with which it is charged, history and faith, fact and legend, poetry and prose, tears and blood, sanctity and desecration – has become so real, that men of vision have anchored the world upon it, from it the world was created, from Even Hashetiya on the Temple Mount...from History: She is the chosen City.[28]

There was never any real doubt, in the mind of anyone familiar with Jewish history, or who had been a living part of that history, that the capital of Israel Reborn had to be Jerusalem. It was inconceivable that it should be otherwise. And, while the translation of this elementary historical-national truth into the hard realities of daily political practice could not be accomplished overnight, it was progressively accomplished over the years–and Jerusalem, capital of Israel, is now an accepted charting on the map of the world.[29]

Looking back on Jewish history, Judea-Samaria has always formed the heartland of this country, with Jerusalem at the centre. Historically, Judea-Samaria's hills and valleys have been the sites of innumerable events of Jewish history in the land, from Bible times down to the 21st century. Jerusalem, Bethlehem, Hebron, Jericho,

Bethel, Shiloh, Samaria and Shechem are just a few of the names linked with some 3,000 years of Jewish history in this area.[30]

Asaph, a psalmist and prophet, pleaded before the Lord on Israel's behalf centuries ago, saying to the Lord of hosts these words: *Your enemies make a tumult; and those who hate You have lifted up their head. They have taken crafty counsel against Your people, and consulted together against Your sheltered ones. They have said, "Come, and let us cut them off from being a nation, that the name of Israel may be remembered no more."*[31] Just in case you missed it, Asaph told the Lord *Your enemies*, even while speaking to Him about those who were Israel's enemies. In essence, Israel's enemies are God's enemies.

Israel, no good would come from your bending back-over to please your friends and the rest of the world. The Lord requires of you, full obedience to Him. The States you look to, will in real trouble, be unable to help you or defend you. Your security is hinged only on the power of the Lord your God. Do not trust in man: *For the Lord has rejected your trusted allies, and you will not prosper by them.*[32]

Jerusalem's title deed is still valid today. Israel, believe this indisputable fact: Jerusalem is Israel's historic and present capital. Likewise, the State of Israel is legitimately established and serves as an important member in the community of nations lending support in crises, as was the case in Haiti following the devastating earthquake that struck that nation in January 2010, sharing valuable intelligence with allies and more so, serves as a place of refuge for the downtrodden and weary...

The Lord promises Israel: *I will take pleasure in doing good things for them, and I will establish them permanently in this land... People will buy fields, and the deeds will be signed, sealed and witnessed. This will take place in the territory of Benjamin, in the villages around Jerusalem, in the towns of Judah, and in the towns in the hill country, in the foothills, and in southern Judah. I will restore the people to their land. I, the Lord, have spoken.*[33]

No doubt the Zionist movement enabled the Jews to do just what the Lord had intended... It is worth emphasising that the promises of God to Israel are everlasting. Only God, the

Sovereign Lord has the power and authority to make everlasting covenants or declarations; those of which no man can rescind!

Therefore, *the Lord made a covenant with Jacob, one that will last forever. "I will give you the land of Canaan," He said. "It will be your own possession."*[34]

Chapter 4

Israel's Relations with Her Interlocutors: Whose Interest must take Priority?

Israel: A Sign for the Global Community

In the earlier three years of Benjamin Netanyahu's reign as Israel's Prime Minister (1996-1999), he made a State visit to the People's Republic of China in 1999. He recounts the President of China Jiang Zemin, expressing his great admiration for the legacy of the Jewish people, who produced such geniuses as Albert Einstein. Further, Zemin added "The Jewish people and the Chinese people are two of the oldest civilizations on earth, dating back four thousand and five thousand years respectively." Netanyahu notes that he concurred, adding India to the list.

The Israeli Prime Minister stated in his response: But there are one or two differences between us. For instance, how many Chinese are there? 1.2 Billion, replied Zian Zemin.

How many Indians are there? About 1 billion.

Now how many Jews are there? Queried Netanyahu.

No answer.

There are 12 million Jews in the world, the Prime Minister told his host.

He relays the reaction to this shocking revelation. "Several Chinese jaws dropped in the room, understandably, given that this number could be contained in an enlarged suburb of Beijing."[1]

Can you believe it? After all the propaganda concerning Israel taking Arab land? One must be aware that the Arabs are more than 300,000,000 strong with 21 States, whereas the Jews in the Israel amount to approximately 6,000,000 with a country that totals a third of one percent of the whole land mass in the Middle East.[2] The other six million Jews are living in the Diaspora.

The Jews were re-gathered to their land for reasons beyond human compression. Two of them being:

i) For the glory of God to be exhibited in the national life of the Jewish people.
ii) For the entire world to behold the glory of God in operation in Israel and by this the nations ought to serve the God of Israel.

Aha, you may say, because this is not consistent with the principles governing international relations. Further, you may argue, States are not governed or created in this fashion. Perhaps not, except for the State of Israel.

Here is the evidence, submitted centuries before it actually happened on 14 May, 1948. God created the State of Israel by His sovereign will and for His own interest:
Before she travailed, she gave birth; before her pain came,
She delivered a male child. Who has heard such a thing? Who has seen such things?
Shall the earth be made to give birth in one day?
Or shall a nation be born in one day? Or shall a nation be born at once?
For as soon as Zion travailed, she gave birth to her children.
Shall I bring to the time of birth, and not cause delivery? Says the Lord. Shall I who cause delivery shut up the womb? Says your God.
Rejoice with Jerusalem, and be glad with her, all you who love her...
For by fire and by His sword the Lord shall judge all flesh; and the slain of the Lord shall be many.[3]

The international community must embrace this paradigm and acknowledge its relevance in the pursuance of the rule of law and international relations. God has been shut out from the affairs of men and this is what He endeavours to change. Henceforth, He starts with Israel and He is coming after your nation next... whether you are willing or not!

God extends His reasoning behind His actions. He tells His prophet Ezekiel:

Therefore say to the house of Israel, Thus says the Lord God: I do not do this for your sake, O house of Israel, but for My holy name's sake... and all the nations shall know that I am the Lord, says the Lord God, when I am hallowed in you before their eyes. For I will take you from among the nations, gather you out of all countries, and bring you into your own land... The desolate land shall be tilled instead of lying desolate in the sight of all who pass by.[4]

Breaking Trust with Israel to Appease the Arabs

The sixty-eight words in the Balfour Declaration is a reminder of broken promises by the Gentiles toward the Jews and this trend of breaking faith remains stridently entrenched, spurred on by exaggerated claims and the pandering nature of the ones who feel inclined to oblige the belligerent antisemitic whose tragic charade at violence leads to a plethora of condemnation against the Jews some of which is nuanced in the rhetoric of friends standing up to friends.

US Foreign Policy analysts Richard N. Hass President of the Council on Foreign Relations (CFR) and Martin Indyk Director of the Saban Center for Middle East Policy at the Brookings Institution wrote at the inception of Barack Obama's taking office as President of the United States in January 2009, an assessment of US foreign policy and its implications, not only for the US but the rest of the world, particularly, the Middle East.

The duo argued: The dependence of the US economy on oil is a key reason that the United States worries so much about the problems of the Middle East in the first place, and US oil consumption also helps extremists in Iran and elsewhere.[5] If the Obama administration could show that there are real payoffs for moderation, reconciliation, negotiation, and political and economic reform, it would recoup considerable US influence throughout the region.[6]

They examined Iran's hegemonic ambitions and quests for nuclear weapons and how the US can engage Iran and at the same time curtail Iran's influence on her proxies: Hamas and Hezbollah and her ties to Syria.

Hass and Indyk claim: The lack of visible progress in the negotiations, however, combined with Israel's settlement activity, has soured them on the Annapolis process. Gaining the renewed involvement of the Arab States will be easier if they see that negotiations are progressing and that settlement activity is being halted. They need to be pressed to fulfil their financial pledges to the Palestinian Authority (PA) and to engage more visibly with Israel throughout the process, not just the end.[7]

Walter Russell Mead reflects on the various players in the peace process. He notes:

Even without the damaging aftermath of eight misspent years (alluding to the Bush administration) the Israeli-Palestinian dispute will not be easily settled. Many people have tried to end it; all have failed. Direct negotiations between Arabs and Jews after World War I foundered. The British tried to square the circle of competing Palestinian and Jewish aspirations from the time of the 1917 Balfour Declaration until the ignominious collapse of their mandate in 1948. Since then, the United Nations, the United States, and the international community have struggled with the problem without managing to solve it.[8]

Mead went on to say further: Unless the Palestinians get enough of what they want from the settlement, the Israelis will not get enough of the security they seek.[9] The question for consideration today, one, most likely has never probably been asked, is: Why haven't the Arabs made room for their brothers in their territories, as Israel has had to do for the Jews who were thrown-out of Arab Middle Eastern States?

Joan Peters argues: Clearly the massive exodus of Jewish refugees from the Arab countries was triggered largely by the Arabs' own Nazi-like bursts of brutality, which had become the lot of the Jewish communities.[10] With reference to history, Peters posits: But the history is long of persecution against Jews by the

Arabs, a chronicle of "intolerable pressure" that had its beginnings in and took its inspiration from the seventh-century book of the creator of Islam.[11]

Peters speaks of a tour she took in the Middle East while working on her book: *From Time Immemorial*, she states: I came to learn that the Arabs weren't the only unfortunates who fled from their homes at the time of the Arab-Israeli War of Independence. Because I'd assumed the Arab refugees from Israel were the "Middle East refugees," I was startled to find that, also around 1948, whole Jewish populations from numerous Arab countries had been forced to flee as refugees to Israel and elsewhere in the world.[12]

Her findings during the course of her research revealed that the United Nations had made a "special" definition for the term "Arab refugee" which lacked universality or did not apply to others. In this instance, the term "Arab refugee" the definition had been broadened to include as "refugees" any person who had been in "Palestine" for only two years before Israel's statehood in 1948.[13] ...the altered "two-years-presence" definition of an "Arab refugee" implied was a direct contradiction of assumed historical factors that are the very foundation of the current Arab claim of "legitimate rights of the Palestinian people to their homeland for a thousand" or "two thousand years."[14]

Howard Grief contends: There is no logical or just reason why Arabic-speaking Gentiles should have 21 States and then be entitled to another on the basis of the existence of a fake nation of Palestinians who have been deprived of the right of self-determination. They never enjoyed that right in any part of the Jewish National Home and the land of Israel under international law, and there is not a single document of international law even today that requires it. In this regard all UN resolutions, whether emanating from the Security Council or the General Assembly, that endorse the right of "Palestinian" self-determination are not classified as international law, despite numerous assertions to the contrary. The latest international plot to re-divide the Land of Israel and establish a so-called "Palestinian State", known as the Road Map Peace Plan, is neither a treaty nor an international agreement nor even a legal document of any sort, but, as its name indicates, merely a plan, the contents of which have not been fully agreed to by one of the parties expected to carry it out – the State of Israel, as is evident from its fourteen reservations.[15]

Furthermore, Grief cites in his work, a note from British official Meinertzhagen's diary, in regard to Transjordan geographical and historical connections to Palestine and why it should never have been separated from it. Meinertzhagen notes:

Geographically, Palestine and Transjordan are one. They should have never been separated nor was their present status ever intended. Transjordan was 'jumped' with the connivance of certain British officials, and Churchill. The artificial partitioning of the Holy Land must be repugnant to many, who, like myself, regard that country as something quite unique and indivisible.[16] In another entry in his diary, this same official stated further: Transjordan should never have been severed from Palestine for *it is Palestine* (Italics in original). Abdullah is a mere upstart, a useless figurehead and could not maintain himself for an instant without British bayonets. He has no more rights to Transjordan (now Jordan) than I have.[17]

The Geopolitical Games: The Neglect of Israel after the Fact

Quite often Lord Balfour is criticised for his historic Balfour Declaration. However, do many people have the courage of this man to stand up to the status quo to do what is right? Who was Lord Balfour?

Arthur Balfour served as British Prime Minister during the period 1902-1906. His Party was the Conservative Party. It was back in 1902 when British Colonial Secretary Joseph Chamberlain sought to upgrade one of their colonies in Africa, Uganda to be precise, Chamberlain offered to place Jews there instead of granting them their inalienable right to return to their homeland. Uganda, he surmised needed settlers.[18] However, this proposal was rejected outright by the Jews in the United Kingdom. Obviously with good reason, it was not the land their God had given to their forefathers and had promised to return them to.

Then, in 1906 Balfour's government collapsed and he failed to win his re-election bid. However, something significant took place during the course of his re-election campaign. He met with Chaim Wisemann, a chemistry professor and a Zionist. After holding a meeting with Wisemann, Balfour appreciated the Jewish people's cause and the reasons for their rejection of Uganda. He wrote:

The scheme... had one serious defect. It was not Zionism. It attempted to find a home for men of Jewish religion and Jewish race in a region far removed from the country where that race was nurtured and that religion came into being. Conversations I had with Dr. Wisemann in January 1906, convinced me that history could not thus be ignored, and that if a home was to be found for the Jewish people, homeless now for nearly nineteen hundred years, it was vain to seek it anywhere but in Palestine. [19]

God granted Lord Balfour another shot at power, this time instead as serving in the position as Prime Minister, he was now the British Foreign Secretary. Consequently, on 2 November 1917, Balfour writes a letter to Lord Rothschild the head of the British Zionist Federation.[20] The letter contained the wording of the now precious words penned by a Gentile, which would eventually usher in the long desired State of Israel after it was accepted by some of Britain's allies a few years later.

The Declaration reads: His Majesty's Government view with favour the establishment in Palestine of a national home for the Jewish people, and will use their best endeavours to facilitate the achievement of this object, it being clearly understood that nothing shall be done which may prejudice the civil and religious rights of existing non-Jewish communities in Palestine, or the rights and political status enjoyed by Jews in any other country.[21]

Meanwhile, Grief submits: It is important to clarify the usage of certain terms or language in the Balfour Declaration in order to fully understand its true meaning. Prior to its adoption by the Principal Allied Powers on 24 April 1920 at the San Remo Peace Conference, the Declaration of 2 November 1917 constituted only a statement of British policy in sympathy with "Jewish Zionist aspirations", as stated in the letter containing the Balfour Declaration that was addressed to Lord Lionel Walter Rothschild, the honorary president of the English Zionist Federation, who was asked to bring it to the knowledge of the Zionist Federation of England, under the presidency of Chaim Wisemann. In its operative and affirmative part, it declared:

"His Majesty's Government view with favour the establishment in Palestine of a national home for the Jewish people, and will use their best endeavours to facilitate the achievement of this object..."[22]

Grief argues further: The intent was clear enough, namely to create a Jewish State in Palestine, as proved conclusively by the Cabinet discussions on the matter, when it was finally presented for approval on 31 October 1917.[23] Subsequently, the British Government was to become the administrators of the very instrument, to guarantee the establishment of the State of Israel as promised in the Balfour Declaration. However, Arab violence was to play a part in corrupting the British officials who eventually decided to neglect Israel. The United Nations forerunner, the League of Nations had given the British the mandate to execute its policies, under what is commonly known today as the Mandate for Palestine.

Since the Balfour Declaration did not resonate with the desires of the Arabs and since Britain's own foreign policy was to further Britannia's influence across the globe, and yet still, since Arab oil would play a critical part in this agenda, those who were at the helm did not intend to assist Israel in her pursuit to migrate to and to settle in her homeland; even in the face of the gravest human rights violation in human experience, the Holocaust. Thus a new policy document was issued, resulting in Britain walking away from Israel at a time when she needed her most.

The new policy was submitted by the Royal Commission and was embraced by the architects of the White Paper. Then as now it is still known as the British White Paper of 1939.

Quotes in the White Paper cite the recommendations and the positions of the Royal Commission, one being this example taken from the text. Section I titled: "The Constitution" notes:

"Unauthorised statements have been made to the effect that the purpose in view is to create a wholly Jewish Palestine. Phrases have been used such as that 'Palestine is to become as Jewish as England is English.' His Majesty's Government regard any such expectation as impracticable and have no such aim in view. Nor have they at any time contemplated .... the disappearance or the subordination of the Arabic population, language or culture in Palestine. They would draw attention to the fact that the terms of the (Balfour) Declaration referred to do not contemplate that Palestine as a whole should be converted into a Jewish National Home, but that such a Home should be founded IN PALESTINE."[24]

Not surprising at the turn of events, there are other instances the international community reneged on its commitments to the Jewish community. Take for example the Versailles Settlement. A series of international conferences were held between 1919 and 1923. They produced a blue print for determining who got what and why.[25]

The case of the Jews was unique because, unlike the other peoples, they were a scattered nation, exiled for many centuries from their homeland. But this in no way affected the judgement of the civilised world at the beginning of this century that the Jews were entitled to a land of their own. Moreover, it was widely recognised that they were entitled to restore their national life in their ancient homeland, Palestine, which up to 1918 was controlled by the crumbling Ottoman Empire... Zionism was accorded the kind of consideration given to other national movements seeking to realise their national goals.[26] Arising from the ashes as it were was the independence of the Baltic region, as part of the promised freedom of Versailles, to the peoples of Central and Eastern Europe. But this has not been the case with the Jewish national restoration. For what was accepted at Versailles as a just solution to the question of Jewish nationhood is today shunned by governments and chancelleries the world over.[27]

They accept, most of them, that the Jewish people are entitled to a State. But they reject the Versailles conception of the size and viability of that domain, preferring to toss the Jews a scrap at best from the original offering. The promise of Versailles to the Jewish people was that it would be allowed to build a nation in the land of Palestine–understood then to comprise both sides of the Jordan River, included the territory of the present-day States of Jordan and Israel. In fact, many people now argue that the Jews do not deserve even 20 percent of Israel, and they demand that the Jewish people be satisfied with a mere 15 percent of the original mandate. This would leave the State of Israel 10 miles wide...[28]

Those who now make such demands, albeit their prominent standing in the international community must be mad!

There is a price every nation pays for its foreign policy initiatives. And Britain paid her price, a costly one. She declined in her global influence by the end of World War II. Her loss in prestige and power has been attributed to such factors, namely; her economic decline, the cost of the war and a number of domestic challenges; in addition, she was most affected by her loss in global influence given the fact that she has had to give up or retreat from the frontline of international politics.[29] However, there may be another factor, one with spiritual implications which comes with the covenant to the Jews. Conversely, America arose to global supremacy and in the course of her rise in earlier years; this nation unyieldingly stood by Israel and supported the lone Jewish State which is truly, the only democratic State in the Mideast.

How can a nation take a 'double-turn' on a people who have supernatural covering? Whether you believe the Scriptures or not, one's wariness does not change the facts. Indeed, the pervasiveness of the conflict and the myriad of challenges may lead mortal men to contrive what they suppose were and often times still is the best solution, but to trample on God's intent so as to do *good* is not the same as doing what's right.

Consequently, every nation should study the past and learn the crucial lessons to be derived there from. Otherwise, your turn is next! God has candidly spoken saying: *I will dwell among the children of Israel and will be their God.*[30] He also says for the benefit of all concerned: *For My thoughts are not your thoughts, nor are your ways My ways, says the Lord. For as the heavens are higher than the earth, so are My ways higher than your ways, and My thoughts than your thoughts.*[31]

Friends and foes of Israel you cannot out-think God. He is Supreme! He has been and will forever be the Lord! His plans, purposes and interests will not be stopped by the actions undertaken by mankind! God's interests must always take priority!

Chapter 5

Facing Challenges within the Mideast:
A Search for New Paradigms

Antisemitism

The global forces are stacked up against the State of Israel as their efforts are well underway to create another Arab State, which would then bring the total to 22 Arab States and "sort-to-give" a "half-a" Jewish State to the Israelites. This is how the international community has resolved to deal with the perennial conflict in the Middle East, saying that a two-state solution is "inescapable" and a necessary outcome. The question is: Why do they all believe that this paradigm will work?

For more than half a century the global mass media, politicians within the international community and the large Arab propaganda machinery have been complicit in their denunciations and condemnations against the domestic policies undertaken by the Jewish government, for the furtherance of their national interest. Doing so aptly portrays Israel's activities in her homeland, illegitimate. Arab fury and orchestrated violence and terrorism against the Jews are well disseminated internationally as Israel is portrayed as a foreign entity on Arab soil. Arabs use of the term "occupation" rather than "possession" is well calculated to ostensibly sustain their overall agenda. The deference given to

the Arabs by Western powers is an enigma. They, Israel's enemies, have accused the Jews of having colonial aspirations and
have also called her a "plant" from the West into the Arab community. All nonsense of course!

Consequently, some like Jordan's King Abdullah II has repeatedly told the great powers that the world's problems are the
result of Israel. Likewise, the Middle East problems are the result
of the Jewish people. No one, absolutely, no one has publicly
challenged the king's antisementic position. There seems to be a
consensus in this regard, albeit after Hitler blamed the Jews for
Germany's problems and that of the world's, there was a similar
deafening silence. Until Hitler's actions took the lives of six million Jews, the powers at the time were reluctant to offend this
tyrant of a leader.

Israel's struggles did not begin with the likes of Hitler nor did
it end when he took his own life. Israel will outlive them all.
There is a saga in the Bible I'd like to recount for you to prove
that antisemitism is vile. There was a man whose name was
Haman the Agagite. He was an aide to King Ahasuerus. King
Ahasuerus' kingdom was quite large, it stretched from India to
Ethiopia and included Persia, today's Iran.[1] When Haman saw
that Mordecai (a Jew) did not bow or pay him homage, Haman
was filled with wrath. But he disdained to lay hands on Mordecai
alone, for they (other officials) had told him of the people of
Mordecai. Instead, Haman sought to destroy all the Jews who
were throughout the whole kingdom of Ahasuerus–the people of
Mordecai.[2]

Then Haman said to King Ahasuerus, "There is a certain
people scattered and dispersed among the people in all the
provinces of your kingdom; their laws are different from all other
people's, and they do not keep the king's laws. Therefore it is not
fitting for the king to let them remain. If it pleases the king, let a
decree be written that they be destroyed, and I will pay ten thousand talents of silver into the hands of those who do the work, to
bring it into the king's treasuries."[3]

What followed should be a warning for all of us. Haman's
despicable behaviour was initially approved by the king, however

circumstance changed for the wicked Haman and eventually he was dealt with. Here's the conclusion of the story.

Queen Esther, the young and beautiful wife of King Ahasuerus told him that should Haman's plot be enacted it would have consequences for her as well.

Then Queen Esther answered and said, "If I have found favour in your sight, O king, and if it pleases the king, let my life be given me at my petition, and my people at my request. For we have been sold, my people and I, to be destroyed, to be killed, and to be annihilated..."[4]

Now Harbonah, one of the eunuchs, said to the king, "Look! The gallows, fifty cubits (seventy-five feet) high, which Haman made for Mordecai, who spoke good on the king's behalf (saved his life) is standing at the house of Haman." Then the king said, "Hang him on it." So they hanged Haman on the gallows that he had prepared for Mordecai...[5]

The antisemite is a person who is debased. He or she blames the Jew for his/her problems and that of the wider community, he/she rejects the Jews right to exercise their freedom of religion, expression, education and the right to exist. The antisemite does not have to be offended personally by a Jew, he/she goes along with the stereotype and labels ascribed to Jews and he/she most often demands the annihilation of the Jewish race.

No doubt, Iran's President Mahmoud Ahmadinejad comes to mind at the mentioned of the term antisemite. Today's major global crisis is not caused by Zionism but by Iran's hatred for Israel and her pursuance of weapons of mass destruction (WMD), which is intended for use against the State of Israel. It will moreover, impact other States in the region and obviously the rest of the world.

Iran has publically stated that the Jewish State must be destroyed. Iran has no qualms showing 'her hand' to the international community because she is well aware that the community of nations is divided based on certain States' national interests. So although the United Nations Security Council is the body with *teeth*: of the five great powers or permanent members with veto power, at least two of can be considered friends of Iran. The remaining ten Member States making up the Security Council are termed non-permanent members. They are elected to serve a two-year term and are elected from regional groupings within the UN.

Ahmadinejad has also repeatedly stated that the Holocaust is a lie. He is mostly hinting that since the Holocaust did not completely eradicate the Jewish race, his nuclear plans will finally annihilate them. His denial, he is aware, will raise the ire of the Jews and some Gentiles, but the real intent and ambitions he seeks to press ahead with is: exactly what he has been doing, testing missiles and building nuclear sites, for use against the Israelis. One should not attempt to prove truth to someone like him. Instead, prepare for battle, because if not this "madman", then the power brokers and the Iran Revolutionary Guard (IRG) do have plans to strike Israel at an opportune time in the future. The Mullahs in Iran are unaware of this fact, like others in the past, they too will be defeated. See, there is precedence!

Prime Minister Netanyahu told the United Nations General Assembly in 2009 that the Iranian regime is fuelled by an extreme fundamentalism that burst onto the world scene three decades ago after lying dormant for centuries. In the past thirty years, this fanaticism has swept the globe with a murderous violence and cold-blooded impartiality in its choice of victims. It has callously slaughtered Moslems and Christians, Jews and Hindus, and many others. Though it comprises different offshoots, the adherents of this unforgiving creed seek to return humanity to medieval times.[6]

He warns the most urgent challenge facing this body is to prevent the tyrants of Tehran from acquiring nuclear weapons. The Israeli leader asks, are the Member States of the United Nations up to that challenge? Will the international community confront a despotism that terrorises its own people as they bravely stand up for freedom?... Will the international community thwart the world's most pernicious sponsors and practitioners of terrorism? Above all, will the international community stop the terrorist regime of Iran from developing atomic weapons, thereby endangering the peace of the entire world?[7]

In March 2010 the Israeli Prime Minister in an address to Christians in Jerusalem told them... No security challenge is more important to our common future than preventing Iran from developing nuclear weapons. I have said before and I'll say again, that the greatest threat facing mankind is the spectre of a militant Islamic regime acquiring nuclear weapons, or the spectre of nuclear weapons acquiring a militant Islamic regime. The first is dangerously close to happening in Iran, and the second may or may not happen in Pakistan. I believe that with the right policies both can be averted.[8]

Netanyahu adds: If Iran develops atomic weapons, the world would never be the same. We would witness a cascade of terrorism across the globe as terrorists would operate under an Iranian umbrella. Look at how much havoc, how much terror they sow now, when there is no such umbrella, and understand what can happen if Iran, their patron, sponsor, supplier and supporter, if that Iran had nuclear weapons. Equally, the region's vital oil supplies could be severely threatened and efforts to prevent the proliferation of nuclear weapons in the Middle East would collapse as one regime after another would rush to acquire nuclear weapons of their own. Worst of all, if nuclear weapons would be given to terrorists, or to terrorist States, a 65 year-old era of nuclear peace would be endangered for the first time. [9]

In another address, this time to the Jewish Agency Board of Governors, Netanyahu provides three major points for consideration to his audience. ... He emphasises: The third thing that we know is that they threatened to use those bombs against us and possibly as weapons of terror against anyone else they choose. This is a formidable combination. When you have no inhibition and you have far-reaching ideological, theological ambitions – the combination of a militant Islamic regime that has the weapons of mass death and could use atomic weapons, not merely to threaten directly but also to use it as weapons of nuclear terror could be a pivot of history. That too is understood in most of the capitals and by most of the leaders that I've spoken to in recent months and over the years and there is a crystallisation of an understanding.[10]

We're at that fateful point. We're at the point where the international community has to decide whether it is serious about stopping Iran. If it is serious about stopping Iran, then what it needs to do is not water-down sanctions, moderate sanctions, sanctions that will only enable people to put a 'V' around the rubric box of sanctions, but effective, biting sanctions that curtail the import and export of oil into and out of Iran. This is what is required now. It may not do the job but nothing else will. And at least we will have known that it's been tried. And if this cannot pass in the Security Council, then it should be done outside the Security Council but immediately.[11]

Have you noticed there is a stilted silence in much of the Middle East on the issue of Iran's pursuits of the bomb? The reason is that most Arab States do not admit that the Iranians have such a goal. See more on this point in the analysis section of interviews I did with key Arab diplomats. Have you noticed also that there is a strangle-hold on what ought to be "biting sanctions"? There is an endless debate on how to punish the regime's ruling elite in Iran and how to safeguard the masses from so much as "hurt," due to the imposition of sanctions. Others argue that sanctions are a waste of time and that they are ineffective. Still others believe that Iran is not pursuing WMDs, rather they express the Iranian's right to build nuclear plants for peaceful purposes. Therefore, Israel seems alone in its cry against the Islamic regime's possible nuclear military capability. This is undeniably a serious challenge, motivated by antisemitism.

The Lord Himself watches over Israel and has given His assurances that He will protect her in the day of trouble from her many enemies. The Scripture notes:

The Lord their God will save them in that day, as the flock of His people. For they shall be like the jewels of a crown, lifted up like a banner over His land...[12] Moreover, the Lord assures Israel ... for he who touches you touches the apple of His eye.[13] He promises the likes of Iran: The Lord Himself will fight against you, and you will be plundered by the people who were once your servants.[14]

Security

The urgent pursuit by one or more regimes to acquire nuclear weapons, more specifically nuclear warheads and bombs, will definitely compromise Israel's national security and this is certainly another challenge within the Middle East.

Also in the Middle East the Jews number approximately six million, within a very small territory, her Arab neighbours outnumber her 50:1. Amazing! She is outnumbered, but not weak!

There is no State in the region which can claim that Israel has threatened their security interests... Instead, Israel which has signed peace treaties with Egypt and Jordan, continually searches for ways she can further peaceful relations with her other neighbours without compromising her people and the State. While Iran has out-rightly called for Israel's destruction, Israel relies on the goodwill of the international community to gather and come up with measures that can discipline this belligerent State. Israel continues to wait.

"Never again" has been the 'promise' of the international community to safeguard Israel as well as other nations from genocide. This phrase has become synonymous with Holocaust Remembrance Day activities. The international community must recall its initial withdrawal and unconcerned manner to the plight of the Jews, until Hitler took Poland, France, The Netherlands, Denmark, Norway, and others surrendered; only then was there much activity and chatter, as to what the multilateral response would be. It was after all these events that they engaged Hitler in war. "They," like "these" now wanted peace via compromise, not war, but war became the inevitable solution. History would show that even while Jews were the main victims of Hitler's Third Reich, other free Jews assisted Britain in World War II. Jews in England, Jews in Israel and Jews in America and Jews elsewhere, helped as financiers, chemists, soldiers, and in other capacities to contribute immensely to the war efforts and the victory of the Allies, who today form the core of the UN Security Council. This core group is now obligated to help protect Israel from bellicose nations.

Time is of the essence! There is a great opportunity for the community of nations to demonstrate that it has the courage and back-bone to stand up once and for all to this impudent State, named Iran, before one life is lost, one inch conquered, one shot fired, before Israel becomes vulnerable. A paradigm shift demands that the nations be proactive, rather than apologetically reactive. One would recall that Jews gave much to the development of mankind in the sciences, and entertainment: in film, music and musical, comedy, and the like, adding to the lifespan and quality of life for individuals through laughter and excellent medical advancements. Therefore, if the nations which have been so amply blessed by the Jews in their midst, fail to respond to this nation's cry for help and protection, then it would be left to their Father in heaven to step-in and defend them and He would not ignore your ingratitude to the Jews.

Appeasement is acquiescence at its basis. History is not kind to British Prime Minister Neville Chamberlain after he acceded to Hitler's demands and he agreed to and divided one of Germany's neighbouring State, Czechoslovakia, which was actually relying on her allies for protection, instead her friends met and divided her territory and "the rest they say is history."

Strategic depth is a security concept which bears particular importance to Israel's national security interests. Moshe Aumann argues: The importance of strategic depth for Israel was underscored in the 1973 Yom Kippur War, when Israel was taken by surprise on both its northern and southern fronts. The threats posed by the advancing Egyptian and Syrian forces was neutralised, to a large extent, by their distance from the heartland of Israel, which allowed the Israeli Defence Force (IDF) the time necessary to call up its reserves, consolidate its forces and prepare its counter-offensive.[15]

Therefore, on the ground, taking Judea-Samaria as examples, they altogether 30-35 miles wide, is hardly more than 2,000 square miles in area (Luxembourg, or the State of Delaware), yet its importance to Israel's security is paramount since its mountains dominate the entire coastal plain. Under conditions of modern aerial and armoured warfare, this topographical reality, coupled with the narrowness of the coastal plain, renders Israel's major industrial and population centres virtually indefensible without security control over Judea-Samaria.[16]

Under the US, Russian, UN and EU plan, Israel's strategic depth would be compromised should they succeed with their promised Palestinian State. The Road Map initiative is not an initiative based on security for Israel, but on the fulfilment of another promise to give the Arabs another State as have already been done vis-à-vis the creation of Jordan out of Palestine.

Israel's withdrawal from Gaza brings one of Iran's proxy's closer "home" to Jewish communities. In my three visits to Sderot, I saw bomb shelters at bus stops, bomb shelters in play grounds, bomb shelters behind houses, all because the residents there have 15 seconds to flee Hamas' rockets. Outside the homes of some Jewish families the walls were filled with holes from shrapnel which came from exploded rockets. The terror there has impacted family relations; men are incapable of providing protection to their families. In many instances men, women and children have become deaf as a result of the explosions of the rockets. Fear has caused skin rashes and has had other deleterious effects on individuals. Families have been torn apart due to tensions and rage. How many foreign countries have not given their security guarantees to Israel? Have they been able to protect these Jews from Hamas? No! Instead, Israel is criticised by the international community who say she uses excessive force in combat against the terrorists. Take for example Israel's War with Hamas in 2008. How can the international community's assurances that things will be different should Israel accede to their mandates to give up Judea and Samaria? Will they then protect the Jews from Hamas in these other areas outside Gaza? When would the international community realise that there is an urgent need for a shift in their policies in the Middle East?

It must be noted that the terror against Sderot and other Jewish communities intensified after Israel's unilateral withdrawal from Gaza in 2005. More than 8,000 rockets have been fired on them between 2005 and 2010; rockets I saw at the Police Station at Sderot were stacked bent and rusted. Sderot is within a "bird's-eye view" from Gaza. The Gaza Strip is approximately one mile from Sderot.

On 9 June 2009, I interviewed a Fire Fighter whose house was destroyed by Hamas rockets on 30 December 2008. Eight rockets fell that day and he was at work putting out fires on other residents homes while his own house was being burnt (I also visited the site of his burnt out home). The house Hamas destroyed was the house this Fireman was born in and was up to then raising his family and taking care of his widowed mother who was 87 years old. Avraham Maman, age 47, married with three children was a 25 year veteran Fireman. His family's life was saved because two days before his house was struck Avraham took his family to one of the bomb shelters in Sderot at the insistence of his elderly mother.

These are serious matters. Israel's major concern is her people living in peace and security and with the likes of neighbours whose passport to *heaven* is murder, it becomes even more critical. Israel ought not be asked, forced, be demanded of, or whipped into compromising her national security interests. None of the great powers would compromise on theirs, so why do they ask a lesser power in a hostile community to do so, knowing that a Palestinian State would endanger and harm the State of Israel?

Prime Minister Netanyahu in his heavily anticipated foreign policy speech in June 2009, a mere two and a half months after his return to office as Prime Minister since 1999, opened by saying: Peace was always the desire of our people. Our prophets had a vision of peace, we greet each other with peace, our prayers end with the word peace.[17]

I am now asking that when we speak of the huge challenge of peace, we must use the simplest words possible, using person to person terms. Even with our eyes on the horizon, we must have our feet on the ground, firmly rooted in truth. The simple truth is that the root of the conflict has been and remains – refusal to recognise the right of the Jewish People to its own State in its historical homeland,[18] declares the Prime Minister.

Further, the Israeli leader told all his audiences: local and international, that Israel must govern its own fate and security. Israel could not be expected to agree to a Palestinian State without ensuring that is was demilitarised. He emphasised that this was crucial to the existence of Israel. "We must provide for our security needs." Netanyahu added further: whenever we discuss a permanent agreement, Israel needs defensible borders with Jerusalem remaining the united capital of Israel.[19]

Land

When it comes to the country, Israel, there are those who have more questions concerning the status of the land than anywhere else in the world. With regard to Jewish towns, cities and villages they label them as settlements so that these Israeli communities will not appear to have any intrinsic value when the international community decides to enforce their call for Israel's withdrawals and their "mandatory expulsions of Jews from their homes in their own State."

Today, since this chapter is designated to finding new paradigms, you'll be introduced to the correct terminology describing Israel's residency in the Holy Land. It is "possession" instead of "occupation."

Aumann, writing in his text: *Land Ownership in Palestine 1880-1948* provides quite interesting statistics on the status of the land as it was constituted in 1948, on the basis of official figures published by the outgoing British Mandatory Administration before Israel's independence. These are as follows:

i). 8.6 percent of these lands were owned by Jews

ii). 3.3 percent by Arabs

iii). 16.9 percent had been abandoned by Arab owners who imprudently heeded the call from neighbouring countries to "get out of the way" while the invading Arab armies make short shrift of Israel.

iv). The rest of the land – over 70 percent – had been vested in the Mandatory Power and, accordingly belonged now to the State of Israel as its legal heir.

v). The greatest part of this 70 percent consisted of the Negev, some 3,144,250 acres, all told, or closer to 50 percent of the 6,580,000 acres in all of Mandatory Palestine. Known as Crown or State Lands, this was mostly uninhabited and or semi-arid territory, inherited originally by the Mandatory Government from Turkey. In 1948, it passed to the Government of Israel.[20]

Moreover, another set of records produced by the Sovereign King of kings confirms that the land Israel now possesses is theirs. He provides precise records of fact, though the text is old, it is not outdated. The Sovereign states that He has the power to determine the ownership of the land, because He is the One who handed down the title deed of the land to the forefathers of the Israelites. Thus the inheritance grants the Jews full powers to govern in the land, plant in the land, live in the land, build homes and places of entertainment in the land and worship their God in the land. Therefore, this should be a closed case. He instructs concerning the contested land, accordingly:

I will bring back the captives of My people Israel; they shall build the waste cities and inhabit them; they shall plant vineyards and drink wine from them; they shall also make gardens and eat fruit from them.

I will plant them in their land, and no longer shall they be pulled up from the land I have given them, says the Lord your God.[21]

Who can contradict the Lord's intent? "Who is wise? Let him understand these things. Who is prudent? Let him know them. For the ways of the Lord are right; the righteous walk in them, but transgressors stumble in them."[22]

Here are a few questions for serious consideration.

i) How's it Jordan was never again called Palestine, after the British gave them nearly 77 percent of Palestine?

ii) How's it Mahmoud Abbas, the recognised leader of the Arabs who claim to be Palestinians, can call the State of Israel, Palestine and he omits Jordan?

iii) How it is there have never been a Palestinian people, separate and apart from those recognised by the Mandate Authority as Palestinian Jews and Palestinian Arabs, so named prior to 1948 given the fact they resided in the land? Who are today's Palestinians?

iv) Is the conflict agenda being driven by the mass media or by the politicians? Whose agenda is it anyway? What are the gains in keeping the conflict sustained?

v) Finally, why do most people have trouble acknowledging and recognising the State of Israel?

In our world, things are never what they appear to be. There is no conspiracy theory being proffered here but one can only conclude that the Arab-Israeli conflict has been based on a *farce* played by certain global interests and their target is Israel. The conflict engages the entire world and without it what would international relations be like? The great powers would then have to solve the troubles in The Sudan and elsewhere in Africa, assist the poor in the Delta, Asia and elsewhere, deal with crimes against women and the girl child, find solutions to the violence caused by small arms and light weapons, and the myriad of other international troubles that go repeatedly unreported or underreported, including murders of Christians in Asia and Africa by Muslims, and so on.

The Arab-Israeli conflict is fuelled by oil resources and it's "sexy". So, would it be resolved? Not in a hurry! As Abbas by his own admission rejected Netanyahu's immediate successor, Ehud Olmert's, offer of 97 percent of the land the Arabs were asking for. Abbas said the gap was too wide. I heard no condemnation to Abbas' folly, yet as soon as Netanyahu was re-elected to office as Prime Minister in 2009, after a decade since he served in this capacity; I recall almost all of Europe's leaders expressing alarm. They were more concerned about the Arabs than the right of the Jews to exercise their constitutional democratic rights, as is expressed as a Western value. These leaders demanded an immediate declaration of recognition of the Two-State Solution from Netanyahu but they did not also demand that Abbas and the other Palestinians recognise the right of the Jewish State to exist.

Aumann, in his closing arguments (in *Land Ownership...*) cites a quotation from an article written by an Algerian-in-exile Abdel Razak Kader. In it the Algerian makes a poignant point:

The nationalists of the States neighbouring on Israel, whether they are in the government or in business, whether Palestinian, Syrian or Lebanese, or town dwellers of tribal origin, all know that at the beginning of the century and during the British Mandate the marshy plains and stony hills were sold to the Zionists by their fathers or uncles for gold – the very gold which is often the origin of their own political or commercial careers. The nomadic or semi-nomadic peasants who in-

habited the frontier regions know full well what the green plains, the afforested hills and the flowering fields of today's Israel were like before.

The Palestinians who are today refugees in the neighbouring countries and who were adults at the time of their flight know all this, and no anti-Zionist propaganda – pan-Arab or pan-Muslim – can make them forget that their present nationalist exploiters are the worthy sons of their feudal exploiters of yesterday, and that the thorns of their life are of Arab, not Jewish, origin.[23]

Obama's Posture

Almost everyone in Israel and even analysts in the United States are saying the Obama Administration has had the 'coolest relations' in several decades with Israel, the US' long-time ally.

He stands tall, supposedly at 6 & 1 ½ feet, his swagger and athletic moves bring him notice. Yes, of course he is currently the most powerful man in the world, as he is the leader of the greatest nation ever, on earth. Barack Hussein Obama is the 44th President of the United States a single but powerful territory with tremendous global influence.

Obama hit the political scene running with the agenda of change. His philosophy of change to US domestic and foreign policy approaches, he anticipates, would improve America's image. This would also certainly bring about a paradigm shift in US-Israel relations. The crucial question is, would Obama's policy shift be helpful to Israel or not?

While Obama was president-elect awaiting to be sworn-in as the next US President, there were numerous editorials and articles written in various places on his posture especially in regard to the Arab-Israeli conflict. One such article by Nicole Jansezian writing for the magazine *Israel Today* commented saying: While Israeli leaders welcomed Obama's election and said they expect the "special strategic relationship" between the two countries to continue, signs of strain quickly emerged. A day after the election, Foreign Minister (of then, Prime Minister Ehud Olmert's government) Tzipi Livini publically condemned Obama's plans to talk to Iran.[24]

Jansezian adds: A poll showed that 76 percent of American voters in Israel cast their ballots for Bush's fellow Republican

John McCain, but American Jews voted on domestic issues and put Israel on the back burner. Polls show that some 78 percent of American Jews voted for Obama.[25]

Meanwhile, in his inaugural address Obama speaking about an era of peace encouraged the Muslim community to accept the new posture his Administration represented. His stance was one of reaching out with friendship. He assured them, then, and many times since that America was not at war with Islam but with extremist elements.

There is a Proverb that provides insight into the differences between man and God. It submits that:

All the ways of a man are pure in his own eyes,
But the Lord weighs the spirits.[26]

One month after Obama took office, Israel's Prime Minister, Netanyahu pledges to work with Obama for peace. The Israeli leader quoted in the Haaretz newspaper stated: I intend and expect to co-operate with the Obama administration and to try to advance the common goals of peace, security and prosperity for us and our neighbours.[27]

Netanyahu also said he wanted to shift the focus of stalled US-sponsored peace talks with the Palestinians away from tough territorial issues to shoring up their economy, an approach their leaders have rejected.[28] The Haaretz recalls that: As prime minister from 1996-1999, Netanyahu clashed with the Clinton administration but bowed to US pressure and handed over parts of Hebron to Palestinian rule.[29]

For weeks after Obama took office there was much speculation in the mass media concerning US-Israel relations and as Netanyahu's visit to the White House loomed on 18 May 2009, his first, since Obama took office and since his own re-election, the pending visit almost sounded as though there was a major storm on the horizon.

In the wake of all this frenzy: reports coming to Jerusalem via European diplomats indicated that some on Obama's team are prepared to live with a nuclear Iran. "Better an Iran with a bomb than the bombing of Iran," they were counselling the president. Meanwhile, Netanyahu's advisers were quietly frustrated that they had to learn such insights second-hand, as Obama had already

made a number of moves in the Middle East without first con-
sulting Jerusalem – a sharp departure from the Bush presidency.
They learned through the press that Obama has secretly dis-
patched Dennis Ross, his special envoy on Iran, to the Gulf States
to discuss strategy. Two senior American envoys also were sent
on another mission to Damascus. In addition, Obama had dis-
creetly asked the Arab League (through Jordan's King Abdullah
II) and the Madrid Quartet to consider revising their respective
plans for ending the Israeli-Palestinian conflict. Finally, Jerusalem
was caught completely off guard when a US official called on
Israel to sign the Nuclear Non-Proliferation Treaty (NPT), a
move that drew into question one of the core elements of Israel's
special relationship with the US – the guarding of its policy of
nuclear ambiguity.[30]

During their four hour long meeting – Obama and
Netanyahu, David Parson notes: As expected Netanyahu stood
fast on refusing to commit to the goal of a Palestinian statehood,
in spite of Obama's insistence that it is the only way forward.
Netanyahu believes the term "State" could be too easily defined
as full sovereignty, and thus he first wants to spell out its security
limitations. This is especially so after Palestinian leader Mahmoud
Abbas made it clear that he has no plans to recognise Israel as a
"Jewish State."[31]

Jan Willen van der Hoeven captures the mood between the
two leaders as they sat together at their 18 May press conference
at the White House. He notes prior to his visit Netanyahu had
sent out word to the US saying: If you don't stop Iran, I'll have
to. Obama responded: Get on with the two-state solution, and
we'll be better able to deal with Tehran.[32]

Furthermore, Netanyahu said "the worst danger Israel faces is
that Iran would develop nuclear military capabilities." "Iran
openly calls for our destruction, which is unacceptable... if Iran
were to acquire nuclear weapons, it could give a nuclear umbrella
to terrorists or worst, could actually give them nuclear weapons.
And that would put us all in great peril."[33] Netanyahu's position
maintains Jan Willen, was that it was necessary to deal with Iran
first, and with the "Palestinian" question later. Obama publically
disputed him saying... "To the extent we can make peace with

the Palestinians – between the Palestinians and the Israelis, then I actually think it strengthens our hand in the international community in dealing with the potential Iranian threat."[34]

Two days after meeting with the Israeli Prime Minister, points from Obama's maiden Middle East speech particularly intended to address his Muslim audience, were in circulation in the media. It was reported that Obama met and consulted with Jordan's King Abdullah II therefore some his initiatives were formulated on the king's viewpoints.

The Obama-Abdullah plan was put together in response to concerns from both Israel and US that the Arab plan was too general and intransigent.

The initiative, which Obama is expected to present in his Cairo speech in three weeks, reportedly sets out conditions for a demilitarized Palestinian state, with east Jerusalem as its capital.

The matter of borders will be solved by territorial exchanges between Israel and the Palestinians, and the Old City will be established as an international zone. The plan also allows for a limited Palestinian right of return.

Reports of the US president's new initiative surfaced as Prime Minister Binyamin Netanyahu was meeting with Obama in Washington earlier this week. During his visit, Obama emphasized his commitment to a two-state solution. Netanyahu reiterated his goal to live side-by-side with the Palestinians, though he did not specifically mention a two-state solution.[35]

At the Cairo University in Egypt, Obama declares that:

We meet at a time of tension between the United States and Muslims around the world - tension rooted in historical forces that go beyond any current policy debate. The relationship between Islam and the west includes centuries of co-existence and co-operation, but also conflict and religious wars. More recently, tension has been fed by colonialism that denied rights and opportunities to many Muslims, and a cold war in which Muslim-majority countries were too often treated as proxies without regard to their own aspirations. Moreover, the sweeping change brought by modernity and globalization led many Muslims to view the west as hostile to the traditions of Islam. [36]

I have come here to seek a new beginning between the United States and Muslims around the world; one based upon mutual interest and mutual respect; and one based upon the truth that America and Islam are not exclusive, and need not be in competition. Instead, they overlap, and share common principles - principles of justice and progress; tolerance and the dignity of all human beings. [37]

Are there really similarities and "shared common principles" between America and Islam on: values, love, life, freedom, liberty, tolerance, justice and human dignity? Thought not!

On the question of Palestinian statehood, President Obama also stresses that:

For decades, there has been a stalemate: two peoples with legitimate aspirations, each with a painful history that makes compromise elusive. It is easy to point fingers - for Palestinians to point to the displacement brought by Israel's founding and for Israelis to point to the constant hostility and attacks throughout its history from within its borders as well as beyond. But if we see this conflict only from one side or the other, then we will be blind to the truth: the only resolution is for the aspirations of both sides to be met through two states, where Israelis and Palestinians each live in peace and security.

That is in Israel's interest, Palestine's interest, America's interest, and the world's interest. That is why I intend to personally pursue this outcome with all the patience that the task requires. The obligations that the parties have agreed to under the road map are clear. For peace to come, it is time for them - and all of us - to live up to our responsibilities. [38]

With regard to the questions of settlements, President Obama's views clash with Israel's domestic position. The Jerusalem Post cites: "The demand for a freeze would have only one quick effect: to create immediate tension between the United States and Israel's new government," wrote Elliott Abrams (the deputy national security adviser under former US president George Bush). "That may be precisely why some propose it, but it is also why the Obama administration should reject it."

Abrams proved prophetic: the issue has indeed created immediate tension with the US, not over illegal outposts - Prime

Minister Binyamin Netanyahu has made it clear he will remove them - but over "natural growth" in the settlements.

The question is why the US is looking for this fight, and why Obama has not heeded Abrams's advice and rejected those pushing him in a confrontation over the matter. [39]

Further, the question being asked is:

But what if Obama, as some maintain, is actually looking for a public fight with Israel on this issue in order to win credit with the Arab world, and legitimacy among the Europeans as a leader who is willing to take Israel on when necessary?

That could be a tricky tactic, because if the US president picks a fight with Israel over the natural growth issue at a time when Israel has declared it won't build new settlements, expropriate land or give incentives to move there, then it could be perceived among some Obama supporters in Congress as being unfairly tough on Israel, especially since various verbal understandings were made over the years that Israel interpreted as a green light for natural growth. [40]

It seems from all indication that the Obama enigma has forced Congress in April 2010 to send a strong message of support to the Israelis given the uncertainity of the long-standing US-Israel bond. The Congressional letters were addressed to Secretary of State Hillary Clinton as a powerful response objecting to the Obama administration shift in US policy. They stress the strong and enduring US-Israel relationship, and object to the current emphasis on pressuring Israel by making demands for precondi-tions in order to entice the Palestinians to the negotiating table.[41] The Congressional letters were signed by 75 percent of the 333 Members of the House of Representative and 76 Senators.[42]

Let's see whether the bond that held US-Israel relations in the past, would still be 'good to hold' or whether it would be loosened at the end of Obama's presidency, following his para-digm shifts.

Overall, the world needs to alter its radical posture against Israel in relation to antisemitism, security, land and Israel's right to exist. Otherwise, the global community's stance would en-courage greater hostilities against Israel rather than their desired bid to end the Arab-Israeli conflict.

Section 3
The Region

Chapter 6

Israel: God's Witness in the Middle East

The Location of Israel is Divinely Orchestrated

Israel is located in the heart of the world and it's the most coveted piece of real estate in all of world history. Only, Israel is not for sale! So the fact that there are others who have laid claim to this territory and are willing to contend for it makes the territory a volatile place. It also emphasises the struggle that Israel faces, as it's inherent in her name.

Whatever happens in Israel does not remain there. Things have a way of spiralling out to the north, south, east and west, affecting all of mankind, those great and small. Some people are quite ignorant about the domestic affairs of their neighbouring countries, yes, those on their immediate borders, but these same people know of Israel and they express their opinion as to what they believe must be done there... they blog on these matters on the internet, airing their views and often assuming the roles as Israel's judge and the Arab appeaser. This shows that not only state leaders have a stake in these matters but the common man as well.

God has never been known to shy away from controversy. The Sovereign Lord knows all things and despite what may appear to be or seen to be coincidental does provide God with the opportunity to advance His interests. It was God who created the whole world and He gave this land in a covenant to Abraham, Isaac and Jacob. He renewed same to Moses and the descendants of Israel that followed. Therefore, there must be a reason for the Jews return to their land.

No! You think the reason is to cause trouble, to destabilise the world, to upset the status quo, to alter the peaceful easy-going trends in the region, well, none of these assumptions would apply.

From the beginning of time, God created mankind so as to form a holy relationship with man; one where He would relate His divine love and shower man with His affection and blessing. It was never God's intent to be at wrath with man. However, things did not remain as God had planned.

Before man was created there was darkness in the world and after man's creation another form of darkness appeared.

The first was physical darkness. *In the beginning when God created the universe, the earth was formless and desolate. The raging ocean that covered everything was engulfed in total darkness, and the Spirit of God was moving over the water.*[1] This condition was changed by God Himself who commanded change and as He spoke that which was corrupted, changed, there was light: the sun and moon, day and night, there was dry ground, seas and oceans were put in their place so that they could function effectively, the ground became fertile and fruitful, and animals, birds and mankind were added to the mix.

The other form of darkness is spiritual darkness. Paul describes the saga of man's existence and he elaborates on the principles which foster spiritual darkness:

God's anger is revealed from heaven against all sin and evil of the people whose evil ways prevent the truth from being known. God punishes them, because what can be known about God is plain to them, for God Himself made it plain. Ever since God created the world, His invisible qualities, both His eternal power and His divine nature, have been clearly seen; they are perceived in the things that God has made. So that those people have no excuse at all! They know God, but they do not give Him the honour that belongs to Him, nor do they thank Him. Instead, their thoughts have become complete nonsense, and their empty minds are filled with darkness. They say that they are wise, but they are fools; instead of worshipping the immortal God, they worship images made to look like mortals or birds or animals or reptiles.[2]

The Middle East is a haven for God's wrath. It is perennially idolatrous and the dominant people there are oblivious to the fact that they are about to face the wrath of God. Indeed, the doctrine of the Arabs is that they serve the *one god*. This god goes by a different name and he is not the God of Israel. How can one know this? Just look at the character of this god, look at the tenets the Arabs espoused about their god! They will argue that they have no idols, but what is not of God and that that which is the object of man's worship and praise is idolatry, and this is sin. The God, everyman, everywhere, is commanded to serve is the God of Israel, who is also known as the Lord!

Cogently, God from the very beginning has had a plan, and in His plan Israel was created to be His priests to the nations and so Israel is back as a State in the region as a witness of the Sovereign God to her neighbours. Though small in number, just approximately 6,000,000 million Jews, they have returned home to show the 300,000,000 million errant Arabs the True and Living God.

How Idolatry Cost Israel Her Home in the Middle East 2,000 Years Ago

The Holy Bible is filled with accounts of God's glory. The glory Israel's forefathers witnessed firsthand in: Egypt, the desert and in the land of Canaan. Yet, something went wrong.

When God had spoken with Abraham about the land He was giving to him there were people living in the land. Nevertheless, God being Sovereign chose to do just what was at His pleasure. The people of the land lived sinful lives and so God in His mercy gave them time to have a change of heart, but they continued in their idolatry. He gave these Gentiles four hundred years to change from their idolatrous ways. God shares with Abraham (whose name at this time was Abram) a plan to fully destroy these people by use of the descendants and heirs of the covenant. God will take Abraham's descendants to Egypt, nurture them there, and subsequently ruin the Egyptian economy because of the way they will treat God's people and then lead the great exodus of the Jews from Egypt. You may recall that ancient Egypt was also an idolatrous nation. The Egyptians believed that Pharaoh was a god among the many gods of the land. With time God fulfilled His plans against the inhabitants of the land of Canaan as He had said. God told Abraham earlier:

Know certainly that your descendants will be strangers in a land that is not theirs, and will serve them, and they will afflict them four hundred years. And also the nation whom they serve I will judge; afterward they shall return here, for the iniquity of the Amorites is not yet complete.[3]

God miraculously releases Israel from their bondage in Egypt, one that lasted 430 years. God gives to Moses, their leader His laws, His statutes, His commands and His judgements which He required that Moses teach to His people. In the handing down of the law God makes a commitment that is amazing. He promises to fight Israel's battles for her. All those she will encounter along the way to the land of Canaan as well as in Canaan. He also takes the time to warn the people against the worship of the gods of those Gentiles. Also key, God commands Israel not to enter into any agreements or treaties with these pagans.

God tells Moses:

I will fight against all your enemies. My angel will go ahead of you and take you into the land of the Amorites, the Hittites, the Perizzites, the Canaanites, the Hivites, and the Jebusites, and I will destroy them. Do not bow down to their gods or worship them, and do not adopt their religious practices. Destroy their gods and break down their sacred stone pillars. If you worship Me, the Lord your God, I will bless you with food and water and take away all your sicknesses... I will make the people who oppose you afraid of Me; I will bring confusion among the people against whom you fight, and I will make all your enemies turn and run from you. I will throw your enemies into panic... I will give you power over the inhabitants of the land, and you will drive out as you advance. Do not make any agreement with them or with their gods. Do not let those people live in your country; if you do, they will make you sin against Me. If you worship their gods, it will be a fatal trap for you.[4]

The territory or State of Israel was meant to be a purely Jewish State. Aliens choosing to live among the inhabitants were to live peacefully with the people of God but it was to remain a

Jewish State in which the God of Israel reigns as their King. There were to be no other gods in the land. Israel was ordered not to tolerate other gods and or people of other gods in their territory! It does apply today! Aha! You may say 'this is all nonsense' or it does not apply to our modern world. Well, God does not change, He is eternal, and He is righteous and He will always be righteous. Consequently, neither Israel nor its city Jerusalem is for Jews and Muslims! Not according to the uncompromising word of God. Its solely Jewish inheritance! God in His jealously will not flex on the notion that there may be some *other god*. He categorically maintains that there is no other God beside Himself!

Prior to Israel taking possession of the land, God establishes the ground rules for prosperity and for maintaining a hold on His property. He stridently reminded the Israelites of His covenants but His words *fell on deaf ears*. Remember it was mentioned earlier that God is not One to shy away from controversy, so when He appointed Jeremiah the prophet to speak to the people about their sin, He tells Jeremiah how difficult the task would be. He says:

Get ready, Jeremiah; go and tell them everything I command you to say. Do not be afraid of them now, or I will make you even more afraid when you are with them. Listen, Jeremiah! Everyone in this land – the kings of Judah, the officials, the priests, and the people – will be against you. But today I am giving you the strength to resist them; you will be like a fortified city, an iron pillar, and a bronze wall. They will not defeat you, for I will be with you to protect you. I, the Lord, have spoken.[5]

Eventually, their idolatry did cause them to be led away as captives to Assyria and Babylon.

In real confrontation God vs. the idols, God uses His prophet Elijah to show the Israelites who is God. This showdown takes place during the reign of Ahab, king of the northern kingdom of Israel. Ahab's wife was the wicked queen, Jezebel.

The territory was divided into two kingdoms following the death of King Solomon: one was the northern kingdom of Israel, called Samaria, and the other the southern kingdom of Judah with its capital being Jerusalem. All of the kings of the northern kingdom engaged in idol worship, each one committing more evil than their predecessors. On the other hand, many of the kings of the southern kingdom in Jerusalem, in Judah, led the people in the way of the Lord, their God.

Jezebel had massacred quite a number of the prophets in Israel, so she could advance in the country her idolatry. Concerning Ahab, the Scripture goes back to the legacy his father left him. It points out that:

Omri (Ahab's father) did evil in the eyes of the Lord, and did worst than all who were before him... provoking the Lord God of Israel to anger with their idols.[6]

Ahab's legacy was just as pathetic as his father's, in fact worst, during his twenty-five year reign. The Scriptures note the following: *Now Ahab the son of Omri did evil in the sight of the Lord, more than all those who were before him.*[7].. *He took as wife Jezebel the daughter of Ethbaal, king of the Sidonians; and he went and served Baal, and worship him. Then he set up an altar for Baal in the temple of Baal, which he had built in Samaria.*[8]

Elijah the Tishbite, of Gilead confronts the king. Not too many brave people are around who would confront a State leader to tell him of God's laws and statutes. First of all, Elijah declares that there will be a famine in the country which would last for three years. This servant of the Living God so declared, and there was no other god that possessed the power to alter, amend or change this edict. Indeed, there was no other god to do so.

When the three year period had ended, God did not grant the return of His dew and rain to a condition that was displeasing to Him, He made Elijah do the unthinkable. Elijah called for a public contest so that God could display His majesty and awesome power before the people. This was to help the people come to the realisation as to who was indeed God.

So Ahab sent for all the children of Israel, and gathered the prophets together on Mount Carmel.

And Elijah came to all the people, and said, How long will you falter between two opinions? If the Lord is God, follow Him; but if Baal, then follow him. But the people answered him not a word.[9]

Consequently, Elijah told the false prophets to kill a bull for a sacrifice to Baal, only, as a caveat he instructed them not to light a fire to the sacrifice. Well, from morning to early evening the prophets of Baal, which numbered more than four hundred and fifty men, were unable to stir their god to answer them. Although they wept loudly, cut themselves and leaped in the air, Baal did not answer. He could not, for he was a fiction of their imagination, he was unreal.

Meanwhile, at the time of the evening sacrifice, the God of Israel displays His glory and He answered the lone voice of Elijah. A lesson can be learnt here, God hears the call of the multitude as well as the individual. After killing his sacrifice, Elijah commands the people to pour water on it and the wood. The area was filled and overflowed all around the altar. Recorded is the prayer of Elijah and God's response. See, by whom the prophet calls on God. Elijah says,

Lord God of Abraham, Isaac and Israel, let it be known this day that You are God in Israel, and that I am Your servant, and that I have done all these things at Your word.

Hear me, O Lord, hear me, that this people may know that You are the Lord God, and that You have turned their hearts back to You again.

Then the fire of the Lord fell and consumed the burnt sacrifice, and the wood and the stones and the dust, and it licked up the water that was in the trench.

Now when all the people saw it, they fell on their faces; and they said, "The Lord, He is God! The Lord He is God!"[10]

After this magnificent act by God, Elijah was emboldened. He ordered the people to capture the false prophets of Baal and he killed them down at the Book of Kishon. This act removed the curse from the land and God lifted the famine and provided for the people.

It's imperative to appreciate this fundamental truth, no country has at any time ever had two reigning kings, two presidents or prime ministers in office at the same time, nor can there be two God (s) at the same time. God has established for the record that He alone is God! And though it's hard to swallow, you have to accept that He has identified Himself as the God of Israel. Otherwise, any other being or thing that is the object of your worship is not God. Consequently, if not God, then you are guilty of idolatry!

Would the Arabs want to put their god on a test with the God of Israel? Would their god answer their pleas? Can he be relied upon?

The Scriptures note that the God of Israel:

Has made the earth by His power; He has established the world by His wisdom, and stretched out the heaven by His understanding.

When He utters His voice – There is a multitude of waters in the heavens: He causes the vapours to ascend from the ends of the earth; He makes lightnings for the rain; He brings the wind out of His treasures. ...

The Lord of hosts is His name.[10]

The Legacy of the God of Israel: Lessons Learnt

The God of Israel had on numerous times and in various fashion appeared to His people. God is real! The tumultuous relations between real-living-people and their God serve as a lesson for us. Israel learnt its lesson and today they make a concerted effort to bow only to the God of their fathers; Him whose name is the God of Abraham, the God of Isaac and the God of Israel.

Pagans worship wood, stones, trees, reptiles, animals, the sun, the moon and stars, great leaders and so forth. Who is He that the Middle East must worship? Henceforth, Israel! Who is He that you and the rest of the world must worship? Henceforth, Israel! For additional support to Israel, are those who love the Lord from among the Gentiles. Israel was given the testimony to bring God's light to the Mideast and the world. God tells Israel:

You are My witnesses, says the Lord, and My servant whom I have chosen, that you may know and believe Me, and understand that I am He. Before Me there was no God formed, nor shall there be after Me.

I, even I, am the Lord, and besides Me there is no saviour.

I have declared and saved, I have proclaimed, and there was no foreign god among you; therefore you are My witnesses, says the Lord, that I am God.

Indeed before the day was, I am He; and there is no one who can deliver out of My hand; I work, and who will reverse it?[11]

God is really not One to back down! He lays down the gauntlet. He sends forth a challenge to the nations, who is he that will oppose Him? This is His fight! He advances:

Thus says the Lord, the King of Israel, and his Redeemer, the Lord of hosts: I am the First and I am the Last; besides Me there is no God... Is there a God besides Me? Indeed there is no other Rock; I know not one.[12]

The testimony of a few witnesses of God's glory is captured here:

1st Account:

Moses, Aaron, Nadab, Abihu and seventy of the leaders of Israel went up the mountain and they saw the God of Israel. Beneath His feet was what looked like a pavement of sapphire, as blue as the sky. God did not harm these leading men of Israel; they saw God, and then they ate and drank together.[13]

2nd Account:

David calls out to God...

In my distress I called upon the Lord, and cried out to my God; He heard my voice from His temple, and my cry came before Him, even to His ears.

Then the earth shook and trembled; the foundations of the hills also quaked and were shaken, because He was angry.

Smoke went up from His nostrils, and devouring fire from His mouth; coals were kindled by it.

He bowed the heavens also, and came down with darkness under His feet.

And He rode upon a cherub, and flew; He flew upon the wings of the wind...

He sent from above, He took me; He drew me out of many waters.

He delivers me from my strong enemy, from those who hated me, for they were too strong for me.[14]

3rd Account:

A Gentile king...

Then Darius wrote to the people of all nations, races and languages on earth:

Greetings! I command that throughout my empire everyone should fear and respect Daniel's God.

He is a living God, and He will rule forever. His kingdom will never be destroyed, and His power will never come to an end.

He saves and rescues; He performs wonders and miracles in heaven and on earth. He saved Daniel from being killed by the lions.[15]

Israel is a beneficiary of God's glory, miracles and mercy. Israel is back in the land given them by God and Israel is left with no other choice but to depend on Him who created them and established them in the Holy Land.

Israel's Prime Minister Benjamin Netanyahu in a meeting in March 2010 in the capital of the United States, Washington D.C., told the gathering; we (the Jews) must defend ourselves against lies and vilifications. Throughout history, the slanders against the Jewish people always preceded the physical assaults against us and were used to justify these assaults. The Jews were called the well-poisoners of mankind, the fomenters of instability, the source of all evil under the sun.

Netanyahu contends further, unfortunately, these libellous attacks against the Jewish people also did not end with the creation of Israel. For a time, overt antisemitism was held in check by the shame and shock of the Holocaust. But only for a time. In recent decades the hatred of the Jews has re-emerged with increasing force, but with an insidious twist. It is not merely directed at the Jewish people but increasingly at the Jewish State. In its most pernicious form, it argues that if only Israel did not exist, many of the world's problems would go away.[16]

Israel is here to stay. God will avenge them of their adversaries. God has offered His services and has to protect His reputation. Just as David called on the name of His God and God shook the entire earth to rescue him from his enemies, God would do much more for the entire nation of Israel.

God affirms His unique relationship with Israel. He says: *Once again they will live under my protection. They will grow crops of grain and be fruitful like a vineyard. They will be as famous as the wine of Lebanon.*

The people of Israel will have nothing more to do with idols; I will answer their prayers and take care of them. Like an evergreen tree I will shelter them; I am the source of all their blessings.[17]

This promise is guaranteed! Remember, Israel's location in the world. It's at the heart! No one can live without their heart. The heart is the instrument that keeps the blood flowing to all the organs of the body. Hence, destroy Israel, you will be destroying your own life... you cannot live without your heart. Israel is the life blood God established for the nations. Israel's encounters with God tell us of His earnest desire for our worship and service to Him alone. No group, enemy or other, will God allow to destroy His people, Israel. They are here at His initiative. Israel is at your heart! Israel's existence is testimony that God is real and that beside Him there is no other God!

Chapter 7

The Region's Dangerous Influence on the International Community

The Entrenched Denial of Israel Ties and Rights

The concerted attempt to annihilate one race of human beings from the midst of humanity is most appalling. It tells us something about human beings. Why would those that hate Israel, hate the Jewish people so much? It is this hatred that has the world in conflict and those human beings who are purported to be decent are caught in the mire as their meagre attempts to resolve the conflict only exacerbates it.

This haunt against Israel stems from the fact that the region is richly endowed with oil and men have used it to corrupt the entire world in order to maintain certain leverage over Israel and the West. Oil is a powerful natural resource. It has been used to power the industrialised countries and take them to higher levels of development unknown to man. Oil has given the nomadic tribes of the desert, stability and affluence. They have become traders and great bargainers and so bargain they do: not only for higher oil prices, but to maintain the status quo in the way they treat women and girls, they use their wealth to buy the luxuries and tastes of the West and to corrupt an entire international system over their row for territory, i.e., for the State of Israel in Arab-heartland.

At the United Nations, despite the subject matter under consideration within the various Committees, be sure the Arabs would insert in their statements some condemnation or a point of reference against Israel. They have deliberately hijacked the international community. As such a "paralyzed" world cannot stand to resist this evil force or influence.

Consequently, powerful nations have insisted that it's in their national interest for them to ensure that there is:

i)   Stability on the oil prices.
ii) Stability in the region so that oil production is not disrupted.
iii) Israel complies with Arab demands, so as to keep Saudi Arabia and the other Arabs happy.
iv) No shift in one's country position in the region so that 'the one that is the hegemon' does not lose it to other aspirants: they all vive to pander to the Arabs.
v)   There are concerted efforts to bar 'hate' speech against these people religion. Whereas who cares what is said of the others?

Look at the Caribbean and Africa. Which Western power has adjusted its foreign policy to meet the demands of these two groupings? None! In fact these 'poor' countries are required to play by the rules these BIG guys write for them. Take for example, Off Shore Banking. The Caribbean wanted to diversify from its dependency on agriculture given its proximity to the United States and that country's dumping policies. US products that land in these Small States are sold cheaply and thus place local farmers at a distinct disadvantage.

Henceforth, despite complaints by the region's leaders to the US about unfair trade practices and dumping, subsidies and other policies that give the US farmers greater advantages over developing countries, there has not been a major shift in these arrangements to level the playing field.

Consequently, the region decided to capitalise on tourism and off shore banking. Well, since then there have been penalties instituted for nationals from rich countries who are found to be and are caught avoiding their tax obligations to their States. Likewise, there are also penalties for these Small States who are suspected of being complicit in violating 'the domestic laws' of BIG nations, ask the Organisation for Economic Cooperation and Development (OECD), some of whose members include the United States, the United Kingdom, Germany, France, Italy, Mexico, Canada and others. The OECD monitors the global economic and social environments and creates the rules under which the state of affairs must be governed.

On the other hand, these same BIG powers adjust their consciences and their policies for Arab oil. Indeed, they are paying with hard currency, but in order to pay cheaply and to obtain oil on demand, they dance to the tune of their Arab trade partners. Unfair, you say? Perhaps!

So Israel is played by the Gentiles as they collectively marry their interests at the expense of hers. Israel's plea is for her right to exist as the lone Jewish State in the world. Is this too much to ask an indulgent, self-aggrandising international community? The gluttonous attempt to swallow up a small and already divided State is the debacle of our times.

What makes the international system unsafe is the fact that among those who have arisen to power there are those who are deficient in the inherent attributes of good leadership. Therefore, policies, initiatives, agreements, treaties and other forms of multilateral frameworks are designed with rewarding or condoning certain interests and punishing others. They are unwilling to upset the international agenda and bring about true change, change based on righteousness, godliness and virtues that come from God. They are afraid to or unwilling to publically acknowledge the presence, existence and holiness of God. Whenever, they attempt to speak about Him, the content is nuanced so that no one would be offended. Meanwhile, God says that He alone is God and beside Him there is none other. He has chosen to identify Himself with Israel and has stated over and over again that He is the God of Israel. Like it or not!

Israel is the object of global scorn and the country under siege! Opposition, false accusations, blame, hateful speech, murder, expulsions and the Holocaust have been some of the crimes committed against the Jews in the centuries gone by, when there was no Jewish State.

Now that there is a Jewish State, many of these crimes still persist today. In addition, Israel must confront the jihadists and Islamic terrorists which are instruments designed to destroy the State of Israel.

There are Arabs who believe that Islam must reign throughout the world and all the *infidels who run-things* in Washington, London, Paris, Brussels, the entire Western civilisation must submit to Islam... at the moment the thrust is being played out as the Israel-Arab controversy but in time to come those who are ambitious would use another paradigm to advance their cause far beyond this region. Nevertheless, their endeavours will be stymied by a greater agenda. God's!

There is Nothing New under the Sun

In this segment we'll take a walk through ancient times and see how the Israelites and her neighbours lived side-by-side each other and you be the judge of how people have treated the Jews then and now, see if the quarrel is really about the size of country Israel currently possesses or whether it's based on other factors.

The story of Nehemiah highlights the cruel opposition and ridicules the Jews faced when they worked amongst themselves for their national interest. Excerpts from the story are as follows:

Nehemiah the Jew was the son of Hachaliah and a captive who was taken to Babylon and now served as the cupbearer to King Artaxerxes. Sometime in the course of his life in the realm of Persia he received visitors from Jerusalem and Judah.

Upon enquiry of the welfare of those who escaped and survived captivity, Nehemiah was told that the people there were in great distress and were reproached. The walls to their beloved city, Jerusalem, were broken down and the gates were burned with fire.[1] Nehemiah was moved with compassion for his country that he mourned and prayed for God's intervention. Subsequently, the king granted him leave to return to Judah so he can rebuild the walls around Jerusalem and replace the gates to the city.

Opposition 1: Mockery-by a coalition of enemies:
But when Sanballat the Horonite, Tobiah the Ammonite official, and Geshem the Arab heard of it (that Nehemiah and the other Jews were rebuilding the wall of Jerusalem), they laughed us to scorn and despised us, and said, "What is this thing that you are doing? Will you rebel against the king?"

Response by the Nehemiah the Jew:
So I answered them, and said to them, "The God of heaven Himself will prosper us; therefore we His servants will arise and build, but you have no heritage or right or memory in Jerusalem.[2]

Persistent Opposition 2- the Enemies from the region:
But it so happened, when Sanballat heard that we were rebuilding the wall, that he was furious and very indignant, and mocked the Jews.[3] Now it happened, when Sanballat, Tobiah, the Arabs, the Ammonites, and the Ashdodites heard that the walls of Jerusalem were being restored and the gaps were beginning to be closed, that they became very angry, and all of them conspired together to come and attack Jerusalem and create confusion.[4]

Response by the Jews
Nevertheless we made our prayer to our God, and because of them we set a watch against them day and night.[5]

Opposition thru' Enticement: 3- Arabs and others
Now it happened when Sanballat, Tobiah, Geshem the Arab, and the rest of our enemies heard that I had rebuilt the wall, and that there were no breaks left in it.., that Sanballat and Geshem sent to me saying, "Come, let us meet together in one of the villages in the plain of Ono." But they thought to do me harm.[6]

Response by Nehemiah the Jew

So I sent messengers to them, saying, "I am doing a great work, so I cannot come down. Why should the work cease while I leave it and go down to you?"[7]

I am sure that this entire scenario does sound familiar. This is an exact replica of today's game plan by the Arabs and their partners. Deny Israel's historical ties, deny her rights and execute plans to stop her progress. It must be stressed that the Jews in Nehemiah's days persisted with their own plans and were undeterred by their enemies. In the end they completed all their work and were able to get on with their lives, following God's commands.

Do not support the argument or believe it when you are told that Israel has 'occupied' Arab land. Jews and Arabs and other nationalities lived in this region for centuries. It has never been an absolute domain of the Arabs. Israel's enemies have always attacked her or sought for ways to destroy her. Even the Lord God himself gave them this instruction whenever they would have to defend their territory. Talk about rules of engagement...

When you go to war in your land against the enemy who oppresses you, then you shall sound an alarm with the trumpets, and you will be remembered before the Lord your God, and you will be saved from your enemies.[8]

In another chronicle in Israel's history, we read of the persistence of Israel's enemies to bring about her defeat and destruction; and how God delivered their enemies into the hands of His people. Here is another highlight:

When the Philistines were at war again with Israel, David and his servants with him went down and fought against the Philistines; and David grew faint.

Now it happened afterward that there was again a battle with the Philistines at Gob.

Again there was a battle in Gob with the Philistines...

Yet again there was a battle in Gath...[9]

Here is a story I love to recall. It's about the technicality of spying. This is espionage at the highest. This is just an example to show you why one ought not to underestimate the power of

God and His influence in the day-to-day affairs of the State of Israel.

The king of Syria was at war with Israel. He consulted his offices and chose a place to set up his camp. But Elisha sent word to the king of Israel, warning him not to go near that place, because the Syrians were waiting in ambush there. So the king of Israel warned the people who lived in that place, and they were on guard. This happened several times.

The Syrian king became greatly upset over this; he called his officers and asked them, "Which of you is on the side of the king of Israel?" One of them answered, "No one is, Your Majesty. The prophet Elisha tells the king of Israel what you say in the privacy of your own room."[10]

It's partially unexplainable; the causes for which Israel's enemies fight against her. To some extent it may be concluded that they themselves are unable to explain their centuries old hatred for Israel. Then, there was no religion called Islam, yet the hatred was as intense as it is today. One cause of the hatred is based on the fundamental principle God laid out when He chose Israel as His own people. Spiritual forces are aligned against God's people by virtue of God's choosing and therefore, every battle against Israel is a battle against their God. And so the international community has picked sides and has chosen to stand against Israel, never mind their rhetoric, God is not fooled by their sayings: *friendship, peace, collective responsibility, justice, a Palestinian State and the like.* He made man and knows the content of their hearts, that's why He could give Elisha, His servant a "heads-up" on the Syrian king's plans. Thus Elisha's actions protected the country.

Israel's Song of Praise

Then as now, Israel's enemies outnumbered her, in size, military capability and global influence. However, there was one major difference between Israel and her enemies, one which is still significant even to this day, Israel's relations with her God.

One cannot separate the Jews from God. For it is for this reason they were established as a nation. Neither can one discount the importance of God in their affairs. Other nations today, in most instances they compromise and embrace multiple gods, or a god that is not the God of Israel. Any national god that is not the God of Israel will not auger well for that nation. Israel's past has attested to this. In the past when Israel trusted God, she enjoyed His protection and blessings. Now, having learnt her lesson, Israel enjoys supernatural favour because of her trust in God. The song below supports this view and it encapsulates Israel's everlasting rights and ties to the land she currently possesses:

Give thanks to the Lord, proclaim His greatness; tell the nations what He has done.

Sing praise to the Lord; tell the wonderful things He has done.

Be glad that we belong to Him; let all who worship Him rejoice!

Go to the Lord for help, and worship Him continually.

You descendants of Jacob, God's servant, descendants of Israel, whom God chose, remember the miracle that God performed and the judgements that He gave.

The Lord is our God; His commands are for all the world.

Never forget God's covenant, which He made to last forever, the covenant He made with Abraham, the promise He made to Isaac.

The Lord made a covenant with Jacob, one that will last forever.

"I will give you the land of Canaan," He said. "It will be your own possession."[11]

Vain Deception to take Israel's Possession

Like his ancestors, the leader of the Palestinian Arabs Mahmoud Abbas, continues to make strife against Israel. He is called a *moderate* by the international community; yet, his public stance decries such a description about this man's character. He jeers at Israel's leadership and rejoices when there is a global verbal assault directed at the people of God. He is delusionary and he maintains the status quo of keeping his people in a beleaguered state so as to sustain international outrage toward Israel. He has even called for jihad when things are seemingly not moving in his favour. He is an enemy of the State of Israel.

The Jerusalem Post, in this report provides a further picture of Abbas:

Palestinian Authority President Mahmoud Abbas will not resume negotiations with Israel unless the Netanyahu government agrees to a complete settlement freeze and publicly accepts a two-state solution, Abbas has told the *Washington Post* in an interview.

And since he does not believe Prime Minister Binyamin Netanyahu will lift his opposition on these issues, Abbas and his leadership expect <u>American pressure</u> to gradually force Netanyahu out of office, the paper reported on Friday. "It will take a couple of years," it quoted one of Abbas's officials as saying.

Abbas was interviewed the day before his Thursday meeting at the White House with President Barack Obama.

Setting out what the newspaper called "a hardline position," the Palestinian leader conditioned a resumption of talks with Israel on Netanyahu's agreement to a halt in all settlement building - a demand being repeatedly stressed by Obama, <u>US Secretary of State</u> Hillary Rodham Clinton and other senior US officials - and formal Israeli government acceptance of Palestinian statehood.

Abbas added that he would not even assist Obama's special envoy, George Mitchell, in trying to encourage Arab states to begin warming relations with Israel until Israel accepted these conditions. "We can't talk to the Arabs until Israel agrees to freeze settlements and recognizes the two-state solution," Abbas was quoted saying. "Until then we can't talk to anyone."

However, the *Washington Post* went on, "Abbas and his team fully expect that Netanyahu will never agree to the full settlement freeze - if he did, his center-right coalition would almost certainly collapse. So they plan to sit back and watch while US pressure slowly squeezes the Israeli prime minister.[12]The Post also provided some insight into Abbas' refusal of Israel's former Prime Minister Ehud Olmert's generous offer to Palestinian Arabs.

Abbas, the article continued, "rejects the notion that he should make any comparable concession - such as recognizing Israel as a Jewish state, which would imply renunciation of any large-scale resettlement of refugees."

Abbas intends to remain passive, he told the paper. "I will wait for Hamas to accept international commitments. I will wait for Israel to freeze settlements... Until then, in the West Bank we have a good reality . . . the people are living a normal life."

Abbas also told the *Washington Post* that former Prime Minister Ehud Olmert accepted the principle of a "right of return" to Israel for Palestinian refugees and offered to resettle thousands of Palestinians in Israel. And he said Olmert proposed a Palestinian state on 97 percent of the West Bank, and showed him its contours on a map.

Abbas said he turned down Olmert's peace offer because "the gaps were too wide." [13]

Abbas is a pernicious "peace partner!"

A fact that is mostly unknown by the people of the West is that the Arabs aspire to control all others, so whether by manipulation, deceit or war; their quest is for leadership. Their religious beliefs may have something to do with this as they uphold the notion that everything else is subordinate to Islam. Their attitude then makes the Arab-Israeli peace process far more tenuous, and Westerners fail to take these perspectives into consideration.

Bat Ye'or in her book: *Islam and Dhimmitude, Where Civilisations Collide* provides insight into the psyche of the Arabs.

Ye'or argues that the *dhimmi* condition, a direct result of *jihad*, is linked to this "protection pact" which suspended the conqueror's initial right to kill or enslave followers of the tolerated religions, provided they submitted themselves to pay the tribute (*jizya*). [14] The general basic principles according the Koran are as follows: the pre-eminence of Islam over all other religions (9:33); Islam is the true religion of Allah (3:17) and it should reign over all mankind (34:27); the *umma* forms the party of Allah and is perfect (3:106), having been chosen above all peoples on earth it alone is qualified to rule, and thus elected by Allah to guide the world (35:37). The pursuit of *jihad*, until this goal will be achieved, is an obligation (8:40). The religions of the Bible, and Zoroastrianism, are deemed inferior as their followers falsified the true Revelation which their respective prophets conveyed to them–this Revelation was considered to be Islam–before Muhammad's arrival. Albeit inferior, these peoples, each a beneficiary of Revelation, have the choice between war or submission to the *umma*, whereas idolators are forced to convert to Islam or be killed. [15]

Now you see why the Arab-Israel conflict remains ongoing. Iran's threat to destroy the Jewish State is in keeping with the belief that Islam; no other religious beliefs must survive or reign in the Middle East, and then the world at large. The Jews presence and existence in the region is an affront to all the Islamic gibberish. The Arabs refusal to recognise the right of the Jewish State to exist is based on their Islamic beliefs. While they glory in their religion, the truth is, Jews have more than religion! They have God on their side! The God of Israel! Indeed, there is only the Lord God who is God. He is the God of Israel... They, the Jews worship the True and Living God, the Muslims do not! The critical question to you is: Which side have you embraced, the side with the God of Israel or the side with the god of Islam?

Thus says the Lord God of Israel:

Turn to Me now and be saved, people all over the world!
I am the only God there is.
My promise is true, and it will not be changed. I solemnly
promised by all that I am: Everyone will come and kneel
before Me and vow to be loyal to Me.
They will say that only through Me are victory and strength
to be found; but all who hate Me will suffer disgrace.
I, the Lord, will rescue all the descendants of Jacob,
and they will give Me praise.[16]

Other Testimonies from the Lord God Himself concerning His status as the only God:

- I am the Lord; there is no other god... (Isaiah 45: 5).
- I created both light and darkness; I bring both blessing and disaster. I the Lord, do all these things. (Isaiah 45: 7).
- The Lord, the holy God of Israel the One who shapes the future, says:
  You have no right to question Me about My children or tell what I ought to do!
  I am the One who made the earth and created human beings to live there. By My power I stretched out the

heavens; I control the sun, the moon, and the stars. (Isaiah 45: 12).

- The Lord created the heavens–He is the One who is God! He formed and made the earth–He made it firm and lasting. He did not make it a desolate waste, but a place for people to live. It is He who says, "I am the Lord, and there is no other god... I am the Lord, and I speak the truth; I make known what is right." (Isaiah 45: 18-19).

Concerning the future of Israel, the Lord God of Israel assures them of His rescue of their race, and salvation of their country. He says:

Thus the Lord says to all His people, when the time comes to save you, I will show you favour and answer your cries for help. I will guard and protect you and through you make a covenant with all peoples.[17] Jerusalem, I can never forget you! I have written your name on the palms of My hands.[18]

Section 4
The Case for Israel

Chapter 8

Israel: Right to Exist – Right to Defend

The Phenomenon of the Blessing and the Curse

"I will bless those who bless you, and I will curse him who curses you; and in you all the families of the earth shall be blessed." (Gen 12: 3)

Article I of the Charter of the United Nations lists the purposes of the Organisation. At Article 1:1 it states that its purpose is:

To maintain international peace and security, and to that end: to take effective collective measures for the prevention and removal of threats to the peace, and for the suppression of acts of aggression or other breaches of the peace, and to bring about by peaceful means, and in conformity with the principles of justice and international law, adjustment or settlement of international disputes or situations which might lead to a breach of the peace.[1]

Whereas, Iran and others seek to engage in acts of aggression against the State of Israel and whereas these acts constitute a threat to regional peace as well as global peace, the international community seems unable or impotent to fulfil its mandate: to indeed maintain the thrust of international peace and to take effective measures to prevent the persistent threat or quash the threat altogether. Instead, of dealing with the violators of peace: those who threaten another State within the community of nations and instead of stiffening punishments against such, as terrorists groups namely, Hamas and Hezbollah and States that sponsor them; the international community reserves judgment against Israel, a democratic State whose governance is based on the rule of law, liberty and justice. They fail to remove these threats to the peaceful existence of the Jewish State and there is no unanimity in the Security Council on steps to maintain conformity with international principles for peaceful co-existence.

The present international instruments were crafted after two major World Wars. Being "war weary" the idealists dreamed of a world where mankind would regard law and order and play by the rules set out by world leaders. They did not see coming, the Arab-Israeli conflict and so now that it's here, what do they do? They look to Israel to make peace. What is peace? Peace for them is that Israel alone would make the hard concessions: relinquish her aspirations to possess all of the land of her forefathers or even the current portion she possesses, relinquish any notion that this is a spiritual deal of everlasting proportions–there is no place for this "kind-of-thinking-in the-real-world," relinquish her sovereignty and security... to the international community. These expectations are "wild." No other State is asked to pay this price for regional or global peace, why should Israel?

You see, they have missed one important fact. This is really not about Israel. It's about God. Yes, God, the Lord! The nations' contempt, unbelief and rejection of Him have been the fuel to the conflict. Because everything they propose opposes His very intent and Word. No man can make peace in the Middle East. Here are a people with different intrinsic values from the rest of humanity. Mankind, without God is evil in heart and so who can make a wicked man consider peace when he's bent on doing harm to his neighbour. Islamists, believe that they must kill to gain global dominance and kill to enter *heaven for great rewards such as women*; whereas, God's posture is love. Man must love the Lord God, love his neighbour as himself, pursue peace, righteousness, godliness and the like; not murder. One party loves life, the other death. One party makes concessions, the other does not. One is the rightful heir to the land, the other is not. Therefore, any call for "comprehensive peace," "viable peace," "the peace process" is all a waste of time. There will be no peace in this part of the world when Islam rules that no Muslim has the authority to enter a peace pact with non-Muslims. The world must stop kidding themselves.

God Himself warns Israel against entering into treaties with those who hate Him. He reassures Israel of His relationship toward them, saying:

"I am the Lord your God; I brought you out of Egypt to be your God. I am the Lord."[2]

God was instrumental in giving to the Israelites this land in the first instance and He, after exercising His powers, once again gave to His people this land. So that His original intent can be established: that He would be their God and they would be His people.

These are the assurances God gave to Jacob concerning the land:

- "The land which I gave Abraham and Isaac I give to you; and to your descendants after you I give this land."[3]
- Then Jacob said to Joseph: God Almighty appeared to me at Luz in the land of Canaan and blessed me, and said to me, 'Behold, I will make you fruitful and multiply you, and I will give this land to your descendants after you as an everlasting possession.[4]

The term "everlasting possession" is not incomprehensible to *the discerning, the wise and the intellectual*. Nevertheless, it means: forever, for all times, throughout the generations and in every generation; yesterday, today and tomorrow; in 2010, 2050, 2100, 2290, 2505, 5555; yes, even then, the land is Israel's property.

Israel has been placed amongst the Gentile nations to be a blessing to them. Israel comes loaded with the "goodies," the blessings already bestowed upon them. Rather than embrace her though, the nations have rejected their "gift" they curse Israel and seek to annihilate her, they have conspired against her saying, that Israel has no inalienable right to exist. What folly! By its very actions, the nations have brought a curse on themselves and will reap what they sow; cursing Israel has brought God's wrath upon the nations because God deems their actions: presumptuous and contemptuous.

The curse of God against Israel's enemies will reverse any of the very mischief they had planned against Israel:

> *The day is near when I, the Lord, will judge all nations. Edom, what you have done will be done to you. You will get back what you have given.*
> *My people have drunk a bitter cup of punishment on My sacred hill. But all the surrounding nations will drink a still more bitter cup of punishment; they will drink it all and vanish away.*
> *But on Mount Zion some will escape, and it will be a sacred place. The people of Jacob will possess the land that is theirs by right. The people of Jacob and of Joseph will be like fire; they will destroy the people of Esau as fire burns stubble. No descendant of Esau will survive.*
> *I, the Lord, have spoken.* [5]

Furthermore, Joel the prophet tells the nations what they do not want to hear:

The Lord says, At that time I will restore the prosperity of Judah and Jerusalem.

I will gather all the nations and bring them to the Valley of Judgment. There I will judge them for all they have done to My people. They have scattered the Israelites in foreign countries and divided Israel, My land.

They threw dice to decide who would get the captives. They sold boys and girls into slavery to pay for prostitutes and wine. [6]

The Lord's blessing is on Israel. The Lord will remember His promises to them. He states further:

> *Then, Israel, you will know that I am the Lord your God.*
> *I live on Zion, My sacred hill. Jerusalem will be a sacred city; foreigners will never conquer it again.* [7]

The right to Israel's existence is amplified in a vision by the prophet Ezekiel. It's a magnificent illustration of the power of God. It took the power of God to revive a scattered people, their language and customs. It also took His great power to restore their land to them. This is an awesome miracle in our life time, yet, one that is globally despised.

Ezekiel tells of his vision in his own words:

The hand of the Lord came upon me and brought me out in the Spirit of the Lord and set me down in the midst of the valley and it was full of bones.

Then He caused me to pass by them all around, and behold, there were very many in the open valley; and indeed they were very dry.

And He said to me, Son of man, can these bones live? So I answered, "O Lord God, You know."

Again He said to me, Prophesy to these bones, and say to them, O dry bones, hear the word of the Lord!

Thus says the Lord God to these bones: Surely I will cause breath to enter into you, and you shall live....

So I prophesied as He commanded me, and breath came into them, and they lived, and stood upon their feet, an exceedingly great army.

Then He said to me, Son of man, these bones are the whole house of Israel. They indeed say, Our bones are dry, our hope is lost, and we ourselves are cut off!

Therefore prophesy and say to them, Thus says the Lord God: Behold, O My people, I will open your graves, and bring you into the land of Israel.

Then you shall know that I am the Lord, when I have opened your graves, and bring you into the land of Israel.

Then you shall know that I am the Lord, when I have opened your graves, O My people, and brought you up from your graves.

I will put My Spirit in you, and you shall live, and I will place you in your own land. Then you shall know that I, the Lord, have spoken it and performed it, says the Lord.

The Lord also told Ezekiel:

Then say to them, Thus says the Lord God: Surely I will take the children of Israel from among the nations, wherever they have gone, and will gather them from every side and bring them into their own land; and I will make them one nation in the land, on the mountains of Israel; and one king over them all; they shall no longer be two nations, nor shall they ever be divided into two kingdoms again.[8]

The world foolishly throws away its blessing in exchange for a curse by their subtle, outright and callous rejection of Israel. Israel has been God's instrument to bless the nations.

The Fulfilment: Israel, one nation, united as God said...

The State of Israel is a dynamic democracy. Its people have voted time and again for political parties to form coalitions so that governance is executed by the majority. They engage in debates both publically and privately, a sign that freedom of expression is not threatened. Its judiciary can be considered the most independent in the world. Israel is a complex society, its people returned from the Diaspora from the ends of the earth yet because of the promises of the Lord that they will be united as one nation with one ruler, and they will return to Him. Yes, even today, Jews continue to make aliyah, i.e., they leave their present abode to take up residence in Israel, just as the Lord has spoken.

Israel is also a sophisticated society. Israel's Prime Minister notes that Israel has per capita more Nobel Prize winners than any other country, than any other people. Israel has the second largest concentration of technological capacity; in terms of venture capital, the highest per capita by far. Israel has scientific publications and they have patents in abundance. Israel, in looking to the future, has the capacity to develop energy from hydrogen, from water, the developments of solar energy and other energies. Israel has the brains, and also the will.[9] Think about what cooperation through bilateral and multilateral relations with Israel could bring to the world. See, I told you that Israel came blessed to be a blessing to the world!

In seeking possible ways to preserve the State of Israel the Prime Minister stresses:

Finding an alternative to oil is a critical matter for the State of Israel must deal with – with regard to geopolitics, security concerns, environmental concerns, to secure the future and to change the world's order of priorities.

Therefore, I repeat my announcement that I am going to establish a national commission comprised of scientists, manufacturers, engineers, businesspeople and government officials, with the goal of formulating a practical plan for efficient development in technologies and engineering in order to replace fossil fuels within the decade...[10] One could see that Israel is rightly getting on with the business of living, making plans for her future and at the same time expressing concerning for the world. Netanyahu concluded his remarks saying:

It is not in our interest alone. The resources need not be exclusively Israel's. Most of the world shares this interest. But Israel has a strong and clear interest in achieving this.[11]

This is indeed a blessing. It would be best if the world could rethink its posture toward Israel and seek genuine friendship with the Jewish State. It will auger well for all of us.

The Right to Defend: Against the Goldstone Report

A little more than one hundred years ago American President Theodore Roosevelt was the winner of the 1906 Nobel Prize. He was represented in Norway for the grand occasion by the American Ambassador Herbert H. D. Peirce. Ambassador Peirce in delivering the President's acceptance speech stated:

It is incontrovertible, as President Roosevelt says, that peace in all its aspects, peace among mankind, peace between nations, peace between social classes, peace between individuals – all are equally important. The one cannot, so to speak, be divorced from the other. If we are to promote civilisation and the well-being of mankind as a whole, we can do it most effectively by securing world peace, for the entire history of the world teaches us that war and devastation are inseparable. The ravages of war arrest the progress of nations culturally, materially, socially and politically, perhaps for generations...[12]

The Arabs have decided that they are willing to pay the price of war. They are willing to embrace the devastation it leaves behind so that that will be the legacy they will leave behind, one of hate, for the younger generations who will also grow up, they expect, to continue the conflict with Israel. This is the status quo in the Middle East, hate breeds war, war leaves destruction, destruction breeds more hate and hate robs all of peace. Consequently, the ongoing conflict robs the region from attaining its full potential which could be only maximised through co-operation with Israel. Therefore, whatever success has been achieved, economically or otherwise these could have been multiple times better had there been a climate of peace and trust.

A collection of statements submitted by Moshe Aumann, from Arab leaders does show the Arabs intent is not to secure peace but to maintain a culture of war with Israel. The list is very revealing. It is as follows:

- It is only for tactical reasons that we carefully stress our Palestinian identity, for it is in the national interests of the Arabs to encourage a separate Palestinian identity to counter Zionism: The founding of a Palestinian State is a new tool in the ongoing battle against Israel.
  - *(Zohair Mohsin, then head of PLO's Military Operation Dept. And member of PLO Executive Council, in interview for Dutch newspaper Trouw, 31 March 1977)*
- The Arab leaders, despite the differences in their approaches, are united in their view that the confrontation with Zionism will not end with the establishment of an independent Palestinian State in a few years' time. On the contrary, the confrontation will continue with the marshalling of the military, economic and political resources of the Arab States, in order to defeat Zionism.
  - *(Shazli al-Klibi, Secretary-General of the Arab League, interviewed on Radio Monte Carlo, 26 November 1976)*
- Our people will continue to fuel the torch of the revolution with rivers of blood, until the whole of the occupied homeland is liberated... not just part of it.
  - *(Chairman Yasser Arafat, AP, Beirut, 12 March 1979)*
- I hope I am making myself clear to everyone everywhere... We have said it over and over again that we refuse to recognise Israel. This is an unchangeable, permanent policy.

- *(Farouk Kaddoumi, head of the PLO's Political Department, quoted by Reuter in Beirut, 9 April 1981)*
- The fulfilment of Palestinian aspirations will be achieved only by the gun. The PLO will never recognise Israel.
  - *(Ibrahim Sousse, PLO representative in Paris, Le Monde, 30 November 1982)*[13]

Also added to the list is PA's Abbas, who argues that:

- Unless all the issues at the root of the Israeli-Palestinian conflict are not solved, violence will break out anew in two or three years.
  - *(Palestinian Authority President Mahmoud Abbas, a Jerusalem Post report on 30 October 2007)*[14]
- I say clearly: I do not accept the Jewish State, call it what you will.
  - *(PA President Mahmoud Abbas, at a preliminary conference of the Palestinian Youth Parliament in Ramallah, published by Palestinian Media Watch on 28 April 2009)*[15]

Meanwhile, Israel's Deputy Foreign Minister Danny Ayalon calls on Fatah to stop the 'culture of hate' against Israel. Ayalon highlighted the fact that hate education and incitement is one of the major problems in the Palestinian Authority. He stresses: Everyone talks about Hamas, which is obvious, but the PA, Fatah and Mahmoud Abbas also engage in incitement and have created a 'culture of hate'. The outcome of a Fatah Conference which Israel helped facilitate, added Ayalon, was very negative which emphasised education to the armed sturggle.[16]

The Deputy Foreign Minister also notes that: The Fatah Constitution still calls for the eradication of the State of Israel and this was reaffirmed during the recent conference. This is a major problem. As long as Israel is not accepted as a legitimate and natural part of this region then we will not see a desire for peace.[17]

The nations have taken God's grace for granted. Modern man has no dramatic, sensational recorded experience of God's wrath been poured out on the rebellious as in the days of Moses. So man tempts God by their refusal to accept Israel's right to exist in the Holy Land and by threats of war and actual attacks on the Jewish State. In the Scriptures, Moses after an incident, said to the people: *When you complain against Aaron, it is really against the Lord that you and your followers are rebelling.*[18] Likewise, when the Arabs complain against Israel and oppose their existence in the Middle East, they and their allies are complaining against God and stand in opposition against the Lord God.

Since Israel's unilateral withdrawal from Gaza in 2005, Hamas gained full control over the territory in 2007. Israel's withdrawal came at the encouragement of the United States and the rest of the international community. Hamas now uses the territory as a launching pad to attack Israeli communities which are within range of their fired rockets. Under the Hamas doctrine, Israel has no right to exist and they, the terrorists, are obliged to provide "resistance" against the State of Israel and they also forbid any peaceful coexistence between Arabs and Jews. Yet, when Hamas' incitement against Israel brought destruction to its own infrastructure there was international outrage against Israel, instead of Hamas. The international community must never forget that aggression against a sovereign State must be dealt with by the State under attack... (and possibly allies of the State), this is every State sovereign RIGHT. War has a price... destruction is inevitable... it's the price the warrior, in this case the terrorist, must be prepared to pay.

Therefore we will briefly examine the Goldstone Report, which came after the Gaza War.

Justice Richard Goldstone, former judge of the Constitutional Court in South Africa and former Prosecutor of the International Criminal Tribunals for the former Yugoslavia and Rwanda, was selected to head the United Nations Fact Finding Mission on the Gaza Conflict established by the Human Rights Council. The mandate "to investigate all violations of international human rights law and international humanitarian law that might have been committed at any time in the context of the military operations that were conducted in Gaza during the period from 27

December 2008 and 18 January 2009, whether before, during or after."[19]

The Mission interpreted the mandate as required it to place the civilian population of the region at the centre of its concerns regarding the violations of international law.[20]

The Olmert government of Israel had had enough of Hamas missiles strikes against Israeli interests. In order to curb Hamas, Israel responded to the assaults on its people and country militarily. Its response code named Operation Cast Lead was a three week military undertaking, designed to weaken the terrorists by destroying Hamas' arsenals and arms smuggling routes. Hamas for its part engaged in an unconventional warfare using civilians as human shields. This strategy led to the death of many persons and gave the Hamas propaganda machine additional impetus as more international condemnation was directed at the Israelis.

The Goldstone Report at paragraph 30: speaks of the number of Arabs killed in the war. Their own findings show that between 1,387 and 1,417 persons were killed, whereas the Government of Israel figures stand at 1,166 dead. Having said that the report goes on to say that the number of the dead "raise very serious concerns about the way Israel conducted the military operations in Gaza."[21] It did not question Hamas' tactics and poor judgement to put innocent people in harm's way. But when is there a war without causalities? One must not forget that these people 'glorify' dying in battle. The report should have stated accurately how many of the dead were terrorists.

The Goldstone Report spoke of Gaza as though it were a normal place under governance by law-abiding officials who execute their mandate under the rule of law and good governance. It is not so. Gaza is sometimes called "Hamastan." This name describes the nature of the place. Hamas is a terrorist organisation that engages in military attacks using rockets and mortar fires against the civilian populations in Israel. Therefore, any institution under Hamas' control belongs, indeed, to the terrorists. However, the Goldstone Report separates Gaza's institutions from Hamas, this step moves to absolve Hamas from their crimes against the State of Israel. Hamas 'run things in Gaza' every institution is under Hamas control, likewise, individuals since 2007.

Goldstone condemns Israel's destructions to two buildings in Gaza. They were the Palestinian Legislative Council building and the main prison. Goldstone refutes Israel's claims that the buildings were used for the conduct of terrorist's activities against Israel. The Mission's response is rejection of Israel's position and concerns. The report goes on to say that the Mission:

i) Finds that there is no evidence that the Legislative Council building and the Gaza main prison made an effective contribution to military action. On the information available to it, the

ii) Mission finds that the attacks on these buildings constituted deliberate attacks on civilian objects in violation of the rule of customary international humanitarian law.

iii) These facts, continue the report, further indicate the commission of the grave breach of extensive destruction of property, not justified by military necessity and carried out unlawfully and wantonly.[22]

One can only remind the honourable judge that this was indeed a war, a response to years of provocation and aggression that involved rocket and mortar attacks by the terrorists against Israel. Therefore, the necessary actions had to be taken to destroy their abilities to maintain this status quo. When the international community treats terrorists as 'most favoured groupings' the terrorists themselves will believe that they do not have to abide by the dictates of international law and boldly attack States, in this instance Israel is the first. This was a war with the full force of the State behind it. When the UN calls it a conflict as stated in the Report, it conveys the impression it was a mere clash with the State of Israel using extra force against its 'playmate.' It is Hamas that has issued a threat to Israel saying that it will destroy the Jewish State... Israel has no such threats against the Arabs.

One must recall the US response to the terrorist attacks against its territory in 2001. The attacks on the lone super power ushered in a new era. One in which the West was forced to take military actions against terrorists, insurgents and "whatever other names for such people," hence the decade long war in Iraq and

Afghanistan, are the first major military responses to international terrorism in the 21st Century. In the case of Iraq, the US struck Iraq's infrastructure with 'mighty bombs,' and the Iraqi army could not fight back, though this was a legitimate army...

The Goldstone Report submits with regard to Hamas fighting in heavily populated areas: The Mission cannot, however, discount the possibility that Palestinian armed groups (they did not say terrorists) were active in the vicinity of such United Nations facilities and hospitals. While the conduct of hostilities in built-up areas does not, of itself, constitute a violation of international law, Palestinian armed groups, where they launched attacks close to civilian or protected buildings, unnecessarily exposed the civilian population of Gaza to grave danger.[23]

No wonder the Israeli government dubbed this Finding "one-sided." The Israel government states that the Report effectively ignores Israel's right of self defence, makes unsubstantiated claims about its intent and challenges Israel's democratic values and rule of law. At the same time the Report all but ignores the deliberate strategy of Hamas of operating within and behind the civilian population and turning densely populated areas into an arena of battle. By turning a blind eye to such tactics it effectively rewards them.[24]

Israel further emphasised that: The one-sided mandate of the Gaza Fact Finding Mission, and the resolution that established it, gave serious reasons for concerns both to Israel and to the many States on the Council which refused to support it – including the Member States of the European Union, Switzerland, Canada, Korea and Japan.[25]

The Goldstone Report repeatedly used terms such as: "this constitutes a violation of international humanitarian law," "such acts are a grave breach of the Geneva Convention and constitute a war crime," in accusation of the democratic State of Israel. Furthermore, the Report specifically maintains this stance of singling out Israel for condemnation. It argues that: the Mission is of the view that some of the actions of the Government of Israel might justify a competent court finding that crimes against humanity have been committed.[26]

Israel, for its part responded to the allegations in the Report saying:

Justice Goldstone as head of the Mission repeatedly insisted that the Mission was not a judicial inquiry and so "could not reach judicial conclusions." On this basis that he justified the inclusion of partisan mission members, admitting that their involvement "would not be appropriate for a judicial inquiry." The Report however is highly judicial in nature, reaching conclusive judicial determinations of guilt, and including 'detailed legal findings' even in the absence of the sensitive intelligence information which Israel did not feel able to provide. These determinations are made notwithstanding the Report's admission that it does "pretend to reach the standard of proof applicable in criminal trials."[27]

Finally, in relation to the Report, Para., 108 addresses Hamas' attacks on Israeli civilians saying that:

The Mission has determined that the rockets (over 8,000) and, to a lesser extent, the mortars fired by the Palestinian armed groups are incapable of being directed towards specific military objectives and have been fired into areas where civilian populations are based. The Mission has further determined that these attacks constitute indiscriminate attacks upon the civilian population of southern Israel and that, where there is no intended military target and the rockets and mortars are launched into civilian population, they constitute a deliberate attack against civilian population. These acts would constitute war crimes and may amount to crimes against humanity. Given the seeming inability of the Palestinian armed groups to direct the rockets and mortars toward specific targets and given that the attacks have caused very little damage to Israeli military assets, the Mission finds that there is significant evidence to suggest that one of the primary purposes of the rocket and mortar attacks is to spread terror among the Israeli civilian population, a violation of international law.[28]

This paragraph in the Report seems to suggest that a terrorist attack on a State's military infrastructure is somewhat legitimate. These are terrorists, not soldiers. They deserve to be punished for their atrocities against the Jewish State.

The Government of Israel notes:

While the Report passes judgment against Israel in respect of almost any allegation, it seeks to absolve the Hamas of almost any wrong doing. The word "terrorist" is almost entirely absent. Soldier Gilad Schalit, now held incommunicado in captivity for over three years, was "captured during an enemy incursion" and the Hamas members that the Mission met with in Gaza are thanked as the "Gaza authorities" for extending their full cooperation and support to the Mission.[29]

It would have been a major success to the Fact-Finding Mission if they were able to obtain the release of kidnapped Israeli soldier Gilad Schalit. But no, Hamas still holds on to him, using him as bait before Israel while the Mission recommends actions to be taken regarding prosecution for war crimes before the International Criminal Court (ICC). Prosecution was recommended mostly, against Israeli officials. Thus the Arabs were especially delighted to endorse this Report to press home whatever leverage this "one-sided" Report handed them. In an update: (Gilad Schalit was eventually freed in October 2011, following intense negotiations by Prime Minister Netanyahu's government. Schalit was held by Hamas for five years).

Right to Defend: Israel's Response

The Goldstone Report recommended that the UNSC should require of Israel under Article 40 of the Charter of the United Nations:

To take all appropriate steps, within a period of three months, to launch appropriate investigations that are independent and in conformity with international standards, into the serious violations of international humanitarian and international human rights law reported by the Mission and any other serious allegations that might come to its attention.[30] Additionally, Goldstone called Israel's non-cooperation with its investigations an obstruction of the work of the committee.[31] Thus establishing in the recommendations narrow timelines for Israel's response in keeping with international law and issued subtle threats of prosecutions of the Government should it refused to comply with their demands. The question is, would any great power stand for this... accepting attacks on its territory and attacks on its credibility? When should a sovereign State defend itself from attacks?

In response to the Goldstone Report H.E. Ambassador Aharon Leshno-Yaar, Israel's Permanent Representative to the United Nations in Geneva, addressed the UN Human Rights Council in Geneva, September 2009 on behalf of his country, saying:

Five years ago, in a remarkable gesture reaching out for peace, Israel removed every one of its soldiers and over 8,000 civilians from the Gaza Strip. We withdrew hospitals and kindergartens, synagogues and cemeteries, leaving only the greenhouses we had struggled to build in the hope that these would be the start of a productive Palestinian society. And you, the States of this Council, applauded this unprecedented measure. You told us in no uncertain terms that in the nightmare scenario that terror would take root, you would back us in our inherent right to self-defence.

Five years later, the greenhouses had been ransacked by Hamas thugs, over 8,000 rockets and mortars had been fired on schools and kindergartens in Sderot and other Israeli towns, and an unceasing supply of weaponry was being smuggled through tunnels into Gaza from terror-sponsoring States like Iran. Israel's urgent appeals to the international community were to no avail, and our attempts to extend a fragile cease-fire were met with new, increased barrages of missiles from Hamas. And all the while the range of the attacks was increasing. Now Ashkelon and Beer Sheva were within reach. One million Israeli children, women and men had to live every moment of their lives within seconds of a bomb shelter.

The decision to launch a military operation is never an easy one. It is even more challenging when we have to face an enemy that intentionally deploys its forces in densely populated areas, stores its explosives in private homes, and launches rockets from crowded school yards and mosques. These are new horrendous challenges, and we sought to deal with them responsibly and with humanity. Yet when we dropped millions of leaflets and made tens of thousands of phone calls to warn civilians in advance of operations, we were witness to the callous and deliberate Hamas

tactic of sending women and children onto the roofs of terrorist headquarters and weapons factories. In such cases, again and again missions were aborted, letting Hamas terrorists escape, Israel protected Palestinian civilians that Hamas had put at risk....
Mr. President

The authors of this "Fact-finding Report" had little concern with finding facts. The report was instigated as part of a political campaign, and it represents a political assault directed against Israel and against every State forced to confront terrorist threats. Its recommendations are fully in line with its one-sided agenda and seek to harness the Security Council, the General Assembly and the International Criminal Court, the Human Rights Council, and the entire international community in its political campaign. In so doing it seeks to inject these bodies with the same political poison that has so undermined the integrity of this Council.
Mr President

Unlike the Hamas terrorists who rejoice with every civilian death, Israel regards every civilian casualty as a tragedy, Israel is committed to fully examining every allegation of wrongdoing. Not because of this Report but despite it...[32]

In March 2010 a report aimed at revealing intelligence on Hamas' war tactics was released by the Intelligence and Terrorism Information Center (ITIC), at the Israel Intelligence Heritage & Commemoration Center, headed by Col. (res.) Reuven Erlich, with the assistance of the Israeli defence establishment. This non-profit organisation is based in Israel and its members are former Military Intelligence officers.

The title of the Report is: *Hamas and the Terrorist Threat from the Gaza Strip. The Main Findings of the Goldstone Report Versus the Factual Findings.* The criticism directed at the Goldstone Report in this Israeli response states the following:

The comparison clearly indicates **four basic flaws** in the way the Goldstone Report relates to the period before Operation Cast Lead:

A. The Report does not deal with the nature of Hamas, particularly its terrorist aspects. It focuses on severe criticism of Israel and presents an openly pro-Palestinian version of the Israeli-Palestinian conflict. It does not deal with Hamas' ideology, its strategy, the military-terrorist infrastructure it constructed, its radical Islamic nature, the way it relates to the West and the pro-Western Arab regimes, the brutality with which it treats its Palestinian opponents, the direction and aid it receives from its headquarters in Damascus, and its record as the terrorist organization which led suicide bombing terrorism against Israel and fired rockets at its civilians over a period of many years. The Report refers to the de facto Hamas administration as a governmental entity ("the Gaza authorities"), and adopts Hamas' false claim that there is no connection between that entity and the military terrorist wing. The facts unequivocally prove that Hamas is one integral system, with a hierarchical leadership which maintains close contact between its political, administrative, security and military-terrorist branches.

B. The Report minimizes the extent and gravity of the terrorist activity carried out against Israel from the Gaza Strip and does not assign responsibility for it to Hamas. It focuses on rocket fire during the six months before Operation Cast Lead and devotes very little space to the rocket and mortar shell fire which began in 2001. It also does not deal with the other types of terrorist attacks originating in the Gaza Strip (including mass-murder attacks in Israel and the repeated attacks on the crossings and humanitarian facilities such as the Nahal Oz fuel terminal). The Report does define the rocket fire targeting the Israeli civilian population as a war crime (during the seven years leading up to Operation Cast Lead about 8,000 rocket and mortar shell hits were identified in Israel territory, killing and wounding civilians and severely disrupting daily life). However, the Report does not assign responsibility for the war crime to Hamas or any other terrorist organization operating in the Gaza Strip (such as the Palestinian Islamic Jihad, which operated side by side with Hamas). Thus the war crime has no address (and no person, institution or organization is held accountable for it). Hamas exploited this basic flaw to shirk all responsibility for the rocket fire, using the Report as a tool for its legal and propaganda campaigns against Israel.

C. As part of its general trend to minimize the significance of the terrorist threat, the Report does not deal with Hamas' military buildup in the Gaza Strip during 2007-2008, which threatened Israel (as opposed to its extensive coverage of the historical development of the Israeli-Palestinian conflict). That was in spite of the military buildup which created a significant threat to Israel and was a gross violation of the Oslo accords between the Palestinians and Israel (the Oslo accords allowed the Palestinian Authority to hold weapons only for the purposes of policing and security). It ignores the various components of the process, including the institutionalizing and organizing of the Hamas' forces into semi-military units (similar to, and inspired by Hezbollah); the smuggling into the Gaza Strip of an unprecedented quantity of advanced standard weapons and raw materials for the manufacture of weapons; intensive training in the Gaza Strip, Iran and Syria; and the manufacture of large quantities of rockets and IEDs. It also ignores the extensive efforts made before Operation Cast Lead to prepare residential areas for fighting, part of its combat doctrine of using civilians as human shields. The effort included stockpiling weapons, constructing pits and other facilities for firing rockets, erecting fortifications and digging tunnels, planting IEDs and mines, and booby-trapping buildings.

D. The Report completely ignores the massive amounts of aid Iran as well as Hezbollah and Syria (directly or through Hezbollah) gave Hamas to construct its military-terrorist infrastructure. Their support was accelerated during the two years preceding Operation Cast Lead and included smuggling long-range rockets into the Gaza Strip, assistance in developing and transferring knowhow for the self-production of rockets and IEDs, assistance in advanced training for hundreds of terrorist operatives and providing broad financial aid (given to Hamas by Iran). All of the above have continued after Operation Cast Lead and make it possible for Hamas to restore and improve the military capabilities which were damaged. The aid includes long-range rockets from Iran which can reach the center of Israel.[33]

The debase mentality of Hamas is unimaginable for people of Western culture and values. Hamas desires to destroy Israel, whether in battle or in image. So their warfare strategy is unconventional and being cognizant that the international mass media sensationalise everything "Arab-Israeli," gives them zeal. Israel can hardly implement strategies of its own to deter the enemy without the international community calling into question the legitimacy of her actions. They are ultimately aiding and abetting the enemy, whose stated goal is to destroy the State of Israel. They must know for certain that God, the God of Israel will not let Israel be destroyed "never again."

The prophet Isaiah says: But Israel is saved by the Lord, and her victory lasts forever; her people will never be disgraced.[34] So Hamas' days are surely numbered.

Moreover, the Israeli Intelligence Report found that:

The main conclusion of this study is that there is an enormous discrepancy between the findings of the Goldstone Report and the factual findings, and an extreme imbalance tipped against Israel in favor of Hamas. The Report systematically relies on selective, biased information, in many cases supplied by Hamas or by individuals and/or institutions controlled by it. The Report analyzes the selective, biased information in a way clearly intended to reinforce the thesis that Israel deliberately targeted civilians (a thesis which supports Hamas' propaganda). We, the researchers and authors of this study, are aware that some of the information we had access to was not available to the

Goldstone Mission. However, it is also clear that the authors of the Goldstone Report consistently avoided using information which was, in fact, accessible, but which did not support its main thesis, or at least presented serious doubts regarding its validity.

The Goldstone Report either ignores or minimizes the serious nature of the terrorist threat from the Gaza Strip facing Israel during the period before Operation Cast Lead (the potential for which still exists). The Report also systematically does not relate to the nature of Hamas or its goals. It also assigns no responsibility to it or any other terrorist organization for the years of rocket fire targeting Israeli civilians. It also does not blame Hamas for its use of Palestinian civilians as human shields. As far as Hamas is concerned, it is absolved by the Goldstone Report of all responsibility for war crimes carried out before and during Operation Cast Lead. Therefore, since the publication of the Report, Hamas has tried to use it wherever possible against Israel and sometimes even against the Palestinian Authority.[35] The Intelligence Report provides insight to the nature of Hamas, the terrorists. The Gaza Strip has been completely under Hamas control since the movement took it over in June 2007 and expelled the Palestinian Authority (which has received international recognition, while the de facto Hamas administration is considered illegal). That was the result of a process begun after Israel's disengagement from the Gaza Strip in the summer of 2005.

The Hamas movement (an acronym for "the Islamic resistance movement") was established at the end of 1987 by Sheikh Ahmad Yassin and based on the social-religious networks (da'wah) of the radical Islamic Egyptian Muslim Brotherhood. His objectives were to give the Brotherhood's radical Islamic ideology a Palestinian-nationalist cast. Its central goals were **the destruction of Israel, the struggle against the Jews and the founding of an Islamic-Palestinian state in its stead, and to** employ terrorism and violence to achieve them. **None of that is mentioned in the Goldstone Report. Hamas' ideology,** as clearly set out in its 1988 charter, states that the Palestinian problem is fundamentally **religious** and not nationalist or territorial, and that it centers around **the conflict between Islam and the so-called "infidel" Jews.** Thus the issue cannot be resolved by political means or by "two states for two people" (a concept vigorously opposed by Hamas, which does its utmost to prevent its adoption), **but only through a jihad** (holy war) **to liberate all Palestine, destroy the State of Israel, and establish a Palestinian Islamic state on the ruins.** According to Hamas' ideology, **all of Palestine, "from the [Jordan] river to the [Mediterranean] sea," is sacred to the Muslim endowment (waqf). Thus none of it can be relinquished, particularly Jerusalem. The charter is laced with antisemitic myths in the spirit of The Protocols of the Elders of Zion** (which are in fact mentioned in Paragraph 32 of the charter). Hamas' ideology is also imbued with deep hatred for the West and its values, **has not been modified since the charter was written** and is expressed in public statements made by Hamas' senior figures, in the Hamas media, literature, theatre, songs, etc. It is also inculcated into the perception of Hamas operatives as well as children and adolescents in the Gaza Strip through the formal and informal educational systems, which endeavor to raise a new generation which will hate Israel and the desire to destroy it.[36] Despite the fact that Hamas won a democratic election, it remains a totalitarian radical Islamic movement which exploited the democratic process to take over Palestinian politics and has no intention of giving up control. That was clearly illustrated a year and a half after the elections, when Hamas took over the Gaza Strip by force (June 2007) in what Palestinian Authority and Fatah described as a military coup. In the year and a half between the coup and Operation Cast Lead Hamas brutally repressed its opponents. Within the Gaza Strip the de facto Hamas administration has gradually enforced its radical Islamic code on the population, establishing what the Egyptians and its rivals in the Palestinian Authority – which fear the Gaza Strip Islamization will seep into their own territories – have often described as an **"Islamic emirate."**[37]

Notwithstanding, a comparison between Hamas and Fatah shows very little difference between the two Palestinian entities. Neither Hamas nor Fatah will be able to bring peace among themselves and the Jews. They both call for the destruction of the Jews and of the State of Israel. Their charters attest to this fact! They both envisage a Palestinian State in place of the Jewish State; they in concert together, refuse to recognise the right of the State of Israel to exist. They both promote a 'culture of hate' in their educational institutions. They both encourage the 'armed struggle' against Israelis. The rivalry between the two is based on one wanting to obtain the "prize" before the other. Therefore, Fatah pretends to be moderate, whereas Hamas is clearly ruthless and willing to openly engage the Israeli government via the use of force and the committal of crimes against humanity, more specifically the Jewish people. However, Fatah has also issued threats of *jihad* against Israel to maximize its leverage. They are all Arabs tutored under the same religion, Islam!

Nevertheless, Israel's Deputy Foreign Minister in an Open Letter to the Arab World in December 2009 stated:

Since the reestablishment of our State, Israeli leaders have sought peace with their Arab neighbours. Our Declaration of Independence, Israel's founding document that expressed our hopes and dreams reads. "We extend our hand to all neighbouring States and their peoples in an offer of peace and good neighbourliness, and appeal to them to establish bonds of co-operation and mutual help." These words are as true today as when they were first written in 1948. Sadly, 61 years later, only two nations, Jordan and Egypt, have accepted these principles and made peace with the Jewish State...[38]

It is surely time to look to the future and break with former intransigencies to create a better future for all the people of the region. Israel has gone very far and is prepared to do its part, but we must be met by a willing partner. Without this, the region is doomed to more conflict and will negate the unity of purpose in the Middle East that is necessary to face the mounting challenges from without and within.[39]

The characteristics of the State of Israel:

- Israel is a small, vulnerable State. It is located in the Middle East where she is recognised by only two of her neighbours: Jordan and Egypt. Otherwise, Israel is surrounded by threats and hostilities from Palestinian Arabs (within and outside of her borders), along with other Arab States who refuse to recognise the right of Israel to exist as a Jewish nation.
- Israel is a democracy. Its governance is based on the rule of law and on the fundamental principles of human rights: freedom of expression, freedom of worship, freedom to make personal choices and so forth.
- Israel's media are free from State's oppression; its judiciary is free from government's interference.
- Israelis are sophisticated and intelligent, friendly and helpful, willing to share knowledge and skills.
- Israelis are industrious and innovative. They have an active civil society.
- Israel, is the world's lone Jewish State, it honours God by nationally celebrating the Shabbat and by the expressions of hope and expectations in His power to deliver them.
- Israel was established by God and shall be kept from any future fantasy in the form of destruction to the State.
- Israel is a modern State and has very productive industries. The country's use of technology is second to none.
- Israel is a success story, successes because of God's influence and guidance.

The world should get use to this fact, Israel is here to stay!

Section 5

An Analysis – The Two-State Solution...

Assessment of Questions put to Interlocutors in the Conflict

Chapter 9

What is the Conflict About?

Prelude

Does the international community know the real cause of the conflict? Whose interest do they advance? Can they say with certainty whether their proposed plans can bring about the desired peace? These thought provoking questions are necessary because many players on the international stage have lent their time, resources and reputation to resolve this conflict.

Having read this book to this point you will notice that the author has incorporated the opinions, views and actions of the parties to the conflict as well as the actions of the international community. Furthermore, you would have also noticed the views of the God of Israel being submitted in this discourse. The reason for the inclusion of the Sovereign Lord is based on the inherent fact that He too is a party to this conflict. It was as a result of His sovereign acts that the Israelis have returned to their homeland. The global initiatives to resolve the conflict will impact His policies, plans and intent. Therefore, from time to time the Lord God's views will be presented as a part of the analysis.

It is pertinent to emphasise that this Arab-Israeli conflict has its roots in generations of hatred by the Arabs for the Israelis. Those who have undertaken the project of *managing the conflict* as well as the ambitious goal to *resolve same* must be aware of this factor. Note also that this is perhaps the very first time the proposed conflict resolution initiatives for the Middle East will take into consideration the perspectives and actions of the Lord God. This is not a religious proposal, for those who will be "up in arms" it is however, clearly prudent to approach any future initiative with the "God factor" in mind. Otherwise, the international efforts will never succeed.

Notes on the approach in the use of identities of those interviewed.

For ease of reference when the author refers to a diplomatic representative, she will instead use the name of the country, rather than the name of diplomat. Likewise, the UN will be used, instead of the name of its representative. In other instances, the surname and title of the individual would be used. In the case of Christian organisations in Israel, the name of the organisation would be used.

For specific details on all those who granted interviews, please go to Appendix 3 of this book.

The Bible relays an account which took place many centuries ago but it holds relevance to this pernicious conflict. The actors included a king, a *'religious man'* and the children of Israel. The 'religious man' was summoned by the king to curse the children of Israel because the king had no regard for the lives of the Israelis. Here is the historical account. See how it mimics today's conflict.

Firstly, God is the only authority that knows what's best for Israel. No one else, no other State has the right to determine what's best for Israel. For God told them: *I alone know the plans I have for you, plans to bring you prosperity and not disaster, plans to bring about the future you hope for.*[1]

The Israelites were on the move in the wilderness and other areas having left Egypt in great victory. A victory in which God Himself played a major role. They now are camping in the plains of Moab east of the Jordan River and opposite Jericho. The king of Moab, Balak son of Zippor saw the vast company of Israelites and he became desperate, so he sends to Syria for a man who feared God, so that this man could collaborate with him to bring about the destruction of the people of Israel. The Syrian's name was Balaam. God spoke to him telling him not do as the king of Moab has requested.

King Balak's envoys brought to the religious man, Balaam, the king's message. They told him:

"I want you to know that a whole nation has come from Egypt; its people are spreading out everywhere and threatening to take over our land. They outnumber us, so please come and put a curse on them for me. Then perhaps we will be able to defeat them and drive them out of the land... God said to Balaam, "Do not go with them, and do not put a curse on the people of Israel, because they have My blessing."[2]

In the end with much persuasion the king of Moab did get Balaam to go to his kingdom but instead of issuing the curse, Balaam blesses the people of Israel four times. The third blessing is summarised for your consideration

The spirit of God took control of him and he uttered this prophecy:

"The message of Balaam son of Beor, the words of the man who can see clearly, who can hear what God is saying...The tents of Israel are beautiful, like long rows of palms or gardens beside the water... God brought them out of Egypt; He fights for them like a wild ox. They devour their enemies, crush their bones, smash their arrows.

The nation is like a mighty lion; when it is sleeping, no one dares wake it. Whoever blesses Israel will be blessed, and whoever curses Israel will be cursed."

Balak clenched his fists in anger and said to Balaam, "I called you to curse my enemies, but three times now you have blessed them instead. Now get on home! I promised to reward you, but the Lord has kept you from getting the reward."[3]

The Analysis: What is the Conflict is about?

The Middle Eastern region is one of the ancient regions still with us in our modern world. And there is a reason for this phenomenon, Israel!

Israel's legitimacy as an independent nation in the region is tied to her history, namely, her inheritance. The Zionist Jews sought to reclaim possession of their land under the direct influence of the Lord, who had on numerous occasions declared that He would return the scattered Jews to their land, the land of their ancestors, the land He had promised to Abraham, Isaac and Jacob and their descendants. God's intent for separating a people to Himself to live in a particular part of the world was based on His intent to provide a model nation for the rest of the region and the world at large. Thus, He did not only select the Israelites, but He also lived among them. They were to live by abiding by His laws because He is holy. The laws which governed their lives were not intended to oppress them but to preserve their lives, as God's holiness and righteousness cannot accommodate sin, the result of sin is death. He is holy! God desired to replicate this model He had established among the Israelites, elsewhere in the world. He wanted the other ancient people to recognise that He was God! The God of the Israelites was and is the only God. This testimony of God holds true even today. Consequently, He returns Israel to the region so that the people of the region would be without excuse and cease their tribalism. They, thru' Israel's presence will come to acknowledge that indeed there is no other God beside the God of Israel. He is the Lord and beside Him there is no other God, in the world!

It must be emphasised that the global community missed their opportunity when the Jews lived in their midst. Except for the United States, which is a prosperous country because of the Jews there and also because of America's historic relations with Israel. For nearly two centuries the Jews lived among the peoples in the north, the south, the east and the west, but instead of welcoming their presence, they persecuted them in most places, thus rejecting the people whom God sent as "light to the Gentiles." So now that Israel, *the rejected people* are back in their own homeland, what happens next is unthinkable, the world follows them there and instructs them on where they ought to live and how much building they ought to do, just so as to accommodate the further division of Jewish land. The State of Israel is not an extension of the former Jewish ghettos of Europe or elsewhere in the world. It's an independent, sovereign State of the Jewish people. Therefore, as a respected member of the international community she should not be oppressed, ostracised and miss-characterised for wanting to exist in her ancestral homeland.

The truth be told, in ancient times, there was no country called Jordan. There was Moab across the Jordan River. There also was the city of Jericho and of course Canaan. After Israel had defeated the kings of the plains of Moab, east of the Jordan River Moses gave as their possession all of Moab, to the Israelite tribes of Ruben, Gad and half of the tribe of Manasseh.

Jordan became a country when Great Britain, during her Mandated Period (between 1917-1948) divided Palestine, the name change was done by the Romans as they moved to replace Jewish identity from the land, in 70 AD. Today's Kingdom of Jordan is located in the very part where the two-and-a-half Israelite tribes lived. The remaining Israelites (there were twelve tribes of Israel), did cross the Jordan River and settle on the west side of the Jordan River (which includes what the world calls today, *the West Bank*, but is known to the Jews as Judea & Samaria). All parts of ancient Canaan were bequeathed to the State of Israel.

Today, ancient Canaan also known as Palestine is the lawful territory of the State of Israel. It must be re-emphasised that the entity known as Palestine was divided by the British and as such by so doing Britain created a new Arab State in 1946, known as Jordan. Jordan is on 77 percent of Palestine. Instead of choosing to name the new State, Palestine, they called the 77 percent of the historical Jewish territory, Jordan. Jordan has become the homeland of the Palestinians and other displaced Arabs.

Since Israel possesses, only, the remaining 23 percent of her territory, the question is: why should Israel suffer a further division for another so-called Arab State?

The Lord tells Moses to sound a strong warning to His people:

When you cross the Jordan into the land of Canaan, you must drive out all the inhabitants of the land. Destroy all their stone and metal idols and all their places of worship. Occupy the land and settle in it, because I am giving it to you. Divide the land among the various tribes and clans by drawing lots, giving a large piece of property to a large clan and a small one to a small clan. But if you do not drive out the inhabitants of the land, those that are left will be troublesome as splinters in your eyes and thorns in your sides, and they will fight against you.[4]

See, how the people actually make Israel's existence a "hellish one" by demanding that the Jews freeze all building programmes; they call it a "settlement freeze." Then despite Israelis unilateral withdrawal from Gaza, Hamas, the Arab leadership there continues to attack Israel. Collectively, Arabs anticipate the destruction of the Jewish State. Their demand for a Palestinian State is a step in the direction toward their goal to destroy the State of Israel. Of late they have "stepped up the ante" by demanding that the Middle East be a nuclear-free zone, in the face of a possibility that the international community should strike against Iran's nuclear facilities. The Arabs, led by Egypt seek to remove Israel's advantage in deterrence in the face of the Obama's Administration *new* US policy on the subject and the US' current tenuous relations with Israel.

Dr Kedar, an Israeli Expert on Arab culture and who speaks fluent Arabic, declares that Arab tribalism is a reality in the Arab world. He provides insight to Arab culture. He states that in the Middle East tribalism is the traditional framework that influences the way of life of the Arabs. He posits that this does not only mean loyalty to clan, which includes ethnic groups and family but includes other traditional frameworks which defines their religious beliefs as Sunnis and Shi'ies.

These traditional frameworks were preserved for centuries, because rulers of the Ottoman Empire did not do anything to weaken the Arab traditional framework. What was required and the Arabs gave it, was Arab loyalty. On the other hand, the Europeans ignored these traditional frameworks when they divided the Middle East. They ignored these, so now the modern Arab States are no longer bound to the traditional frameworks; instead, loyalty must now be directed to the State at the expense of their traditional frameworks. However, the people remain loyal to their own traditions.

Consequently, Kedar argues, the modern Arab State is a failure. The Arabs have no loyalty to such State symbols as: Flags, Anthems and the like. These States are governed by one framework which took over the States. For example, Jordan and Saudi Arabia are viewed as dictatorships. No one is elected on a democratic basis. There is gross suppression of Human Rights of individuals, in order that intelligence could be garnered for the State leaders own survival, this is also the case in Syria.

Dr Kedar provides two contrasting paradigms to support his argument:

1. Take for example the successful Gulf States in the Emirates. Every Emirate is a tribe, no one fights. They make fortunes out of oil. They are also small States.
2. Iraq, on the other hand, is a large State. It has more oil than the Gulf. It was and still is a failing State, due to the fact, its tribal society now lives under different conditions than those in the Gulf.

Dr Kedar further argues that wealth is an outcome of societal stability, not an outcome of natural resources.

Furthermore, he points out a very dangerous trend in Arab community. He states that in order for State leaders to maintain a hold on their people they use Israel as a constant threat to their society. By so doing they are able to consolidate power because using Israel as an enemy enables them to put aside quarrels. Israel is not merely an enemy, but she is an eternal enemy. Syria and others need an external enemy in order for their regimes to survive. Therefore, Israel is serving these regimes by being in the region. She is their external enemy. Israel is a "fig leaf" to cover their unwillingness to give up power. Accordingly, Israel is viewed by the Arab people from their Islamic point of view. In their opinion, Israel is not a nation it is a part of a religion. So wherever they might be found in the Middle East, to the Arabs, the Jews are not a nation, only a religion.

Consequently, the Jewish aspiration to create a Jewish State is unheard of. In the Arab psyche, there is no Christian nation, so why should there be a Jewish nation. How can the State be legitimate? Even if the Jews define their nationality by being Jewish – Jewish religion has lost its validity, since Islam came to the world. Islam came to replace the old religions of Jews and Christians. The Koran does not cede to other religions. Therefore, the Arabs belief is that all other religions lost when Islam came to the world.

Dr Kedar adds further that according to Arab beliefs: Judaism doesn't mean anything anymore. The land under conflict was declared in the 7th Century a WAQF. It means the land is a holy endowment for Islam, forever. This land belongs to all Muslims, all over the world. Nobody can change this. *This belief will be tested!*

Here is where the Sovereign Lord comes into the debate. His actions have certainly proven that He alone is God and consequently, He has returned the people of Israel to their land and will keep them there. If this is a battle between Himself and Islam, then He has served notice, He alone is the Lord. He is the God of Israel and will stand by this declaration and prove it.

For thus says the Lord God: Indeed I Myself will search for My sheep and seek them out.

As a shepherd seeks out his flock out his flock on the day he is among his scattered sheep, so will I seek out My sheep and deliver them from all the places where they were scattered on a cloudy and dark day.

And I will bring them out from the peoples and gather them out from the countries, and will bring them to their own land; I will feed them on the mountains of Israel, in the valleys and in the inhabited places of the country.[5]

In addition, that's not all, God tells us:

Hear the word of the Lord, O nations, and declare it in the isles afar off, and say, He who scattered Israel will gather him, and keep him as a shepherd does his flock.[6] God adds, *people of Israel, I have always loved you, so I continue to show you My constant love. There is hope for your future; your children will come back home. I, the Lord, have spoken.*[7]

Meanwhile, Major-General Robert Mood, Chief of Staff of the United Nations Truce Supervision Organisation (UNTSO), headquartered in Jerusalem, states that it's possible to give 25 good answers as to what the conflict is about. However, if one looks into the conflict itself, it's about land.

It's about the historic rights of the Jews to a nation State – to land in this part of the world. It's about the emotional and historical connection to this land for those who were driven away in 1948. It's about the right of the international community to establish a State on the land in this part of the world – without asking the consent of those who live there. The answer is land!

The UN also adds that taking a look at the equation the conflict also includes the peoples' history; it is also about religion, water and culture. Therefore, the reason why the conflict in the Middle East is so hard to be resolved is due to the complex interaction between the issues.

The UN further states that there were two protracted facts driving the perspectives and emotions:

i) Demographics. This makes it hard for the Israelis to accept the refugee problem.
ii) Poverty. Extreme poverty is fed by religious fanatics. On the one hand, trial and discontent, on the other hand, the self-chosen victimisation approaches.

Consequently, the UN's mandate is an open-ended mandate with comprehensive peace as the end-state. It's a regional mandate based on the formal commitment with Egypt, Jordan and others. Even when bilateral peace is achieved the UN's mandate to maintain the comprehensive peace among the parties: Jordan, Egypt, Lebanon and Israel, would still be valid. The role of the UN is to assist. The problems and solutions are owned by the people but the UN is to assist, to have a consistent, long term engagement which would lead to comprehensive peace.

Moreover, Germany asserts that the conflict is about two peoples fighting over the same land.

The difference is for one people, is the outcome of the last 2,000 years – a colonised people – under foreign rule. The other people have lived in the Diaspora under foreign rule. This has caused the Jews to have a different mindset from the Palestinians.

The Jews have been often persecuted, which they have withstood and resisted through the Holocaust and other experiences when Europe tried to annihilate them. Thus, they came to Palestine, where they met people who were also traumatised; the outcome of which we as an international community have to help the parties resolve the conflict by getting involved and presenting a clear idea of what a practicable and equitable solution of the conflict would be, submits Germany.

Furthermore, Germany contends that at the end of the day, there is no just solution to the problem. The one-State solution would not be workable in the foreseeable future. There is no complete justice for Palestinians or Palestinian refugees and Jews. The land has to be split to address the key concerns of both sides.

On the contrary, Member of Israel's Knesset Danny Danon argues that the conflict is a war of religion and it has no connection to the land.

Israel is the only democracy! Israel does not come from the Islamic regime. Nothing Israel does will help promote the peace process. Take for example, the hostile reaction from Gaza to Israel's peace efforts.

Meanwhile, veteran Israel Member of Knesset and Cabinet Minister Benjamin "Benny" Begin (*son of former Prime Minister Menahem Begin, who signed the peace treaty with Egypt's President Saddat in 1979*) also shares his views about the conflict.

Begin argues that not too many people are cognisant of the true nature of the conflict. He relays that it's the unwillingness on the part of the so-called PLO and Hamas, to recognise the right of Israel to establish their home in the land of Israel. Palestine is the idea the Roman Emperor in 136 AD used, as he sought to erase from memory the term Judea and Samaria, as he did with Jerusalem – which was given a name after a Roman god. The Emperor also decided that Judea and Samaria would become part of Greater Syria. It was a clever move. Only, he didn't erase it from our memories.

He examines the ploy by the Arabs and their strategies to continue in their refusal to put an end to the conflict with Israel. Begin says that the Olmert government in 2008 made a dangerous offer to the Palestinians which they rejected. The amazing answer – Abbas said, the gaps were too wide. The PLO cannot say that any offer on Israel's part would end the conflict. The PLO has refused to accept that the Jews are a nationality, except they acknowledge, it's a religion.

Begin emphasises that the Jews are not only religion, but we also comprise a nation. This is indeed a unique situation. This uniqueness is not recognised by the Arabs. This is the root of the conflict. They, the Arabs, would not agree to foreigners roaming on their *sacred land* in large numbers. It has nothing to do with Jewish communities and towns in Judea and Samaria.

On the other hand, Egypt states that the conflict has two layers:

i) The presence of Israel in the heart of the Arab world.
ii) The West is trying to dominate the Middle East based on its geographic location, oceans and proximity to Africa. However, the geopolitical reason is oil. Albeit oil is not a major factor due to the possible decline in the demand for oil as alternative sources of energy are obtained. They were more interventions in the Middle East before the discovery of oil.

Egypt emphasises that the "shorter layer" i.e., the cause of the conflict is due to the presence of Israel in the Middle East. Egypt pointed out that the discrimination against the Jews in the 19th Century resulted in the Zionist Movement wanting a place for the Jews. Hertzog, the father of Zionism first wanted to send the Jews to Latin America. However, the British sent the European Jews to the Middle East, under the British Mandate.

As a caveat, what Egypt did not say was that the British did not fully assist the Jews fleeing the Holocaust in Europe. Many Jews, in the time of their distress were denied entry into Palestine by the British, even as they had nowhere else to go. The British, to appease the Arabs, limited the number of Jews who sought refuge in their ancestral homeland, turned some back to their death, and others they took to Cyprus.

Egypt contends further that Lord Balfour promised the Jews to help create a "National Home." Egypt laments that Balfour promised land he didn't own, to a people who were not his people. He continues, Britain was the superpower and had a Mandate over the land. Consequently, this encouraged an influx of Jews into Palestine. They were buying lands, the people there did not know that the Jews planned to take over Palestine.

Egypt proclaims that Palestinian Arabs and the rest of the Arab world are against Jews living in the land.

Egypt emphasises that the Jews are not a race (a people), but a religion, whereas, Egypt posits that Arab is a race. Palestine, Egypt exclaims, belongs to the Arabs.

In order to enlighten all Arabs and in particular the Egyptians, see the Lord's opinion on this matter:

Even before modern day Egyptians considered themselves Arabs (their forefathers may not have had the same opinion), the Jews were a people and remain so. The Lord told Moses, to deliver a people, not a religion. To claim that the Jews are not a people is a deception. They are a people, they are relevant and they have an inherent right to live in the State of Israel, yes, with Arabs as their neighbours. Thus the Lord says:

Therefore say to the children of Israel: I am the Lord; I will bring you out from under the burdens of the Egyptians, I will rescue you from their bondage, and I will redeem you with an outstretched arm and with great judgements.

I will take you as My people, and I will be your God. Then you shall know that I am the Lord your God who brings you out from under the burdens of the Egyptians.[8]

It's obviously very hard for the Egyptians and the other Arabs to describe the Jews, because they are trying to affix to the Jewish people, their culture and their relationship with their God, a natural interpretation. However, this is a spiritual matter and cannot be discerned with a carnal mind. Note that I did not say it's a religious matter.

The Lord says to Israel:

I will contend with him who contends with you, and will save your children.

I will feed those who oppress you with their own flesh, and they shall be drunk with their own blood as with sweet wine. All flesh shall know that I, the Lord, am your Saviour, and your Redeemer, the Mighty One of Jacob.[9]

Israeli Minister for Social Affairs and Services Isaac Herzog (*son of former President Chaim Herzog and grandson of former Chief Rabbi Isaac Herzog*) states that Israel is the only democracy here in the region. Israel upholds the rule of law and the Supreme Court is independent. He stresses that Israel is a unique place on earth. Its peoples have made aliyah from over 140 countries.

Herzog emphasises that Israel has always stretched her hand out for peace with her neighbours. He states further that there are existing two coalitions in the Middle East.

i) Israel with moderate countries and Fatah
ii) Syria, Hezbollah, Hamas and Iranian extremists.

Herzog opines that the conflict is over land and the right to self-determination with religion as an underlying factor. It can be considered *a clash of civilisations*. Though difficult, it can be solved.

Herzog points to the phenomenon of antisemitism. He argues that the fight against antisemitism will never end. The scars of antisemitism are huge and deep. Antisemitism he posits is all over the world. It's lurking, it mixes with *antiIsraelism*. It's presented as allegations against Israel, such as violations on Human Rights, and Saudi Arabia is funding some of these allegations and programmes.

Palestinian Ambassador of the Observer Mission to the United Nations Dr Riyad H. Mansour submits that the Mideast conflict is all about the policies and actions of the Zionist Movement, in collaboration with the British; creating a tragedy of the Palestinian people.

Dr Mansour stresses that this has led to the occupation of Arab lands in Syria, Lebanon and Palestine. He says also that the Zionist Movement succeeded in planting settlers and establishing a State. As such it has put the Arab States in a state of war and has led to the destruction of Arab national homeland, while creating millions of refugees. However, despite this tragedy, the Arabs have not lost sight of the vision for a home for the displaced Arabs, that since the early 1970s they have been advocating a two-State solution.

The Scriptures certainly refute Dr Mansour's positions. Firstly, the Jews are not settlers, nor are they occupiers of other peoples land. Secondly, Israel too has had to settle displaced Jews, Jews who resided in Arab territories and had to flee after their expulsion, upon the creation of the State of Israel. Thirdly, the Jews have returned to the land God promised to their ancestors and them.

Grief an international law expert (he was not interviewed) argues that after Palestine was specifically created at the San Remo Peace Conference on 24-25 April 1920, as a mandated State to be the Jewish National Home as set out in the Balfour Declaration, and officially placed under British mandatory administration on 1 July 1920, the name "Palestine" became intimately associated in the worldwide public mind with the Jewish people, certainly not with the local Arab inhabitants. The ethnological, legal and linguistic association between Palestine and the Jews in terms of nationality existed because both Palestine and the Jewish National Home were created for each other at the same time under international law, and both terms referred to the same geographical territory (Palestine and the Jewish National Home) were not then defined, but they were understood to include all territory historically conquered, settled and governed by the Twelve Tribes of Israel and their descendants in the first and second Jewish Commonwealths, i.e., "from Dan to Beersheba." As a result, the national designation of "Palestinians" was primarily attributed to the Jews of Palestine. This perception was supported by Article 7 of the Mandate for Palestine which reads as follows:

The Administration of Palestine shall be responsible for enacting a nationality law. There shall be included in this law provisions framed so as to facilitate the acquisition of Palestinian citizenship by Jews who take up permanent residence in Palestine.[10]

Moreover, Peters (*she was not interviewed*) indicates that:

When "Palestine" was referred to by the Arabs, it was viewed in the context of the intrusion of a "Jewish State amidst what the Arabs considered their own exclusive environment or milieu, the 'Arab region.'" As the late Egyptian President Gamal Abdel Nasser "screamed" in 1956, "the imperialists' 'destruction of Palestine' " was "an attack on Arab nationalism," which "unites us from the Atlantic to the Gulf.' "

*Ever since the 1967 Israeli victory, however, when the Arabs deter-
mined they couldn't obliterate Israel militarily, they have skilfully
waged economic, diplomatic and propaganda war against Israel. This,
Arabs reasoned, would take longer than military victory, but ultimately the result would be the same. Critical to the new tactic, however, was a device designed to whittle away at the sympathies of Israel's
allies: what the Arabs envisioned was something that could achieve
Israel's shrinking to indefensible size at the same time that she became
insolvent...*

*As a more effective means of swaying world opinion, the Arabs
adopted humanitarian terminology in support of the "demands" of the
Palestinian refugees," to replace former Arab proclamations of carnage
and obliteration.*[11] (The Arabs themselves created their own
refugee crisis by demanding that Arab citizens flee Palestine as
Arab armies invaded with the goal to obliterate all Jews from the
newly independent State of Israel).

*Consequently, Grief posits that the constant use of the name
"Palestinian" to denote a separate Arab nation in the land of Israel is
fraudulent since no such nation has ever existed, either in the days of
antiquity or in modern times. This is evidenced by the fact that not
once in the literature of the ancient world does the word "Palestinian"
ever appear as a proper noun to describe a nation of that name or an
individual member of such a nation.*[12]

Libya, for its part contends that nobody can say that there
were no Jews among Arabs in the land. They were small in
number, claims Libya, and because of their agony and what happened to them in Europe, Europe was trying to help them find a
homeland. They searched in Libya, Uganda and elsewhere before
the Balfour Declaration granted them their home in the region.

Libya further submits that the State was a Palestinian State
before the British gave the Jews the right to live in the land. He
questions, if the Europeans had a problem with the Jews in
Europe, why send them to this place, among Arabs and Muslims?

Libya stresses that the problem in the area is the Palestinian
problem or cause. All Arabs are supporting the Palestinians. They
are advocating for peace, he claims. The Arabs want the international community to demand that all the parties make peace. He
pointed to Israel's military capabilities and shamelessly claimed

that the Palestinians were only throwing stones at the Israelis. *What about Qassam rockets and missiles?*

Libya calls for the Palestinians to be granted their right to return to live among the Jews.

A message for Libya from the Lord God Himself concerning Israel:

Therefore, behold, the days are coming, says the Lord, that they shall no longer say, As the Lord lives who brought up the children of Israel from the land of Egypt, but, As the Lord lives who brought up and led the descendants of the house of Israel from the north country and from all the countries where I had driven them. And they shall dwell in their own land.[13]

Turkey views the Middle East as one of its major foreign policy priorities. Its geopolitical and historical ties with Israel and Arabs are strong.

Turkey seeks a just and lasting peace in the region and also seeks to improve economic relations which would then usher in a stable and peaceful region; which would benefit Turkey.

The Palestinian question has been promoted as the key problem by all. However, Turkey believes that all tracks should be revitalized. Turkey opines that the inter-related conflict ought to be dealt with more comprehensively; that Turkey played an important role as a mediator in the Syrian-Israel talks and had come very close to reaching an agreement however, the military action in Gaza (in 2008), disrupted the talks. The other tracks include: Israel-Lebanon; Israel-Palestinians and the Israel-Syrian tracks. Turkey believes that the whole process should be undertaken simultaneously.

Turkey says that it is expecting a peace agreement between Syria and Israel and if they can make progress, this track can positively impact the other tracks. Turkey is ready to continue to provide its auspices between the Syrians and the Israelis. Western governments support this process as well as: the EU and the US.

Turkey emphasises that the active engagement of all the international community is very important to put pressure on both sides, to fulfil their responsibility, that there are no alternatives to a negotiated solution. The situation in the region is still fragile;

however, Turkey welcomes President Obama's speech to the Arab community in Cairo (in 2009) as it raises hopes for the region.

Turkey believes that a real opportunity is now, and that the peace process should be revived as soon as possible. Likewise, Turkey calls for concrete results of this approach on the ground.

Jordan says that she first concluded a peace treaty with Israel in 1994. Since then Jordan has had very good co-operation with Israel. Nevertheless, the Arab-Israeli conflict remains unresolved. Consequently, unless the core issues: the Israel-Palestinian tracks, as well as the Israel-Syrian and the Israel-Lebanon tracks are resolved there will be no peace, says Jordan.

Jordan, for its part tries to bring the parties together based on her own experience, which is important in moderating the process. Jordan seeks to assist both sides. However, Jordan supports the Palestinian aspirations and dreams in having their own State, based on UNSC and UNGA Resolutions, and within the framework of the Quartet's Road Map vision and the Arab peace initiative that offers Israel complete peace and diplomatic relationship after withdrawal from *occupied territories* and the establishment of a viable Palestinian State.

Israel sees the initial rejection by the Arabs to the United Nations Partition Plan as a critical element in the Arab-Israeli conflict. Whereas the Jewish side did accept the plan, the Arabs instead rejected same and on the wings of Israel's Declaration of Independence the Arab world declared war against the Jewish State. No sooner the State of Israel was declared on 14 May 1948, the Arabs struck on 15 May 1948.

The Arabs continue to deny the right of Israel to exist as a State for the Jewish people. While on the one hand, Israel is building a remarkable country, on the other hand, Israel has to deal with those who confront it. Added to this is the threat from terrorism. This is a new ingredient in Israel's specific conflict. It has been very apparent in the last few years.

Israel signed peace treaties and has diplomatic relations with Jordan and Egypt. Israel's vision is to have peace; to share peaceful borders with her neighbours. Israel does not desire to have enemies on her borders. Israel does not desire to see armies flowing across the borders, but peoples flowing from one country to another – doing business, sharing values and knowledge and experiences, not weapons. Israel desires to win co-operation with her neighbours, it's a waste of time not to do these things. However, Israel laments, that the vision is not broadly shared.

Likewise, Israeli diplomat Moshe Benzioni who serves as Political Adviser to the Mayor of Jerusalem states that throughout the Middle Ages the Jews had the similar structure: they had a national institution and a common language. Today, Israel is the national homeland for the Jewish people.

Benzioni alludes to the fact that within the Jewish community the majority believe that peace is important, but for peace to be achieved, then, there will be major compromises. Peace will be to everyone's value. A minority says no! The vast majority is willing to make a compromise. Dating back to the 1947 UN's Partition Plan, Benzioni recalls that the majority of Jews was willing to take the compromise.

Unfortunately, the Arab side, continues the diplomat, for the vast majority, rejected the UN's Plan. Arabs see any concession as weakness. They view the conflict as a zero sum game. In the end they want the whole land. They see compromise as forced on them out of weakness. They see concessions as harmful to them. The Arab side sees every concession as a loss – they gain – we lose, that's terrible. The vast majority of Arabs consider that Israel is not a legitimate entity. For the Arabs they can't say that their god made a mistake. Therefore, they will not compromise for peace. Consequently, in the long run this does not lead to a negotiated settlement. The Israeli side is willing to make concession, willing to make compromise.

Professor Eldad and Member of the Knesset states that most people think that this is a territorial conflict. If this were a territorial conflict the solution would be to divide the land, draw a border. We tried it – dividing or partitioning the land, the first attempt in 1922. In 1929 the Arabs reigned terror and shed Jewish blood all over Palestine: in Hebron, Tel Aviv, almost everywhere. The British catered to the Arab demands to appease the Mufti.

Great Britain was granted a Mandate in 1917. The Arabs refused to co-operate with the mandated authority in the matter. The British then, in order to fulfill a promise to Saudi Arabia gave ¾ of the Jewish homeland to the Arabs, and the outcome is now Jordan.

Subsequently, the 29 November 1947 Partition Plan didn't work. The Arabs rejected the whole idea. They said they would not accept a Jewish State in the region.

After providing a brief overview into the Arab-Israeli conflict Prof. Eldad then reiterates that Israel does not suffer from a territorial conflict. It's a religious War. The Arabs, according to their beliefs, this is forever a WAQF land. Once occupied by Muslims, so forever they cannot have any foreign rule over the land. Therefore, they will not tolerate a Jewish State, no matter how small it is. For example, Iran has no territorial conflict with Israel, yet Iran threatens the Jewish State.

It's not the settlements that bother the Muslims, its religion.

The greatest success of the Arabs is to create an image that there was a Palestinian State. There is no *Palestinian nation*. There is only Arab nation. *A Palestinian nation* is the creation of the colonial powers. The world now recognises a Palestinian people. Conversely, the world does not recognise that there is a Palestinian State already in existence, which is Jordan.

There are 98 percent Palestinians in Jordan, with a couple thousands of Hasmites from Saudi Arabia, argues Eldad.

Prof. Eldad asks the question, why does the US support the Palestinian demand? He concludes that the US has lots of troubles. He adds that the US is facing war in Afghanistan, facing serious problems in Iraq, facing the Iranian threat to create nuclear weapons, facing North Korea (though a non- Muslim country), dealing with Pakistan's internal threats to her nuclear weapons.

Therefore, to solve these threats, to create a coalition of the moderate Muslims States against the extreme; some moderate States tell the US that the key to solving the US' problems is to solve the Palestinian problem first, in order to get their support to put pressure on Iran. Those who are leading this demand for a Palestinian State are Egypt and Saudi Arabia.

For many years, during the Cold War, Israel was seen as a Western base. Israel was the stronghold, the fortress for Western civilisation. After the Cold War, Israel's importance deteriorated. During the Cold War, the US had plans to stop Russia's influence in the Middle East. Russia had influence over the Arabs and supplied them with weapons.

Today, for the US, its commercial interests in the Middle East takes precedence.

Furthermore, the time that has elapsed since the Holocaust means the "guilt feelings" are no longer there.

Importantly, the US has declined in her support for Israel. Prof. Eldad repeats, yet again the changes in US-Israel relations. He lists:

i)   The fall of the Soviet Union
ii) The growing interests of the Arab world
iii) The time lapse of the Holocaust. These changed the balance of US support for Israel.

The Editor of The Jerusalem Post Christian Edition Gershom Gale advises that the conflict is a modern version of a family conflict: Ishmael vs. Isaac. Whereas Jews have lived in other lands, they have never claimed any part as theirs. Indeed, Arabs have lived in Palestine without any rights to the land. They moved in some time ago and now claim it as theirs. So when the Jews came back they found these Arabs living in their houses...

Muslims, he says, love death and will defeat those who love life. They worship death.

Territorial claims are used to foster a greater Arab goal. Islam has the notion to rule the world. Therefore, once they had control of any land, and have lost same to the infidels, they are commanded to get it back. So in their estimation the State of Israel is either Muslim or is going to become Muslim.

Although the US Department of State did not provide a view on what the conflict was about. The Department did say how the conflict impacts the US relations with States in the region:

The US opines that the situation in the Middle East is volatile and complex but that the President and Secretary of State have made it clear that difficulty cannot cause the United States to turn away. To the contrary, they recognise and have said that peace and stability in the Middle East are in US national interest.

Further, the President knows that achieving this goal will be difficult, but he also has said that he will not waiver in his persistent pursuit of a comprehensive peace in the Middle East. For that reason, he has dedicated himself and his Administration to the resumption of Israeli-Palestinian negotiations and to the creation of an atmosphere that maximises the prospects of success.

With regard to the Administration's vision for the region, President Obama and Secretary Clinton have stated their desire to use engagement with all countries in the region to address issues of mutual concern. The US is not engaging for engagement's sake, but rather to advance the interests of the US and their allies. The US remains committed to their goal of helping the nations of the Middle East move towards prosperity and a lasting peace.

The President has appointed Senator George Mitchell as his Special Envoy for the Middle East Peace. The President has been explicit from that day on: our goal is a lasting peace between Israel and its neighbours and a two-State solution with a Palestinian State living side by side in peace and security with the State of Israel.

Now given the attitudes, beliefs and the inherent religious factors driving the Arabs, there is no way in the future Arabs would live in peace and security with Israel as a non-Muslim State, even if the great powers were to succeed in creating the long-awaited Palestinian State.

In the final analysis the Arab-Israeli conflict is about the rejection of the True and Living God, the Lord God of Israel. It's driven by satanic forces in opposition to God. People are the pawns in this spiritual warfare.

It's God of Israel vs. the god of this world.

The ancient peoples of the Middle East had their god, *Baal,* and many other gods. However, the God of Israel demonstrated to those people then, that He alone is God. Today's Middle Eastern peoples have another god before the Lord God of Israel. The god they serve is not the same as the God of Israel, no they are not the same. Israel's God has revealed His character and He differs from the god the Arabs speak of. The God, the Lord of Israel has categorically stated that He alone is God and beside

Him there is no other. The Lord God reiterates unequivocally that there shall be no other gods before Him!

The Lord says, come together, people of the nations, all who survived the fall of the empire; present yourselves for the trial! The people who parade with their idols of wood and pray to gods that cannot help them – those people know nothing at all!

Come and present your case in court; let the defendants consult one another. Who predicted long ago what would happen! Was it not I, the Lord, the God who saves His people?

There is no other god.

Turn to Me now and be saved people all over the world! I am the only God there is.[14]

The opposition to the presence and rule of God is demonstrated in several ways:

- The emphasis on the supremacy of a particular religion.
- The antisemetic trends, manifested in the refusal to recognise Israel's right to exist as a Jewish nation:
  - o The malice, hatred and contempt directed at the Jews
  - o The plans to isolate the Jews globally, weaken their resolve to preserve their heritage and then to destroy the Jewish State.
- God, for His part will demonstrate His capability to keep Israel in the land of their inheritance. The land He gave to their ancestors and to their descendants, the present Jewish population. He will also cause all the peoples of the world to come to the realisation that:

This is the purpose that is purposed against the whole earth, and this is the hand that is stretched out over all the nations.

For the Lord of hosts has purposed, and who will annul it? His hand is stretched out, and who will turn it back?[15]

Chapter 10

Is the Two-State Solution the Only Viable Option for Mideast Peace?

The Nub for Finding Mideast Peace: World Opinion!

Security for the State of Israel is as paramount as life itself. Without adequate security, the State of Israel could suffer terrible devastation. This must never happen!

Unlike other countries, Israel is surrounded by neighbours who seek her demise. Some are actually engaged in a "proxy" war with her through their terrorist associates, namely, Hamas and Hezbollah.

In 2006 the UN stopped the war which was underway between Israel and Hezbollah. Peacekeepers were left behind in Lebanon to prevent Hezbollah rearming. This terrorist entity has not only rearmed with long range missiles and other lethal weapons, but has issued a challenge to Israel, threatening a future war; confident that its arsenals will bring about the defeat of Israel. This shows that the UN's policy to interfere in halting wars between Israel and her enemies in the Middle East and providing peacekeepers to keep the peace is an embarrassing failure for the International Organisation. Hezbollah should never have been allowed to rearm. Lebanon should be held accountable, Syria and Iran as well.

Henceforth, Israel cannot trust the "mantra" of the international community, that, to support the creation of another Arab State in its own 'backyard' would guarantee its own security and the prosperity for the entire region. Peace does not come thru' weakness. Security guarantees in the future would mean nothing except Hamas and Hezbollah are disarmed and are prevented from attacking Israel under the guise of "resistance" as their actions are really acts of war. These two Iranian proxies and friends of Turkey must be contained otherwise they will give impetus to other "minor league players" to join forces to seek to destroy Israel.

Whereas the Arabs strategic goal is the destruction of Israel, Israel seeks the preservation of the Jewish State. The international community has interpreted the conflict to mean that in order for there to be a peaceful region, the Israelis must make concessions and adopt *confidence building measures* (whatever this means), more or less without reciprocity. Should Israel grant these concessions, they would not only endanger the Jewish State but serve to advance their enemies interest, which the Jews have repeatedly stated would lead to the destruction of the State of Israel.

The Arabs have been unwilling to accept Israel's presence in the region. They want the Jews out, whereas, the Jews want to stay in their homeland. The Jews are prepared to live peacefully with their Arab neighbours, but as in the case when Jordan captured Judea and Samaria, the Arabs ordered all Jews out of their midst. The Arabs will gladly expel the Jews from Israel should they gain leverage over the Jewish people. The Jews have indicated their willingness to compromise further for the sake of peace, the Arabs have refused to make compromises on their part, and Abbas usually reaffirms his commitment to preconditions before sitting down with Israel, despite calls from Israel to talk without preconditions.

The perennial climate of war in which the Jewish people find themselves impact their economy as scarce financial resources have to be directed at intelligence gathering and defence. Israel's economy has accomplished much, and much more could be attained should she find peace a realistic resolution to the conflict with her neighbours.

Meanwhile, the policy of appeasement thrust upon Israel allows her to send the wrong signals to the Arabs. To some extent Israel is keeping the conflict alive by being forthcoming, i.e., adopting the policy of appeasement as a desirable instrument to resolving the conflict. Going along with the international community's thrust is detrimental to Israel's national interest. The policy of appeasement actually brings about war. Most nations hate war, they are not really willing to fight their enemies, and this sends signals of weakness and enables the other side to increase its demands. Thus Abbas could proudly reject Olmert's generous offer of 97 percent of what the Arabs demanded. Instead, he later boasted that the three-percent gap remaining was too wide. Yes, the man rejected all 97 percent of the "goodies" Olmert offered him including: territory and the return of Arabs.

When Israel removes its citizens by force from their homes so as to accede to international pressure, they are actually making room for war as such moves empower the Arabs. Consequently, an attack against the Jewish State becomes imminent. In game theory such moves create the right motivation, the right incentives for war. Those who shout peace are the war mongers. They do not want peace! Therefore, if Israel wants peace, Israel should prepare for war! It's a principle the enemy understands only too well. As a former US president stated years ago "speak softly, carry a big stick." When the players see that Israel will hold its ground, they will be more likely to willingly reach a co-operative outcome. Israel ought to send the Palestinians a strong signal saying "if you don't co-operate with me today, then I won't with you tomorrow." The goal is to co-operate today for tomorrow. The Arabs must learn this! They must also be called upon to make concessions, real concessions toward Israel. Then the parties would have no need to go to war, otherwise, they will eventually be driven to war.

US Representative Congressman Doug Lamborn states that the first step towards peace in the Middle East is for Arabs and Muslims to recognise Israel's right to exist. After this, then, the global community can structure the pursuits or give consideration for a Palestinian State.

Meanwhile, Israel asserts that her country has signed two peace agreements with neighbouring States: Jordan and Egypt, and as a consequence, does enjoy relative success to a certain point. However, with the Palestinians, instead of seeking peace with Israel, they instead introduced terrorism. This caused a setback. Albeit Israel believes that there are prospects for a real genuine hand outstretched, for real genuine peace.

Israel expects that the Palestinians will deal with their deep rooted hostilities toward the Jews. The peace that Israel expects is one that goes deeper than "cease-fires". The very last Arab should be cognisant of what peace is, therefore, Palestinians should instead seek a permanent, long-lasting peace, seek an irreversible cease-fire and seek to promote mutual interests with the Jews. The Palestinians should also abhor violence and terrorism, they also need to stop thinking that these instruments would bring about their desired results.

Israel is confronting her challenges on two-fronts: fighting terrorism and engaging in negotiations with moderates. Israel's aspiration for the region is one in which Israel is able to share of her skills and experiences(science, medicine, education, et al) with not only the world but with her neighbours. However, Israel emphasises that the Jewish State has to be recognised as an integral part of the region so as to foster regional peace and security. The region must no longer be defined by war and conflict, but become renowned for peace, common values and common success.

Cogently, the United States maintains that it is committed to a just, lasting and comprehensive peace in the Middle East. That includes resolution of the Israeli-Palestinian conflict. The US' goal is two-States living side by side in peace and security – a Jewish State of Israel, with true security for all Israelis; and a viable, independent Palestinian State with contiguous territory that ends the occupation which began in 1967, and realises the potential of the Palestinian people.

It must be noted here that the Jews in 1967 re-conquered its historical land from Jordan in war, after Jordan had captured same in war, 18 years prior. It was Jordan that occupied Jewish cities: Judea and Samaria and a part of Zion, i.e., Jerusalem.

In order to help create a climate in which productive negotiations can begin and succeed, the US continues to call on Palestinians to end incitement against Israel, to maintain the progress on security reform and institutional development, and the US continues to emphasise that America does not accept the legitimacy of continued Israeli settlements and calls on Israel to take additional steps to improve the daily lives of Palestinians. Furthermore, the US urges Arab States to take steps to reach out and engage Israel directly. These steps, the US believes will help create an atmosphere in which productive negotiations can begin and succeed.

In addition, the US has asked Arab governments, in the context of the Arab Peace Initiative and Israeli and Palestinian action toward peace, to take meaningful steps to demonstrate that a peaceful and prosperous future for all of the region's people is possible.

Dr Kedar declares that the problem for Israel with its neighbours is not a problem of land, but a problem of existence. The world knows about struggles over territories – India and Pakistan over Kashmir, Britain and Argentina over the Falkland Islands. Here in the Middle East, the fight over territory is a secondary matter. The main fight is existence, because the Arab world does not recognise Israel's right to exist. The Arabs claim to the 1967 borders is a deception, because they did not recognise the right of Israel to exist even before 1967, look back to 1948 and prior. In Arab view even Tel Aviv is occupied. The fact that the Jews live in the land and have become masters of the land is against Sharia Law (Islamic Law).

Dr Kedar points out the second deception by the Arabs. He says, in the West peace recognises the independence and sovereignty of each other. However, in Islam, peace is totally different. Peace is normal relations between communities who live together under Islamic rule. In their tradition this is the only peace which exists. Theoretically, there cannot be peace between Islamic States and the infidels because everybody should enter under the umbrella of Islam.

This fact is unknown in the West, laments the professor.

Therefore, through the eyes of Islamic culture the conflict is much deeper than territory.

Dr Kedar says that the two-State solution wouldn't work.

He advances that the Arab world presents this phenomenon for more than 60 years, only to keep this problem bleeding, in order to push to repossess Israel when they can. Israel should keep in its hands the rural areas to ensure these hills do not become terrorist's hills. He suggested further that the areas where Arabs live could be based on the Gulf paradigm, where they live according to their tribes, because they know how to live with each other.

Moreover, Prof. Eldad argues that some Europeans now see that Israel will endanger its people if there is a Palestinian State, but they don't care. They forge ahead saying: we will sign a treaty to protect Israel if she is attacked. Therefore, now more and more pressure is being placed on Israel – it's dangerous.

Some major cities in Israel are 30 or 40 km away from the border – the whole country is under fire. It doesn't matter if its home-made fire, it's enough to terrorise a whole State.

The other side uses terror activities; this makes it very difficult to fight. The situation is: Terrorists groups vs. The State.

Prof Eldad emphasises that the reason the State of Israel was created is so that: we could defend ourselves. We only trust ourselves. Nobody came to help us in Europe, until much later, in the Holocaust, and similarly in 1967. He submits that previous US Administrations have gone so far as to drag their feet, for example when Abba Eban of the Ministry of Foreign Affairs went to the US to seek help, US President Johnson told him: if you act alone, you'll be left alone.

Begin maintains that Jews must be allowed to live and raise their families in their homeland of Judea and Samaria; where their prophets prophesied, kings walked, etc. It's absurd to expect otherwise.

Begin also states that for many people, the conclusion is very grim. The moderates support a two-State solution with the Arabs alongside Israel. Plans to return refugees to their actual homes will then establish one-State, an Arab State with a Jewish minority.

The Cabinet Minister does not see an end to the conflict, while the leadership of Israel's neighbours maintain the same attitudes they have held for decades. Furthermore, he states that the State of Israel flourishes despite the conflict. It flourishes in culture, education, the arts, and so forth. He reiterates that despite all its problems Israel is still a flourishing society. "Time is in favour of those who make good use of time," concludes Begin.

Nevertheless, Minister Herzog of the Labour coalition argues that he unequivocally supports the two-State solution.

He states that Israel will achieve peace and this will give Israel a qualitative edge. He says that Israel has accepted the paradigm of dividing the land. It requires the Palestinians to accept once and for all that the Jewish State will exist. However, he acknowledges that Gaza has remained as a major thorn and he did not know how it can be resolved.

Herzog posits that if there were no two-State solution, analyse the alternative, it would be the end of Zionism. The Palestinians have a right to self-determination. Israel should be innovative and bold. He stresses that the international community should support Israel in this. He concludes that the Clinton proposals of 2000 are still there and are still viable today.

On the other hand, MK Danon states that he strongly opposes a Palestinian State in Judea and Samaria. Israel, he says will receive more Qassam rockets, only this time they will land in the centre of the Jewish State. He contends further that Israel seeks a partner. But there is no partner on the Palestinian side to rule and stand behind agreements. He adds that if today's Palestinian leaders were to go to Gaza, Hamas won't let them out.

He suggests that the vacant land which is located in Judea and Samaria should be under the sovereignty of Israel. However, Danon did stress that this should not include the Arab cities where most of the Palestinian people live, but that they should be linked to Jordan in a type of a confederation. Gaza, he emphasises should be connected to Egypt, thus the burden of solving the conflict will be to Jordan and Egypt as well.

Danon expressed concerns at the fact that Arabs are building freely whereas rules that are in place restricted the Jews. With reference to the US, Danon states that it will take them some time, they will see we don't have a partner. It will happen! Concerning the Europeans, he declares that the EU is sponsoring terrorism. The money they give to the Palestinians goes toward terrorism. And he identifies Iran as a major threat to Israel.

Furthermore, Benzioni argues that most Israelis are uncomfortable with the American two-State solution which also proposes the division of Jerusalem. It gives away too much, he stresses. Most Israelis are waiting for the Palestinians to indicate genuine acceptance of Israel's right to exist. The feeling is there will be a "giant Gaza" rather than a small Gaza. Israel needs clear and positive indicators that the people who are willing to make compromises are in control, i.e., to live in peace with Israel. He commented that any division would be very difficult because of the zero sum view: a lack of compromise would make peace almost impossible.

He further points out that in the Jewish culture open debates are allowed. However, no such concept exists among the Arabs. Those Arabs are killed who might want to voice compromises. The people in Palestinian controlled areas don't dare express verbal ideas or free thinking. Arab societies are still closed, and as a consequence their societies are limited. This attitude helps them to refuse to see that the other side might have some merit.

Again because of the lack of compromises the refugee question becomes a political tool. There are no compromises; there is a lack of flexibility; a lack of acceptance of peace for 60 years. Their *attitude* only makes the problem less solvable. Nevertheless, there is hope for a settlement that would bring a win-win solution, concludes Benzioni.

Meanwhile, Maj.-General Mood contends that the issue of the Palestinian State is not a part of his mandate. It is that of the Special Coordinator of the Office of the United Nations Special Co-ordinator for Lebanon (UNSCOL). However, now that it's on the table, the two-State solution was proposed because of demographics. Israel is the nation State of the Jews – they will not compromise on this. The Palestinians Liberation Organisation (PLO) constitutes a threat to some Arab countries. However, the insistence of Israel that this land is the nation State of the Jews excludes other people. Consequently, governments in the region use this to serve their own domestic agenda.

Germany states that her relations with the State of Israel is a special one. Germany took the position years ago to make this relationship very strong, for historical reasons. Germany also has relations with the Arabs. German relations with both sides serve as a balancing act. The Middle East is a neighbouring region to Germany and it's an important region. Everything that happens in the region has implications for the rest of the world. Germany has achieved the position as a trusted partner in the region. She:

- Mediates to support both sides
- Does not exert pressure
- Encourages each side to find solutions

Germany does support the proposed two-State solution for two peoples living side by side. Germany is a part of the Quartet; its position is reflected in the Quartet's statements as that of the EU as well.

Furthermore, Germany expects that Israel must stop building and expanding... A perquisite to create an atmosphere to persuade their Arab friends to create a sustainable peace process is that Israel should refrain from taking actions which would undermine her credibility. To the Palestinians, Germany urges them to continue the path they begun in 2007, under the Fayyad government. Germany expects that they will continue to fight incitement, to end violence against Israel, take steps to:

- Take away illegal weapons
- Disarm private citizens
- Demilitarise the society
- Amnesty
- Build Palestinians institutions
- Improve security and justice.

Senegal has chaired the Committee on Palestine at the United Nations since 1975. This 23 Member Committee was created by the General Assembly. The country itself has a Jewish community and an Israeli Embassy. Senegal also has North African and Arab communities. Therefore, Senegal sees itself as very balanced.

Senegal views that from an historical perspective Jews, Arabs and Africans are the three groups that have suffered and need to work together. Senegal sees itself playing the role to bridge the gap between Palestinians and Jews and between Arabs and Jews.

Senegal, contends that the two-State Solution is very good; the best solution. However, Senegal sees the one-State as ideal, but notes that it would be very difficult to have *them* in one State, but suggests that it would be good for the future.

Additionally, Senegal wants to continue to speak to both sides. She has asked that the conflicting parties to work toward peace and recognise each other.

Moreover, Turkey does support a two-State solution. Turkey shares the vision with the Arab community in the Arab League, the Arab Peace Initiative as well as the Saudi Initiative. Turkey also expresses support for the UN Security Council Resolutions, the Madrid Principles and the Road Map Initiatives.

Turkey demands that the international community peace solution should be based on the land for peace principle. Turkey also calls for the division of Jerusalem based on the establishment of an independent Palestinian State

Turkey believes that Israel has a right to live in peace and security within its recognised borders. Turkey says that they expect Israel to adopt a positive approach and all Arab countries are awaiting concrete steps.

Turkey expresses concern about rifts among Palestinian groups and calls for national reconciliation and urges that cooperation should be a priority among all factions. Turkey supports Egypt's efforts in trying to bring Fatah and Hamas together in unity. Nevertheless, Turkey expressed disapproval at Hamas rocket attacks against Israel, and says that Hamas should be integrated in the political structure. Hamas has the responsibility to meet the expectations of the international community, contends Turkey.

Egypt also supports the two-State solution, saying that there is international support for this. Egypt also calls for clear borders. Egypt argues that the two-State solution was nothing new. Admitting that Arabs first rejected it, but now they support it.

Egypt asserts that Israel should engage in serious negotiations to give Palestinians their rights. Egypt also insists that Israel must stop alleged aggression and act as a State and not as a militia. *Egypt claims that Palestinians unite and engage seriously with Israel on broader issues of settlement.*

Additionally, Egypt declares that Arab nations have nothing against the Jews as a people. The problem, Egypt says, is with Israel and Zionism, where the expansion aspiration is well rooted.

Egypt further states that Israel should give the Palestinians their land in return for peace; and reveals that the Arabs do provide cover to the Palestinians through the legal track.

Jordan fully supports the Palestinian National Authority along with the PLO. Jordan believes that they are the only legitimate leadership organizations equipped to represent the Palestinian people. Jordan actively participates in the Quartet meetings and intends to help the Palestinians achieve statehood. Jordan affirms that she maintains an historic role in protecting and managing the holy shrines in the areas it had occupied for 18 years which are now remaining in Palestinian areas over in Judea and Samaria.

Jordan believes that the region has wasted a lot of resources in conflict and insists that the resources could have best served to develop the human resources in the region. Further, it's in Jordan's national interest that a comprehensive peace be concluded very soon. This would hold out the prospects for regional development in joint ventures, develop water resources and so forth. Water is a political issue, States have to come together to agree on how to utilise this resource at their national levels.

The core of Jordan's foreign policy: No peace without two-States. It's in Jordan's national interests. Jordan further explains that this issue falls at the heart of Israel's national security interests and notes that it's in Israel's interest that the two-State solution is established according to the Road Map. That it would help in ending the frustrations and fury in the region.

Jordan further argues that a solution *by division of the land* would deny international terrorists a reason to build a case on. International terrorists try to build their case in the absence of a political settlement. Jordan asserts that the Palestinians hate that international terrorists are taking advantage of their national aspirations.

Jordan is willing to bring this conflict to a peaceful threshold and to assist the Palestinians to develop their national institutions in preparation for their own national State.

Libya contradicts its Arab brothers by insisting on not two-States but one-State for both peoples to live together in a democratic State.

It doesn't take a magic wand to see what is behind Libya's position. A democratic State with Arabs outnumbering the Jews would quietly ruin the Jewish aspirations for their own State. It's a ploy to destroy the Jewish State by the ballot box.

Libya contends that the UN accepted Israel and forgot about the Palestinians when they divided Palestine. It's not right! It's not fair, insists Libya.

Libya also argues that they are not against the Jews, nor are they against the Palestinians negotiating with the Jews. However, Libya stresses that there will be no peace until the US and EU countries help Israel to come to a compromise and insists that there must be a right of Palestinians returning to Israel. Libya believes that without the US exerting pressure on the Israelis to accept the Palestinians there can be no peace. Libya concludes, saying, this is not easy but its views have to be considered.

Dr Mansour of the Palestinian Mission to the UN argues that since the 1970s they have been advocating a two-State solution. The Palestinians, he says, are prepared to have their State on 22 percent of historic Palestine.

Based on the finding in previous chapters (especially Chapter 5), this means that the Palestinians are saying that the Jewish State must be on the remaining one percent or go someplace else. This would not do. Jordan controls 77 percent of the said Palestine, whereas Israel had control of the remaining 23 percent of Palestine but has since withdrawn from places such as Gaza, 80 percent of Hebron and other areas due to international treaties and pressures. Perhaps that's why he calls for the remaining 22 percent as he may be saying that they currently have one percent. His call makes it clear that they want all of the entity of Palestine, which is all of the State of Israel.

God will have none of this! This is the real story behind the conflict, the greed for Jewish territory! In the Arab world it's all of Israel or nothing! In God's word it's none of His land and even what they have now they will lose to Israel!!!

Dr Mansour maintains that this is their vision! He elaborated that there is global consensus on the two-State solution; and advanced that now the international community needs the political will so as to realise the Palestinian State. He denies that the two-State initiative begun with the Quartet. He says that it dates back to 1947, and everybody now accepts this notion.

Meanwhile, an Israeli spokesman in Jewish Hebron, David Wilder argues that the Arab aspiration is not Israel as such, getting control of Israel is one goal, but their ultimate goal is to govern the world under Islamic rule and influence. The Muslims, he submits, aspire to control Washington, London, Paris, Berlin, return to Madrid, and control the rest of the world. He laments, that while the Arabs are allowed to build unrestricted on the land, Jews are confined, contained, as in parts of Europe sometime ago. Wilder insists that the land belongs to the State of Israel.

Gale concurs and submits that the Palestinians do not want a State of their own. The Palestinians are here as agents, left in the land by Jordan and others to make a case for occupation after the 1967 war. Gale does not believe that the Jews have the right to give away land. He calls for the Arabs to recognise the right of Israel to exist. He also urges Israel to impress upon the Arabs its strength and in a sense this will give Israel peace.

He points out that in 1948 the Jerusalem Post was bombed, several employees were injured and two were killed by the Arabs in the attack.

Cogently, the Mayor of Jerusalem Nir Barkat believes that contrary to the Obama's Administration, Jerusalem must remain whole, as the united capital of Israel. He points out that Jerusalem comes from the root word in Hebrew, shalem. The Mayor continues: if you put a shovel in the ground anywhere in this city, you find Jewish roots. For thousands of years Jerusalem has been the heart and soul of the Jewish people. Beyond that, there is no example in the history of the world of a split city that works. Dividing a city is focusing on the differences, while he is focused on the common denominator and bringing together all residents of the city.

Mayor Barkat speaking about his vision for Jerusalem concludes: three thousand years ago, Jerusalem was a destination site for pilgrims from around the world. It was a place each person yearned to visit at least once in their lifetime. He wants to open Jerusalem once again for the world to enjoy and he invites all to come to experience Jerusalem.

In conclusion, the proposed two-State solution is doomed to failure. The parties have divergent views and the international community persistently ignores this reality. One party, the Jews, desire to survive. To them life is important and given the opportunity to exist in their homeland, they could make an invaluable difference to the region and the world at large. The other, the Arabs, have collectively called for the destruction of the Jewish State. There is consensus on this among them, so no Arab State has publically condemned this call. In fact proxies are being used to oppress the Israelis right now and serve as "thorns in their sides."

Yet, the international community insists that the only viable option is to divide the Jewish State so as to usher in an era of peace. This move will never bring peace in the Middle East! What is needed in the region is a stronger Israel holding on to her territory including all of Jerusalem; not a division of territory.

The international community must take a step back and rethink the situation clearly. Not because an opinion is popular makes it a viable one. Someone needs to be pragmatic. The reality is that the same Arabs, now called *Palestinians,* are called by this name because they serve the Arabic, Turkish and Persian interests. Interests that are clearly articulated: the destruction of the Jewish State and the removal of Jews from the region.

A further division of the State of Israel is a further violation of God's intent and plan. And this act will not go unpunished. Hegemonies will change, powers will be weakened, economic woes will be further escalated, natural disasters will increase, and more and more plagues will be unleashed from the heavens. Just remember what happened to ancient Egypt when she tried to stand-up to God. God unleashed His plagues on that territory and humbled the Egyptians. Don't mess with God!

Moses, the great Hebrew leader submits this account for our reflection:

The people of Israel left Egypt on the fifteenth day of the first month of the year, the day after the first Passover. Under the Lord's protection they left the city of Rameses in full view of the Egyptians, who were burying the first-born sons that the Lord had killed. By doing this, the Lord showed that He was more powerful than the gods of Egypt.[1]

Therefore, to force Israel to capitulate to the Arabs will force God to show the entire world His might and power. He is all powerful and He will defend His great name before you His enemies, and establish His glory before His people, Israel. He is committed to doing so. He is prepared to show that He is the only God in the Middle East and the world as a whole! Therefore, mortal men take heed; do not divide God's land, again!

The ancient prophet Zechariah announced a promise God gave to him for His people. He says:

The Lord Almighty gave this message to Zechariah:

I have longed to help Jerusalem because of My deep love for her people, a love which has made me angry with her enemies.

I will return to Jerusalem, My holy city, and live there. It will be known as the faithful city, and the hill of the Lord Almighty will be called the sacred hill...it's not impossible for Me.[2]

God does not concede to men, men concede to God! Therefore, take note that God has exposed the kingdom of darkness' operation against His heavenly kingdom. The Arab-Palestinian-Israeli conflict is designed in the "spirit realm" to make God look a liar. However, God will fight to defend His holy name. He will defend Israel! Consequently, men everywhere, the current status quo will not remain the same for long. God says:

I, and I alone am God; no other god is real. I kill and I give life, I wound and I heal, and no one can oppose what I do.

As surely as I am the living God, I raise My hand and I vow that I will sharpen My flashing sword and see that justice is done. I will take revenge on My enemies and punish those who hate Me.

My arrows will drip with their blood, and My sword will kill all who oppose Me. I will spare no one who fights against Me; even the wounded and prisoners will die.

Nations you must protect the Lord's people – He punishes all who kill them. He takes revenge on His enemies and forgives the sins of His people.[3]

Further, Moses' parting words to the people of Israel serve to testify of God's intended faithfulness which is relevant to them today; for blessings are timeless. He says:

Israel, how happy you are!

There is no one like you, a nation saved by the Lord. The Lord Himself is your shield and your sword, to defend you and give you victory. Your enemies will come begging for mercy, and you will trample them down.[4]

Chapter 11

Christian Alliance: Building Bridges; Strengthening Ties with Israel

Encouraging Christian-Jewish Relations

Helping Israel, secured the future of the prostitute Rahab and her family from certain destruction in Jericho city. Here's an account of a woman who in "ancient times" recognised that her destiny, survival and future were tied to her support of Israel. Albeit she was a woman of ill-repute, she however, recognised that the hour of her salvation was near and took hold of same; seeking to save not only herself, but her kindred also. This is truly the purpose of Israel... thru' them we received redemption... The Scriptures relay the woman's story as follows:

The Israelites are encamped in Moab, today's Jordan, where the two-and-a-half Israelite tribes: Ruben, Gad and the half tribe of Manasseh had settled their wives and children, along with their animals and then they joined with the fighting men of the other tribes to lead the children of Israel into Canaan. However, they must pass thru Jericho. Therefore, Joshua sends two spies to Jericho. The intelligence machinery in the city learns that there were two Israelites in the city and a city wide search begins for the two men. The men find refuge in a most unlikely place:

When they came to the city, they went to spend the night in the house of a prostitute named Rahab. The king of Jericho heard that some Israelites had come to spy out the country, so he sent word to Rahab: The men in your house have come to spy out the whole country! Bring them out!

Before the spies settled down for the night, Rahab went up on the roof and said to them, "I know that the Lord has given you this land. Everyone in the country is terrified of you. We have heard how the Lord dried up the Red Sea in front of you when you were leaving Egypt...We were afraid as soon as we heard about it; we have all lost our courage because of you. The Lord your God is God in heaven above and here on earth.

Now swear by Him that you will treat my family as kindly as I have treated you, and give me some sign that I can trust you... Don't let us be killed!"[1] As you would expect, Israel kept her promise to Rahab.

However, before the Israelites reach Jericho, they have to cross the Jordan River. The Lord showed them His mighty power once again as He did at the Red Sea: though by different rules of engagement He demonstrates His mighty power over the environment, and was able to achieve the same purpose, thus resulting in the Israelites ability to cross the Jordan River. *Because of this everyone on earth will know how great the Lord's power is, and you will honour the Lord your God forever,*[2] Joshua told the people.

The story continues:

... Then all the army went straight up to the hill into the city and captured it.

With their swords they killed everyone in the city, men and women, young and old. They also killed the cattle, sheep and donkeys.

Joshua then told the two men who had served as spies, "Go into the prostitute's house, and bring her and her family out, as you promised her...

Then they set fire to the city and burned it to the ground, along with everything in it, expect the things made of gold, silver, bronze, and iron, which they took and put in the Lord's treasury. But Joshua spared the lives of the prostitute Rahab and all her relatives because she had hidden the two spies that he had sent to Jericho. (Her descendants have lived in Israel to this day).[3]

Today a number of Christians have made it their personal goal to go to Israel to serve the people there. They too have heard of God's mighty acts among His people and have decided that they will serve the Lord God of Israel, by living among the Jewish people and serving them.

Christian service comes at a time when America wants less to do with God. Americans are pressed repeatedly to accept the notion of separation of *Church & State* as though living right is burdensome or wrong. Nevertheless, even though Israel is a Jewish State, the nation welcomes the support given it by Christians. The Christian community makes up a large part of the tourism enterprise to Israel and lobbying groups such as Christians United For Israel, based in Texas, and Chaired by Pastor John Hagee, speak of the love and desire of Christians to support the people of Israel as well as the State.

Aumann in his book (cited earlier: Conflict & Connection) argues that Judaism and Christianity: Two millennia of estrangement and hostility, rancour and hatred, persecution, conflict and strife may finally have come to an end. It has taken a human Holocaust to accomplish that – a Holocaust followed by a miraculous re-flowering of Jewish nationhood. But it appears to be happening now. Our generation is witnessing a swelling tide of new thinking and new speaking in Christendom. It began slowly, quietly, haltingly and more than fifty years ago. But with every passing decade, every passing year, it gains momentum, spreading from Church to Church, from denomination to denomination, from country to country across continents. It promises – yes, we refer to a promise, not an accomplished fact – to revolutionise the Christian-Jewish relationship, to transform a two-thousand-year legacy of bottomless animosity into a totally fresh era of mutual respect, harmony and fraternal co-operation.[4]

Aumann continues: Another thing needs to happen before the connection that has been made can be pronounced permanent – indeed, irreversible: *The theological revolution that has been set in motion in the Church needs to find its appropriate echo on the Jewish side of the Jewish-Christian spectrum.* It needs to be acknowledged, so that the Jewish partner in this dialogue can bless the change and encourage those who have been instrumental, on the Christian side, here too it is, first of all, a matter of education. People cannot be expected to relate to what they do not know; ignorance needs to be replaced by awareness and knowledge.[5]

Christians have ample opportunity to serve and support Israel given the conflict and strife Israel faces from day to day. The Christians are now the *Watchmen on the wall,* set there to ensure the survival of the Jews as a nation so that "never again" will they suffer another *Holocaust*. The following provides a reflection of the views and accounts of Christian organisations in Israel.

Understanding the Conflict and the Price of Service

She is petite, and it's a miracle she is alive. Rev. Dr Petra Heldt hails from Germany, but she has lived in Israel for more than 20 years. On 30 July 1997 while shopping at the Shook (market) she became a victim of a terrorist attack on innocent civilians. She was burnt all about the body, and was hospitalised for five weeks in the intensive care unit at the Hadassah Hospital in Israel. A number of other victims died. In her survival she has been able to help so many other victims of terror. She was among 10-15 burn causalities that day and was treated by the best, Prof. Dr Eldad and other specialists. Today, the Rev. Dr Heldt has fully recovered and there are no signs left of that horrific event. She is resilient and is determined to continue serving Israel.

The Rev. Dr. Heldt is the Executive Secretary of the Ecumenical Theological Research Fraternity, located in the Jerusalem University Compound. In an article written by her and Malcolm Lowe they explain the purpose of this institution.

The Ecumenical Theological Research Fraternity in Israel, from its inception in 1966 until today, has constantly observed and evaluated developments in Christian attitudes toward Judaism in official statements by various Christian churches, starting with the Second Vatican Council...[6]

Dr Heldt expresses concern at the fact that the academic world is following the false line of the mass media. She argues that both Jews and Christians are victims of the same system, which is the Muslim jihad. It was through jihad the Muslims conquered territories of both Jews and Christians. Islam, she emphasises is a religion based on war!

Dr Heldt explained at length the Muslims attitude to those nations they conquered. The conquered became *Dhimmies*. This means that the people were now under the jurisdictions of Muslims and they were governed by the Islamic legal system: the Sharia Law. Using another term she submits, the *Dhimma*: is a dictate that a Muslim conqueror dictates to Jews, Christians and Zoroastrians. To refuse is to face certain death. The *Dhimma* is a genocidal contract. Muslims call it protection as part of the Sharia Law. This law impacts: Poll Tax, Land Tax and Free Tax. The *Dhimmies* do not enjoy any civil rights. This has been the tradition in the Middle East since the 7th Century. This law prohibits non-Muslims from owning land and it also prohibits complaints.

Consequently, based on the Sharia Law no Jew has the right to own land or to exist. On this basis the Muslim believes that he is doing the right thing/the legal thing.

No wonder Arabs have a problem recognising Israel: their Sharia Law serves as a basis for sustaining the Arab-Israeli conflict.

Dr Heldt maintains that even today Islam believes this is a right and they will never cease.

Therefore, she argues, if there is no change in the Sharia Law, the conflict would remain ongoing. The conflict is a Muslim war; one that Muslims conduct against non-Muslims countries.

She sees Israel prospering! Israel has come back because it's written in the Bible and 16th, 17th, 18th and 19th Century Christians supported the return of Jews to their own land. Her own organisation does support Israel in research and teaching capacities: they are however, affected negatively by ongoing conflict due to the lack of adequate funding.

Dr Heldt sees more wars in the region. She posits that Muslims can never stop fighting. Their ambition is to destroy others. She adds that Jerusalem is not important to Muslims. It's only important because of Jewish and Christian interests in the city. In order for there to be peace: Palestinians would need to give up jihad. Israel would have to continue to be themselves.

Finally, Dr Heldt does not see a resolution of this conflict in her lifetime; nevertheless, she does have hope, since the Lord can do anything.

Malcolm Hedding, Executive Director of the International Christian Embassy Jerusalem states that the Christian Embassy is the biggest pro-Israel organisation in the world. The Embassy was established more than 30 years ago and its annual Christian Celebration, the Feast of Tabernacles is celebrated around September-October every year and is the biggest tourist event bringing large number of people from around the world to Israel.

Some 14 million people signed a petition drafted by the Christian Embassy, endorsed Jerusalem as the capital of Israel.

The Christian Embassy is a multifaceted organisation, it engages in diplomatic initiatives and advocacy. They have been actively engaged in lobbying the United Nations General Assembly (UNGA). In one instance the Christian Embassy served a global petition to the UNGA in which there was a call for the indictment of Iran's President Mahmoud Ahmadinejad who has called for the destruction of the State of Israel. Ahmadinejad's call is tantamount to a declaration of genocide against Israel, argues Hedding. The Christian Embassy has also addressed the European Parliament.

The Christian Embassy is the non-governmental organisation (NGO) that speaks to global constituents. Its reach is larger than that of some countries. Its activities involve garnering diplomatic support for Israel.

Internally, the Christian Embassy assists all the population groups in Israel and the region. They give out aid according to the demographics of the country to the Jews, Druze, Palestinians, Christians and so forth.

The Christian Embassy has a highly trained staff in its media department. They partner with The Jerusalem Post to produce the Christian Edition Monthly Magazine. Their magazines are distributed around the world and are in 10 foreign languages including: Chinese, French, Danish, German, and others. The Christian Embassy also sponsors a radio station which can be accessible on line as well.

In one of his articles, Hedding addresses a sensitive component of Christian-Jewish relations. The article titled: Armageddon now? Seeks to remove the strident distrust Jews may have for Christians motivation to assist them. He argues that:

Time and time again one hears the accusation that Christians view the modern restoration of Israel as a stepping stone to the final battle of Armageddon, in which countless Jews will perish. Supposedly, this is what motivates Christian Zionists to side with Israel at present while ultimately wanting to accelerate 'the end,' and with it the second coming of Jesus.

As a consequence, the Jewish world is being warned to stay away from such Christians, since their support is based on a dark eschatological agenda.

Conversely, Hedding points out that: the accusation levelled against Christians in this regard has its roots in the Hebrew Scriptures and not the Christian Scriptures. Armageddon (literally the "hill of Megiddo") is only briefly mentioned in the New Testament in Revelation 16, and even then without any great detail.[7]

Therefore, Hedding clarifies:

Also as a matter of record, most Christian Zionists do not support Israel because of some future eschatological blow-up. No, they support Israel because of the past. That is, 4,000 years ago God made a promise to the Jewish people through the Patriarch Abraham that Canaan would be their everlasting possession. This promise He ratified by a covenant.

This effectively means that Israel's presence in the Holy Land is not because of prophetic considerations, but because of God's faithfulness to the promise He made to Abraham... This Abrahamic covenant is also clear about the fact that Israel exists for the blessing of the world (Genesis 12:1-3), and thus Christians bless her and stand alongside her because they have been profoundly enriched and blessed by her. In short we are grateful and seek to demonstrate it. There is no other agenda.[8]

The Christian Embassy also has outreaches to Darfur Sudan. They work alongside other Christian based organisations to bring relief to the millions of Christians in that part of the world.

Shifting gears, Hedding took a look at Arab policy towards Israel. He doesn't see Arabs changing their attitude toward Israel. He adds that the Western world is misled, as Islam is a religious civilisation based on the acquisition of land. Any track of land that becomes a part of Dar-al-Salam must never be given up until dooms day as this is an affront to Islam.

Furthermore, according to Islamic beliefs they will not change for the West, they believe that the land has to be returned to Islamic sovereignty. Their honour has been offended by the existence of Israel. Likewise, Islam does not offer peace to anyone. Peace in the Islamic world does not mean tolerance. Peace is when Islam has total sovereignty over all, and then, they will give the conquered people *peace*.

The Christian Embassy sees the winds of change blowing thru' the EU and America. The reason for this is the wider global agenda. These partners of Israel, will sell out a tiny country – no bigger than New Jersey or a game reserve in South Africa. They are rushing to achieve their own agenda. They have big constituency of Arabs in their own States and these Arabs are willing to riot. The Arabs are also a large voting bloc in the EU and these issues present challenges to the EU, likewise the US.

Antisemitism in the EU is largely due to a proliferation of Arabs in Europe, especially in France and the United Kingdom.

The Christian Embassy concluded by asserting that Israel will not be removed. The God of the Bible will vindicate His word, His identity, His Messiah. Israel has a glorious future!

Hedding hails from South Africa and has been serving in the capacity of Executive Director of the International Christian Embassy for more than 12 years.

Meanwhile, on Wednesday 20 May 2009, I was invited to attend a Press Conference. It was sponsored by the Catholic Church leadership following the Pope's visit to Israel.

Pope Benedict XVI had been visiting the Holy Land for four days, 11-14 May 2009. During the Press Conference the church leaders including His Beatitude Fouad Twal, Latin Patriarch of Jerusalem; reviewed the Pope's visit and addressed matters of concern to the Church.

The Church spoke of the Palestinian homeland and stated it has a role, though not political, it encourages the people to accept each other so as to create the conditions for peace and says that it is prepared to help win or facilitate the possibility for peace. Additionally, they noted their right to encourage new efforts toward peace.

The Church leadership also indicated that the *Holy Father*, the Pope, supports peace among the two peoples. They also advised the media delegation from Gaza to remember the Pope's advise to keep silent. He urged: Silence to remember, silence to hope and silence to pray. They also reiterated the fact that the Pope said "no more antisemitism."

Speaking about the Pope's views they noted that the Pope was happy to see that there was goodwill among the groups in Israel. He also recognised that the matter was complicated and pointed out that that was why he preferred to keep silent and pray. He is a pastor, his visit was pastoral, they emphasised. While admitting that the Pope did make some political statements the Church leadership noted that he could not avoid the political affect that surrounded his visit. Nevertheless, they reiterated that the Pope came as a pilgrim to the Holy Land and during his pilgrimage he encouraged the Christians to remain in the Holy Land. They expressed the hope that the Pope's visit did give a boost to encourage the people of the Church living in the Holy Land.

Regarding the political dimension, the Church pointed out that the two-States were necessary for peace and good relations. In response to the question: Is there a role for the Church in advancing this peace process? The Church leadership replied that there were moral and ethical roles. Theirs is to demand for peace and also to demand for Israel to live in secure boundary. The Church leaders appealed: Let us recognise Israel and affirm the right of the Palestinians.

Shlomo Mordechai in an article titled: *The Star of David and the Cross*, examines the Pope's positions toward the Jews and their right to their homeland, Israel. He argues:

Yet belief in the patriarchs and prophets does not mean endorsing God's promises to and through them that the Land of Israel would be the inheritance of the Jewish people...

Here the Gentile Church joins hands with the nations (*goyim* or Gentiles in Hebrew) to divide the Land between Jews and Muslims. This begs the question of why the leader of the world's one billion Roman Catholics would endorse Muslim control over the holiest places in Christendom.[9]

This is indeed baffling!

Meanwhile, Malcolm Hedding writes in an article following the Pope's visit, of his personal dismay at the Pope's silence on the Church's responsibility for the vicious antisemitism committed against Jews in Europe "down thru the centuries." However, Hedding points out that despite this, the Evangelical Christians – today the fastest-growing stream of Christianity – who have sought to fill that prophetic role... to profess the Christian world's corporate guilt for our church's dark history of antisemitism, and to repent for these great moral failings. This repentance has been honest, sincere and without condition...[10]

The founders of Christian Friends of Israel Ray and Sharon Sanders have spent 25 years in service to the Jewish communities in Israel. This American couple sold their home to attend Bible College and received the requisite training to facilitate their performance. They manage a large staff and Ray, the International Director in this organization, shared his views concerning the conflict and its impact on Israel.

CFI opines that they don't think the Arabs want to live in peace with Israel, although it is Israel's desire to live in peace with her neighbours. CFI further posits, given what takes place on the international scene, with regard to the influence of both the Americans and the Russians; they both do play integral roles, here, in the Middle East. However, their interests are competing, and these differences do not make for peace.

God gave this land to Abraham and to his descendants. As Hamas tries to delegitimize Israel, Satan is trying to nullify God's word. This is a spiritual conflict! Nothing unites the Arabs like Israel as a common enemy. CFI asks: How could one live in peace with a group of people who teach their people to kill others? They live for martyrdom; they honour those who die as martyrs.

CFI states that whatever offers Israel tries to extend to her neighbours fail; because her enemies are not interested in peace with Israel. Their goal is the destruction of Israel. To initiate peace, the other side has to lay down their arms. They don't realise the benefits of peace, that the benefits could be phenomenal. The reality, however, is that the Palestinians don't want peace. Their map shows the entire Jewish State. Likewise, American pressure will make Israel totally indefensible.

The Arabs, maintains CFI, need to acknowledge that Israel has a legitimate right to her land and that the Jewish people have a right to be here. The Arabs need to focus more on development, but instead, their goal is the destruction of Israel!

In addressing Christian-Jewish relations, CFI notes that the Jews suffered a lot at the hands of Christians. Their organization, i.e., CFI, does not engage in evangelism of Jews, but they serve the Jews and this has a tremendous impact on the Jews. Over the years CFI has distributed millions of dollars worth in aid to Jews in Israel including: Holocaust survivors, Ethiopian Jews, newlyweds, Jews that are disabled as a result of Hamas rocket attacks in Sderot and its neighbouring environs, to the IDF and others. They also try to educate the Church across North America and Asia about their responsibilities toward the Jews.

CFI reiterates that the Arabs have made a conscious decision not to live in peace with Israel, so long as they have that mentality, there will be no peace in the region.

Finally, CFI urges the Church to pray for peace. Noting that Arab animosity toward the Jew is deep seated. Too much bloodshed, too many scores to settle, laments Sanders. In the end, the Prince of Peace is the only One who can bring peace, concludes the CFI leader.

While, Bridges for Peace did not grant an interview, I was taken on a tour of their headquarters and their food bank, from there they issue tons of food, clothing and so forth to Jews in need. They have a Rabbi on hand to ensure that all foods are up to kosher standards.

Jan Willem van der Hoeven, Director of the International Christian Zionist Center (ICZC), was also a co-founder of the International Christian Embassy in Jerusalem and he is the author of the book: *Babylon or Jerusalem*. Jan Willem is passionate about Israel and he hails from The Netherlands. Jan Willem submitted selected materials from his work: *Islam Not Territories* for consideration as interview notes, for this book.

The ICZC submits that the cause of the conflict is Islam, not territories.

He argues because neither the West nor Israel, generally speaking, wants to be seen as being against another man's religious beliefs, there is widespread reluctance to face up to this problem! It is not done in our so-called tolerant society, i.e., to criticise the tenets of a whole religion which comprises one billion adherents, and yet it is impossible to really solve the present Middle East conflict without facing up to this overall problem!

The ICZC reiterates the system of belief of Islam: Islam believes that it's the final revelation of *Allah*, superseding all previous beliefs it has a high built-in characteristic of intolerance. Furthermore, Islam has conveniently divided the whole world into two spheres: '*Dar al-Harb*' and '*Dar al-Islam*.' Dar al-Islam being the house or region of peace that means all lands and peoples have been already conquered by Islamic forces; and Dar al-Harb being those lands and people in the world that still need to be conquered by Islam which is, therefore, the whole remaining world.

Noting also that: Once the forces of Islam conquer a land or territory, it is to remain under Islamic dominion forever ('for generations'), and it is a mortal affront to the supremacy of Islam when such territories would ever be lost to the dominion of Islam and revert to previous – infidel – ownership as was the case in Palestine. It was a Muslim controlled territory (under the Muslim Turks and later the Muslim Arabs) reverted by the decree of the UN resolution back to its previous owners: the Jews.

The forces of Islam need to be made aware of this Scripture:

Joshua and the people of Israel defeated all the kings in the territory west of the Jordan, from Baalgad in the valley of Lebanon to Mount Halak in the south near Edom. Joshua divided this land among the tribes and gave it to them as a permanent possession.[11] This Scripture shows that Israel was given permanent ownership over the territory, an act by God's divine will; whereas mortal men, enemies of God subsequently declared the same land theirs forever. Mortal men have no authority over the word of God and they cannot change His intent.

The ICZC argues further that the acceptance of *jihad* or 'holy war' comes easy to Islam. From its inception Islam has been a warring and very bloody, subjugating religion, which has not blushed at the use of war and terror but glorified it as the absolute will of their god.

This, then, is the main problem. As long as Islam remains intolerant of really accepting any other group of people on an equal basis – rather than as dhimmies to be subjugated by Islam – there can never be a real peace with an Islamic power! Only on the basis of 'submission' (which is what Islam means) to its stated superiority and dictates. This awaits the whole world including the secular, often irreligious West, contends ICZC.

Please note: Sharia will be the Law under which the Palestinians will govern themselves. Most assuredly, the Islamists will overthrow the so-called moderates… Nevertheless, there is a greater law at work: the governing laws of God, a blood covenant He made with Abraham. This will never cease to take effect!

The ICZC expresses concern that the Arabs thru' their oil wealth and enormous spread of their religion through thousands of Mosques and millions of Muslim adherents all over the world, their Islamic leaders believe the day has come to wipe out the humiliation – of their defeat in Europe by the armies of Charles Martel – and now, conquer Europe, and all the West. Cogently, these territories in Europe will become *'Dar al-Islam'*: Which means, Europe will become a part of the house and possession of Islam.

The ICZC states that: If it is true that the root problem of the Middle East conflict – or the Arab-Israeli conflict – to be found in the tenets of Islam then we have to address these tenets as the main reasons. Just as we in Europe would have to address the tenets of Nazi ideology as being the main reasons and culprits for the terrible massacres and destruction all over Europe. We cannot say – as some indeed have done – that because people believe a certain ideology or even religion therefore we have to accept and respect this. This is probably the gravest error of our time! All in the name of so-called tolerance the wicked or fanatics then triumph!

Touching on Jerusalem, the ICZC argues that: Islam did not originate in Jerusalem, it originated in Mecca and Medina on the Saudi Arabian Peninsula! Not once is Jerusalem mentioned in the Koran, whereas the Bible mentions Jerusalem over 600 times. Therefore, Jerusalem is not in the same sense important to Islam, as it is holy to Judaism and Christianity.

In elaborating, the ICZC contends that the reason Islam built the stunning golden Dome of the Rock on the Jewish Temple Mount was to express its repudiation of Jewish or Christian claims of sanctity, thus usurping the right to all Jerusalem, which the Muslims call 'el-Quds' which means – the holy city of Islam because Islam conquered it!

Finally, the ICZC in its Manifesto submits that:

"... We believe, then, that even as the Jewish people in 1922 established an organisation called the Jewish Agency to bring their State into being and secure it, so we as believers from the nations need a mother centre, or agency, in Israel, from which the whole Christian movement can be inspired, instructed and activated to become an agent of support for Israel in all aspects."

In conclusion, the Evangelical based organisations in Israel eagerly express love for the Jewish people. Their daily presence and outstretched arms serve to tell Israel that they are not alone! These Christians have made amends for the Church's past crimes and are prepared to support the people of God never mind the price they pay: in time, with material resource and with their lives! They are committed to going all the way with Israel, in the good times as well as in the bad or difficult times!

Chapter 12

Existential Threats to the State of Israel will Undermine Global Security

Arabs must accept Israel's Presence

The consensus among Arabs is that Israel must be destroyed! The international community is in dire need for a doable solution so as to usher in an era of peace, but rather than playing the role of Arab benefactor, they should instead be Israel's advocate. This is the way to peace, the long awaited global peace.

It's absolutely important for the international community to be realistic and realise they do not need a two-State solution, now, or in the future. They need to take into consideration the tiny size of the Jewish State and regulate that all the homes and properties the Jews left in the Arab States when Jews fled, let these be given to their Arab brothers who are allegedly displaced. The global leaders should also insist that there is enough territory elsewhere in the region to make comfortable homes for all Arabs. Then the region would be on the road to peace. For in so doing the international community will help the Arabs return to and reunite with their tribal roots.

Israel has accepted the two-State initiative, but she should not have accepted it as a whole or in part as the much hyped two-States solution, where two peoples live side by side, is impractical! Instead the Arabs want the Jews out! The Jews are staying put, they are not going anywhere, take it or leave it!

Israel has always pushed for peace. Their attempts at Mideast peace have not worked. Take for instance, the Gaza removal. The Jews withdrew from this area unilaterally, in 2005, what have they gotten in return, peace? No, they have been bombarded with home-made as well as Iranian made weapons; they also got a "bad rap" from the Goldstone Report and to date, no peace, instead, threats of more conflict. Did the international community hear the drum beat of war? Have they heard Iran's threats lately or Hezbollah's? The truth is an Israel under attack, would not spare this global village. Israel is too integral to our world, and the international community should accept this never-thought-of-idea: a threatened Israel means a threatened world, all the players will be involved, and all will be affected. This is the manner in which God will choose to get glory over the nations: He will arise to defend Israel and at the same time weaken the very instruments and support networks the international community has come to rely on for survival. God's response would be hostile to those who treat Israel with hostility, it would be pleasant for those who treat Israel kindly, and each nation would be rewarded according to their actions.

Consequently, a major paradigm shift is what is urgently needed at this time. It can be done using a very simple approach. Protect your interest by protecting Israel's!

The international community should work with Israel to convince the Arabs to accept the Jewish presence in the Middle East. The more you talk about peace, the more the Arabs demand concessions, the more difficult the problem becomes. A lot of damage has been done to Israel by way of the various international treaties, agreements and plans; all envisioned to increase the 300,000,000 (million) Arab population's influence over the small Jewish race and State. These measures did not succeed. So why keep on pushing ahead with the rest of the doomed-to-fail policies?

The Arabs must accept the Jewish presence. They must accept the right of Israel to exist and to live in the Holy Land, their only homeland.

To the Arabs: the way to secure peace is not to tell the Jews they'll be destroyed, or they must get out, or further still, demand that they give up land! Instead, the way to secure peace is to accept the Jewish State and establish co-operations with the people of Israel. Jordan and Egypt can achieve much more than they already have. Having signed peace agreements with Israel they should be the advocates for these measures to be replicated in other Arab countries when they speak in the Arab League or at the United Nations. They need to take leadership and then they will see more benefits coming to their respective nation States. Otherwise, if they remain silent when calls are made for Israel's destruction or lead in seeking Israel's isolation, they are complicit!

Currently, Jews are suffering from decades of hateful education in Palestinian schools. The glorification of terrorists who have murdered Jews is a practice that must stop. The Abbas machinery and the Hamas leadership are competing to foster hatred of Jews among the very young. Yet, when these very children are ill, they are treated by Jewish doctors in Israeli hospitals. Hatred never pays. Hatred undermines the health and wellbeing of those who are filled with hate. Haters are losers! Their hatred will destroy them, not those who are the object of the hatred. The Palestinians will end up destroying themselves because of their own deceit and hatred!

Any attack against the Jewish State "the heart of the international community" will undermine global security!

The Iranian Factor

The Iranian threat is treated with askance by some entities in the Arab world. While Israel remains their immortal enemy the Arabs seem unwilling to pay heed to the dangerous aspirations of one of the members of their Muslim family. It is widely believed that should Iran strike Israel, militarily, Iran would be fulfilling the collective goal of the Islamists in the region—the destruction of the Jewish State. However in reality, Iran does have additional goals; goals which in the end might prove harmful to the entire region, to Jews and Arabs alike.

Iran is dominated with the Shi'ite brand of Islam, whereas most of the Arabs and Muslims in the region are adherents to the

Sunni principles. Iran was once a global power under the Persian-Mede Empire. Iran entertains the aspirations to return to its former glory and its hegemonic ambitions are a part of its foreign policy strategies, whereas, Egypt sees itself in this role as well. Additionally, Turkey also has similar aspirations; therefore, aside from the much published Arab-Israeli conflict, there is simmering below the surface a deliberate campaign among Arabs, Turks and Persians as to which nation State will emerge as the leading entity in the region. Saudi Arabia is also a contender. The State that emerges will have the backing and support of the great powers. The great powers are themselves split according to geographical locations. So an Egyptian or Saudi hegemonic State would have the backing of the United States, the United Kingdom and France. An Iranian or Turkish hegemonic State will be supported by Russia and China. Why Turkey? Turkey has for sometime been moving slowly away from its Western allies to a take on a more Islamic stance and "all things being equal," a move from the West is a move toward Russia.

However, for the time being, Iran has the world's attention. Iran has openly called for the destruction of the Jewish State. Iran has done so at the United Nations in New York and in Geneva, in other multilateral arenas as well in bilateral talks. What Iran doesn't know is this:

The Lord will appear above His people; He will shoot His arrows like lightening. The Sovereign Lord will sound the trumpet; He will march in the storms from the south.

The Lord Almighty will protect His people, and they will destroy their enemies. They will shout in battle like drunken men and will shed the blood of their enemies; it will flow like the blood of a sacrifice poured on the altar from a bowl.

When that day comes, the Lord will save His people, as a shepherd saves his flock from danger. They will shine in His land like the jewels of a crown.[1]

At the time of writing this section of the book, May 2010, the United Nations Security Council (UNSC) was giving due consideration to a new UN sanction "with teeth" to bring Iran into conformity with the demands of the international community. The Obama Administration scored a scoop when the other four great powers signalled their intention to support the new UNSC Resolution under consideration, albeit Russia and China may attempt to weaken the Resolution in favour of Iran. These two have much to lose from a very strong UNSC Resolution against Tehran – they both have economic and other ties with the Islamic Republic.

Cogently, Iran being the creators of the game of Chess made a very strategic move and announced same on Wednesday 19 May 2010. The move done to influence the UNSC Resolution by having her friends "water it down" as Iran seems to want to impress upon them that she is keen to follow the rules of the game; Iran announced that Turkey and Brazil will collect the fuel from her reactors which the international community fear if left in Iran could be converted to the bomb. Iran denies she has such intent, nevertheless, she does have motive: her plans to destroy Israel and her denial of the Jewish people suffering the Holocaust.

A question that needs be considered is what price Israel will have to pay for this? Obama had publicly disputed with Netanyahu about Iran. Now that he has decided to take on Iran, what would Israel have to give? What confidence building measures would Israel have to proffer to facilitate Middle East peace? Would the Arabs finally accept Israel's presence and right to territory in the region? You (the reader) will have the benefit of determining the end game as time moves on.

Meanwhile, Member States were asked questions about the Iranian threat to Israel and the region as a whole. The following are the responses obtained:

The United States argues that: both we and our allies remain deeply concerned about Iran's nuclear programme and we continue to hold frequent discussions on the subject.

The US also emphasises: although we have stressed our preference for dealing with the Iranian nuclear programme via diplomacy, we have also made clear that our offer of engagement with Iran is not open-ended and stressed that we are ready to take strong new steps should Tehran fail to respond to our offer. We have also made it clear to all our allies that our desire to seek engagement with Iran will not come at the expense of our long standing relationships in the region.

Meanwhile, Dr Mansour (the Palestinian Rep to the UN) states that the international community thru' the Security Council is discussing the nuclear capability of Iran. He adds that the issue of nuclear capability is not seen as a threat to most of the Arab States. And that the international community is clear, with calls for the Middle East to be free of weapons of mass destruction (WMDs). He stresses that Israel refuses to be a party to the Nuclear Non-Proliferation Treaty (NPT). He calls for Israel to open its weapons facilities and submits that as long as Israel continues to have nuclear weapons, it will encourage a nuclear arms race.

In continuing Dr Mansour continued to focus on Israel rather than on Iran. He adds that the Palestinians were against any country having nuclear weapons since these do not lead to peace.

He emphasises that the objective is disarmament in the Middle East.

Dr Mansour has probably forgotten that there is a regional concerted move to destroy the sovereign State of Israel. Therefore, what Israel has stated is that she will not attack any State first... but Israel must have a measure of deterrence. To remove this would spell destruction for Israel as well as undermine the rest of the world's security interests.

Contrary to what the Palestinian representative stated, Egypt admits that Iran is a threat to all Arab States, because it has expansionist ideals. Tehran is trying to meddle in Arab affairs. They are Shi'ites!

Egypt adds however, historically, Iran has no issues with Israel and maintains that there is no justification to this fear.

On the other hand, Germany says that they have to make sure that the international community is serious about dealing with Iran's nuclear programme. Germany insists: we don't want Iran to acquire nuclear weapons and submits that Bahrain, Egypt, Kuwait, Jordan and others fear a nuclear arms race. There is also the fear of terrorists having the "dirty bomb." Germany advances that Iran feels threatened by the US and Israel. The Iranians believe that the Americans have evil designs in the region. They feel extremely threatened by the Americans who have surrounded them. They recall US position on Iraq and so they feel threatened.

Germany believes that Iran is not going to give in to the demands of the international community; they are going to have a bomb for defence purposes. Germany declares that the Iranians are proud! Outside of the Turks, they, are the only ones who could pull off the bomb. They are very proud. They believe that they deserve to be a world power once again. They feel that Iran must be a great nation in the region, they feel threatened!

Germany opines that Iran does not want to go down the road as Iraq. There are three points Germany provided to prevent Iran going nuclear:

i)   Credible threat of sanctions
ii) Have engagement and sanctions at the same time. Consider Iran's interests. In any scenario peaceful negotiations, not the use of force will create real progress in the Middle East.
iii) To create a regional framework that would include Israel, the Arab States and the Palestinians.

Germany believes that the only way to isolate Iran is to draw the Arabs States away.

With regard to Arabs relation with Israel, Germany says that there is a lot the Arab States can do. It's important for them to make it clear that they seek peace and they are ready to normalise relations with Israel. They need to be more pro-active. Germany needs to see Arab States make this a key feature of their foreign policy.

Turkey shares border with Iran, and has a border agreement with Iran which dates back to 1699.

Turkey does not want Iran to acquire nuclear weapons. However, like other countries Turkey stresses that Iran has a right to use nuclear power for civilian purposes, but not militarily.

Like Egypt, Turkey also expressed concerns at Iran's hegemonic ambitions in the region and states that this is destabilising. However, Turkey says that she doesn't support isolation and that they welcome the new approach of the Obama Administration toward Iran. Turkey emphasises that in their bilateral relations with Iran they have urged Tehran not to turn down this hand of friendship the US has extended.

Turkey adds that Iran is an important neighbour and they would like a peaceful Iran to co-exist with them. Turkey purchases oil from Iran and states that Iranian products should be integrated into the international community. On the other hand, Turkey shares the same concerns with the international community. Turkey does not want a nuclear armed Iran. Turkey declares that her nation objects to any nuclear weapons in the Middle East, and states that it's their vision that the Middle East be free of nuclear arms, seeing that nuclear arms do present a direct threat to Turkey's security interests. Consequently, Turkey is against a nuclear armed Iran.

Additionally, Israeli Cabinet Minister Benny Begin states that the Egyptian-Israeli peace treaty was a great achievement. (Begin's father, as Prime Minister of Israel had signed the treaty with Saddat of Egypt during the Carter Administration). Begin stresses that the growing threats from Iran in recent months have intensified the demand for a two-State solution, which Egypt speaks to. Begin believes that Egypt's position stems from the growing threat coming from Iran. Iran's strategy is to operate through its proxies Hamas and Hezbollah, both of whom pose a threat to the Egyptian regime. Egypt is challenged internally by the Islamic Brotherhood of which Hamas is an offshoot.

Israel's Security should be Global Interest

Miriam of Sderot, a Social Worker in the Ministry of Social Affairs Department who has more than 15 years of experience, outlines the effects of the conflict on the approximately one million people in the firing range of Hamas rockets. She states that everyone is badly affected by Hamas attacks. There is no difference for the old or young, male or female. As a consequence of the terror the residents there face serious health challenges, including deafness, there are not enough jobs. Low employment opportunities affect the income of families and the living standards of the people. Consequently, aside from security, finances are the top need of the people. Most importantly, security guarantees will enable them to return to normalcy, after which they'll be able to once again go on to be productive citizens in Israel.

The officials of Sderotmedia.com, a non-governmental organisation, run by two young men, state that there are 20 different types of Hamas rockets. A number of terror groups in Gaza compete in attacking Israel and because of Iran, their missiles range have extended and can affect residents down in the Negev Region as well.

These examples serve to remind the international community that terror does affect real people. It affects their mental and physical health, their ability to perform on the job; it affects productivity and job creation, in the long term it affects whether the government allows residents to remain in volatile areas or whether they are removed as a result of acts of terror against the civilian populations.

Israel is a small State and cannot afford acts of terrorism against its people or territory. Small States have a number of vulnerabilities and so does Israel. There is not enough wriggle-room to flee terrorist attacks, thus acts of terrorism are intended to jeopardise the continued existence of the Jewish State.

The international community can no longer sit by saying to Israel "be divided" and then you'll have peace. It's time for the community to make the tough decisions, calls to divide Israel is a cop-out. They all know that this act will not bring peace, yet they press ahead. They say it's in their national interest to secure peace, but they do not consider Israel's national interest.

Here is news for everyone, Israel's national interest is to exist in peace and security in her homeland, and be recognised by her neighbours, this is her inalienable right!

Israel's interest must be that of the global community. The international community must not ask Israel to make compromises which can be injurious to her existence.

Walid S Abu Alhalaweh, an Arab Public Relations official in Arab dominated Hebron states that they are funded by the EU and as part of their efforts to stop Israel's control of Hebron they import "Palestinians" from neighbouring communities. He says that they also move Palestinian families within Hebron from densely populated areas to less populated areas or to uninhabited buildings so that Israel's military cannot possess them.

The movement of persons in the Arab world to Israel or near Jewish communities is all part of a broader strategic game plan by the Arabs to establish claims to the Holy Land. Their goal is to get Israel out so that they can come in! Israel will not be moving out!

When challenged, if no one comes to Israel's aid, God Himself will help Israel. Brigadier General Michael Herzog in the Introduction of the book: *The War of Atonement, The Inside Story of the Yom Kippur War*, by Chaim Herzog, his father, contends that:

The October 1973 Arab-Israeli War (known in Israel as the Yom Kippur War, namely the War of Atonement) was a breaking point and watershed in the history of the Arab-Israeli conflict.

It was the last multi-front comprehensive war waged between Israel and its Arab neighbours, although the Middle East was still to witness further serious outbreaks of violence and military confrontations.[2]

The War of Atonement put under severe scrutiny Israel's security doctrine, that had first been shaped back in the days of David Ben-Gurion, Israel's first Prime Minister, and prevailed ever since. This doctrine was designed to provide an answer to the fundamental reality of the few against the many, to Israel's difficulty in keeping a large regular army on its borders and of withstanding a protracted war as well as the possibility of a simultaneous offensive against Israel on several fronts. The Israeli concept of security was therefore based on the fundamental elements of deterrence (relying also on American backing), early warning, air supremacy to provide a brake and response in the face of a surprise attack, a sophisticated organisation of reserve units capable of being rapidly mobilised and reaching the front in time (due to early warning), taking the battle into enemy territory and striving for as rapid a decision as possible.[3]

Although this doctrine was a great success in the past it failed in 1973. Herzog provides a number of possibilities for consideration as to why Israel's strategic doctrine failed then. Nevertheless, Israel had to fight for her survival following the surprise attack led by Egypt. By the same token, there are plans afoot to attack Israel in the future. In fact, Hezbollah's calls to Israel to prepare for war and Hamas' insistence on its right to maintain the *resistance* against Israel are just some indications of how volatile the Mideast is and will remain. Similarly, a Middle East in turmoil will mean that the world will be in turmoil. The nations still rely heavily on the region for their oil supplies and "therein lies" their dilemma.

However, the God of Israel will come to her rescue. He also has a strategy for future battles in the region. He plans to reign down His judgement on His enemies and guess whom He plans to use as His instrument? Israel! He tells His people Israel:

You are My battle-axe and weapons of war: for with you I will break the nations in pieces; with you I will destroy kingdoms...[4]

God's glorious promise to Israel is worth being drawn to the attention of the international community. God will see to it that His people remain in the earth! They will not be wiped off the face of the earth. The Scriptures note:

Thus says the Lord, who gives the sun for a light by day, and the ordinances of the moon and the stars for a light by night. Who disturbs the sea, and its waves roar

(The Lord of hosts is His name):

If those ordinances depart from before Me, says the Lord,

Then the seed of Israel shall also cease from being a nation before me forever...[5]

Finally, there was a righteous Gentile in "ancient times" named Job. During his period of trouble his friends accused him of wrong doing and he himself doubted the love of God, and challenged God, he spoke evil of the day of his birth and questioned the purpose of his suffering. Then one day the Lord spoke to him saying:

Who is this who darkens counsel by words without knowledge? Now prepare yourself like a man; I will question you, and you shall answer Me.[6]

In the end Job answered the Lord and said:

Behold, I am vile; what shall I answer You? I lay my hand over my mouth.

Once I have spoken, but I will now answer; yes, twice, but I will proceed no further.[7]

May the nations stop in their tracks and precede no further with plans to divide the State of Israel, for God will do to them as He did to Pharaoh, He will resist them and humble them before all mankind. Pharaoh thought to himself that he was "the man" but God showed Pharaoh that it was He the Lord, who was the ultimate, the Sovereign Lord! Despite all the laws that govern the international community, the international community is ultimately accountable to God. This is a fact! Every nation, man, woman and "in-between" will stand before God!

In the end the Lord showed the rulers of Egypt who oppressed His people that He responds to the cry of His people. During the time of Israel's deliverance God revealed a strategic plan against the Egyptians to Moses:

For Pharaoh will say of the children of Israel, 'They are bewildered by the land; the wilderness has closed them in.'

"Then I will harden Pharaoh's heart, so that he will pursue them; and I will gain honour over Pharaoh and over all his army, that the Egyptians may know that I am the Lord."[8]

Similarly, today's world leaders will come to acknowledge that the God of Israel, He is the Lord! He will defend and protect His people Israel from all their enemies! He will gain honour over the international community because of His mighty deeds!

Section 6

The Ulterior Motive

Chapter 13

The End Game – Halt to the Peace Process

The World vs. Israel

Let's say there are 6.7 billion Gentiles and 12 million Jews in the world today as of May 2010. Then the ratio would read; 558 Gentiles to one Jew (558:1). The Jews are vastly outnumbered! Yet to the chagrin of most, the Jews are united and successful, they are brilliant and innovative, despite the challenges to their existence, they have preserved their identity through the centuries. The world's preoccupation with the Jew is not limited to their country, but it includes also, their abilities. This should not be surprising: the Jews are living under the blessings of God; the God of their forefathers whose legacy of commitment to His people is undeniably rare and unending.

The Jews have their home in the Middle East. Their country's name is Israel. Despite changes to the name of the geographical location in the past, Israel has been their homeland *from time immemorial*. Their fore parents have been laid to rest there: Abraham, Isaac, Jacob, Joseph, Boaz and David, and others. Among the women are Sarah, Rachel, Leah and Ruth. Through these men and women the Hebrew race was propagated. Their burial places are still here with us to this very day.

The Jews are under immense global pressure to give up land to an errant race, the Arabs, who already possess mass volumes of territory in the region. These people have no regard for fact or for history. Their denial of Israel's historic ties to the Holy Land is astounding. Their penchant for lies and deceit has made a mockery of the "peace process". It's all a game of TIME. Waiting for the inevitable, War!

Former Israeli Ambassador to the United Nations Dore Gold posits that in regard to the Arab-Israeli conflict, often policy makers suffer from a kind of myopia when looking at the underlying reasons for problems in the Mideast; they focus exclusively on this conflict, and have become riveted to the Palestinian issue in particular. Consequently, disproportionate diplomatic energy is invested in Israeli-Palestinian diplomacy at the expense of addressing larger regional issues, such as the 1979 Iranian revolution or Saddam Hussein's threats to Kuwait in 1990. Indeed, these major Middle Eastern developments came as complete surprises to the Carter administration and the first Bush administration, which were so mired in the details of Arab-Israeli diplomacy.[1]

Gold further emphasises that: For many Arab radicals, hatred of Israel stems from its being perceived as a Western outpost. They resent the many European incursions into the Middle East, from Napoleon's 1798 invasion of Egypt to the British and French colonial regimes throughout the Mideast. Al-Qaeda's training manual introduces its members to its historical grievances by starting with the fall of the Ottoman Empire to the Allied powers after the First World War, the dissolution of the office of caliph (successor to the Prophet and spiritual head of Sunni Islam), and the rise of secular regimes in the Arab and Muslim world.... in any case, Israel, which is not mentioned in the al-Qaeda manual, is a small thread in a much larger historical tapestry.[2]

On the other hand, Libyan President Muammar al-Qadhafi in his White Book, titled: ISRATINE proposes a single state for Jews and Palestinian Arabs. Inclusive, the return of Palestinian refugees.[3] Qadhafi argues that: A Jewish State alone is exposed to the Arab and Islamic threat, but a mixed State comprising

Muslims, Jews, Arabs and Israelis would never come under the threat of Arab or Muslim attack.[4]

Redefining Comprehensive Peace: A Nuanced idea

The caveat "there is no comprehensive peace" has been bandied about whenever Israel stands up like every sovereign State does. The Arabs try to imply that they are for peace and more importantly, comprehensive peace. However, what is comprehensive peace, in their context? Comprehensive peace, the Arab way, is based on the principle that the one remaining State in the Middle East, now under Jewish control, be unconditionally and unilaterally governed by Arabs, advancing the Islamic dogma.

The so-called Arab moderate, Mahmoud Abbas, the leader of the Palestinians, states that he does not recognise the Jewish State and maintains that the entire country is Palestine, albeit he conveniently leaves out Jordan which belongs to Palestine as a geographic entity. Qadhafi, Libya's leader issues calls for a one-State solution with the anticipation that the Jews will be ultimately outnumbered by Arabs and Muslims and thus, another Arab State in which Jews will reside as *dhimmies* (as was the case elsewhere in the Middle East, in Yemen, Morocco, Iran, Iraq, Turkey, Egypt, Syria, and others). Jews no longer reside in most of these countries because of expulsions and the confiscations of their properties. Most likely, this is the part of their "final solution" to "wipe off the Jewish State" from the map of the Middle East. Fortunately, today, the Jews are masters of their own State.

If comprehensive peace is not attained via the diplomatic route, and if Israel continues to insist that Jerusalem shall remain their undivided capital, and if Israel does accede to international demands from the community of nations: to remove security check points and road blocks which will endanger her national security interests, and if Israel continues to build new homes for her citizens on State lands, then Israel will be attacked by a coalition force for another war. Israel ought to prepare for war and must not accede to her enemy's whims and fancies.

Israel's Arab neighbours: are arming themselves "to the teeth." These Arabs will not go to war against each other, but they will, with each other, against the Jewish State, Israel. How can the great powers of this world exercise grave double standards against the Jews? While they are arming the Arabs with the latest and very sophisticated conventional and unconventional weapons they are at the same time offering the State of Israel verbal guarantees of protection. These Arabs are spending their fortunes garnered from oil sales and donors money to purchase billions of dollars worth of weapons, such as: ballistic missiles, tactical guided missiles, anti-ship cruise missiles, and the like. Their aim is to destroy the State of Israel, and build on her ruins another Arab State, this particular goal is viewed as unstoppable by those who have invested in it. This is their "final solution" of the Jews: the annihilation of the Jewish people. This is the sum-total of Israel's struggle with men. Hence, the peace process will be halted by Israel's enemies in pursuance of their destructive agenda.

Tactical questions for Israel's considerations:

a. Would Jerusalem cease its global crusade against a nuclear pursuing Iranian regime?
b. Would any portion of Jerusalem be given up for peace?
c. Would Israel live side-by-side in peace and security with an Iranian as well a Syrian proxy Palestinian State?

Facts from ancient history that should motivate the Israelites:

i) Israel's leaderships never capitulated to their enemies. Joshua led Israel's fight for possession of Canaan, then David and Joab and Gideon fought to preserve Judea; and now this generation will have to fight to keep Israel in the family-the Jewish family.
ii) Israel's enemies now, are not unlike those in ancient times – they are really the descendants of those who hated Israel then, same tricks, same spirit.
iii) Israel's rich history is plagued with war. But her leaders then, trusted in their God and He led them to victory. The record would show that Israel only suffered defeat when she did not consult with or trust in her God: the God of

Abraham, Isaac and Jacob. Most of the men who led were very courageous men, take King David for example.

iv) Israel never secured peace from a position of defeat. Israel secured peace after conquering her enemies.

Reasons why the peace process is a vain exercise:

i) Israel is expected to yield her sovereignty to the Arabs, including all aspects of her past – all the legacies the ancients left to this generation.

ii) Israel's historical ties to the land existed before the Arab invasion which came after Roman rule, and this fact cannot be ignored.

iii) It is genuinely believed that Israel is outnumbered and has lost her qualitative military edge and therefore her own weapons supply does not serve as a point of deterrence. All this is interpreted to mean that Israel is weak, that she can be fully destroyed, returned to captivity and once again exiled. Not true!

iv) Scarcity of the vital natural resource, water.

v) Antisemitism coupled with jealously.

vi) There already exist two sovereign States in Palestine: one a Jewish State, the other, an Arab State, called Jordan.

vii) Apart from Egypt and Jordan which have recognised Israel's right to exist, all the other Arab States have adamantly refused to recognise Israel. Similarly, the Palestinians have refused in previous negotiations to make concessions to recognize the State of Israel as the Jewish State. This will be the key "sticking point" in any future "land for peace" negotiations.

Here is the Lord God of Heaven's position:

- God does not grant approval to the division of His land, for any peace initiative.
- He opposes any solution which further divides His land.

- He reiterates that He has given this land to the children of Israel and it is He who has brought them back to this land, from the four corners of the earth.
- Those who claim that the land is theirs and have refused to live in peace with the children of Israel must leave the land for other lands, i.e., for the land of their brethren, in the region. It is the best peace solution.
- Jerusalem is not up for grabs. It is the undivided capital of the State of Israel... it is also the city of the great King, the Lord of hosts... it's not the domain of other gods.

Never mind the pressures on Israel, there must be no division of the land for peace. God gave the land to Israel and their descendants, forever. The aliens among them must live peaceably with the children of Israel – as they have no legitimate claim to this land, no inheritance with Israel. Israel is a Jewish State, one in which the Sovereign Lord reigns as King of kings!

The Lord God of Israel urges the nations to stand down from oppressing Israel. The nations' interests in the Mideast; likewise, their policies and initiatives for Middle East peace do contradict with God's own plans and policies. His intent is that Israel should possess the land of their forefathers, and live in it in peace and security with Jerusalem as their undivided capital. Whereas, the international community's plans to foster peace by diving God's land. The policies of the nations are therefore in conflict with God's interests. Thus He is angry with the nations.

Declassified Materials

The intelligence gathered from the Scriptures reveals a number of critical factors that must be taken into consideration immediately. Two of those would be mentioned in this section, they are as follows:

1) For the day of the Lord upon all nations is near, as you have done, it shall be done to you; your reprisal shall return upon your own head.[5]
2) And the Lord answered the angel who talked to me (the prophet Zechariah), with good and comforting words. So

the angel who spoke with me said to me, Proclaim, saying, 'Thus says the Lord of hosts:

I am zealous for Jerusalem and for Zion with great zeal.

I am exceedingly angry with the nations at ease; for I was a little angry, and they helped–but with evil intent.

Therefore thus says the Lord: I am returning to Jerusalem with mercy; My house shall be built in it (i.e., the Temple), says the Lord of hosts, and a surveyor's line shall be stretched out over Jerusalem.

And again proclaim, saying, Thus says the Lord of hosts: My cities shall again spread out through prosperity; the Lord will again comfort Zion, and will again choose Jerusalem.'[6]

Finally, second to the Holy Bible, there may be more literature written on the Arab-Israeli conflict than any other subject matter, from the briefs by governments, to analyses by countless personalities in the mass media. This author did not join the long list for the sake of submitting another perspective, but her cause is greater. It's because of the threads in the tapestry...

God the Lord, who appeared to Abraham as God Almighty called Abraham, and Abraham answered the call and moved with his wife and possessions to the place where God led him. This country was then called Canaan and God took the liberty and exercised His right as Creator of the world to give to Abraham and his descendants this land. This land which is now known as Israel!

The world has missed the initial purpose for God's actions then and they have missed it yet again, today. The entire world was idolatrous, then, as it is now. Men have been doing what seems right in their own eyes from the very beginning and they persist to do so, even to this very day. Hence, Israel! God chose them by initiating the birth of these people under special circumstances, having Himself arranged the birth of Isaac to Abraham and Sarah, who were well advanced in years. She was approximately aged 90 and he approximately 100 years old when Isaac was born.

God did so to show that everything about the Jews would be exceptional. He built them as a nation, He ruled over them and was instrumental in them obtaining the land in the first and second and now the third instance. Would you not stop and think and give God glory? For this is God's doing. He gave the land to Israel because He chose to do so. This act in itself makes it supernatural. Stop! See! Listen! He is God! All other gods are idols! And by Israel being where God wants her to be at this time, makes it all the more important for men everywhere to remove their "blinders" and leave Israel alone. See their God is sitting in His glory, awaiting your worship.

God wanted a paradigm shift in the world. He wants all men to acknowledge Him and worship Him, so He created the people of Israel to lead us in the way. However, instead of serving the God of Israel, the nations have continuously persecuted the people of God, for one reason or another in every generation: in ours it's been opined that it's the creation of the State of Israel is the issue. This argument has caused men everywhere to again miss God. The nations have gone after other gods and they try to make their gods relevant by dying for these idols and creations of their imagination... However, if God wanted to remain a mystery why then would He end the Scriptures on this note?

The throne of God and of the Lamb will be in the city (Jerusalem), and His servants will worship Him. They will see His face, and His name will be written on their foreheads.[7] *The greatness and the wealth of the nations will be brought into the city. But nothing that is impure will enter the city, nor anyone who does shameful things or tells lies. Only those whose names are written in the Lamb's book of the living will enter the city.*[8]

The God of Israel, He is the Lord! It is He who created the world and everything in it. He chose Israel and gave her the land of Canaan, today's Israel, for her eternal possession. Jerusalem is God's Holy City! These things God did for the glory of His holy name.

Epilogue

As long as the State of Israel faces threats from enemy State actors and their proxies – bent on fulfilling their intent to destroy the 'People of the Book,' i.e., the Jews – the Mideast will remain in turmoil.

The threat is to the existence of the Jews and of the State of Israel, and, this is swallowed up in the global quest to divide the land so that a Palestinian State can be established, as a universal solution toward global peace.

Israel, the lone Jewish State in the world, does have a right to exist but this right is being challenged. While, every sovereign State has a right under international law to protect its country and people, Israel is not at liberty to duly exercise this right under international law. Whenever she confronts her enemies, there is most likely some "fall out" and she is "backed into a corner" and has to defend her military actions, while her findings are most often ignored on the premise that Israel cannot truly prosecute herself, the international community faces its own dilemma of bias, with the mass media overtly supporting the Arab cause and the UN Human Rights Council (UNHRC), being a "sham unit" of the UN, where credibility is sorely undermined because most of the Member States on the Council are unfit to stand in judgement of Israel given the fact they conduct their States' affairs under the principles of *dictatorship* and in such environments governance is by the "rule of force" not the "rule of law."

The international community which has a moral responsibility to protect Israel from destruction collaborates with her enemies by pressing Israel to further give territory for the creation of another Arab State. The geographical entity known as Palestine has already been divided by Britain to create Jordan. The remainder is now the territory of Israel. Nevertheless, the United States insists, that it is in their national interests to create a State called Palestine (to be carved out of Israel which is currently a very Small State), thus robbing the Jewish State of not only territory, but its security and dignity. Consequently, whatever troubles befall Israel in the future, should the great powers manage to divide the Holy Land, then, God will hold the international community to account. Because what will follow will not be peace, but war.

This Arab-Israeli conflict is being sustained because of bias and conflict of interests: the world vs. Israel, which inevitably results in the world vs. God, as it was He who established the State of Israel. The Scriptures say of God:

With the merciful You will show Yourself merciful; with a blameless man You will show Yourself blameless;

With the pure You will show Yourself pure; and with the devious You will show Yourself shrewd.[1]

To the international community: remember, your promise to Israel, "never again." Do not let the State of Israel disappear. Do not divide her land any further. She is counting on each nation to stand with her, do not betray Israel. Do not oppose God in your unbelief, leave His land alone!

To Israel: do not be afraid, the God of Abraham, Isaac and Jacob is faithful! He will not neglect you. He is concerned about your well-being and security. He is very interested in preserving the status of Jerusalem. He will not renege on His obligations to keep you and protect you. He will rescue you from all your enemies. You will see Him in His glory, just as your forefathers did because His love for you is eternal. You are God's precious offspring, the fruit of His ingenuity!

Your prolific search for peace along with non-reciprocal concessions has over the past 60 years failed. Please be reminded that the people who live in your land abhor your presence and with excessive penchant they stridently seek your destruction, aided and abetted by the international community. The universal support the Arabs have garnered places you in a difficult position globally, nevertheless, don't bend or bow albeit you stand more-or-less alone. If you accede to a Palestinian State it would be to your peril. In the Book of Judges 2: 1-2 the Lord sent an angel to your forefathers to remind them of a warning He had previously given to them. The angel told the people the Lord's words: *... I said, I will never break My covenant with you. You must not make any covenant with the people who live in the land...*

God has heard your cry; He has seen you struggle against your foes; He has destined you to win!

God's Communiqué

God has been generous in His mercy toward man, but as He watches from His throne in heaven, century after century, He sees His people Israel murdered, brutalised, abused and falsely accused of being the destabilising factor in the international community. God has now decided to openly deflect any strategic initiative that would allow Israel's enemies to gain the upper hand over His people. God knows that Israel is small in number and will not be able to stand against a mighty global alliance, therefore, like in ancient times He will score victory over the international community by fighting on Israel's behalf.

The State of Israel will outlast Lebanon, Jordan, Iraq, Libya, Turkey, Iran, Russia, and many, many others.

America:

God calls on you to choose one of the two sides of this conflict. His interests preclude you from "hugging both parties" it must be either the Jewish State or the Islamic Alliance. Not both! By your choice you will continue to stand as the world's lone superpower, or fall there from.

The Palestinians:

Those who call themselves Palestinians will be overthrown before Israel.

Europe:

The Lord is going to settle "old scores" against you; the blood of tens of millions of Jews "cries out" to Him for justice.

Egypt and Syria:

God will plunder your nations. Damascus will be totalled, afterwards, both of you will repent of your crimes against Israel. You will leave the Arab alliance to foster lasting friendships with Israel.

Russia and China:

Beware! The kingdom of heaven will deliver your great armies to tiny Israel.

Then all the peoples of the world will know that the Lord God of Israel is the Lord! He will do these things for His name's sake and His glory!

Selected Photographs: The Jewish Experience, and of my visit to Israel

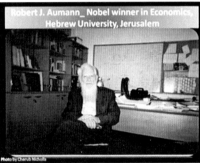

Mom Lola and Dad Norman Cohen (Cher's adopted Israeli parents)
Photo: Abigail Klein

Ray and Sharon Sanders
Directors of Christian Friends of Israel, Jerusalem

Christian Friends of Israel

Sharon Sanders (Co-founder of Christian Friends of Israel) with Holocaust survivor
Photo by CFI

Cherub visits Ministry of Social Services in Sderot
Cherub's Photo

Moshe Benzioni, Political Advisor to the Mayor of Jerusalem, standing in the Old City
Photo by Cherub Nicholls

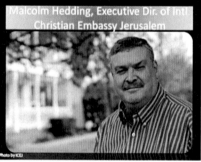

Malcolm Hedding, Executive Dir. of Intl. Christian Embassy Jerusalem
Photo by ICEJ

Rev Jan Willem van der Hoeven, Dir. of Int'l Christian Zionist Center, Jerusalem

Photo by ICZCJ

Jewish Historian Aryeh Routtenberg & Friend Chaim Mandel

Photo by Cherub Nicholls

Christian men in robes in Jerusalem

Photo by Cherub Nicholls

Arab man on his donkey next to an ancient wall in Hebron

Photo by Cherub

Cherub sits on the stairs to the Dome of the Rock, on the Temple Mount in Jerusalem

Cherub's Photo

Cherub stands on the stairs to the Dome of the Rock, on the Temple Mount in Jerusalem

Cherub's Photo

Cher and women praying at the Western Wall

Cherub's Photo

Church of Holy Sepulchre

Cherub's Photo

Messianic Jewish Woman and Arab Christian man on Mount Carmel

Photo by Cherub Nicholls

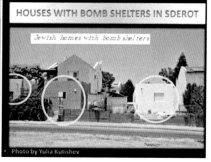

HOUSES WITH BOMB SHELTERS IN SDEROT

Jewish homes with bomb shelters

Photo by Yulia Kutishev

Appendices

Appendix I

A Dialogue – The Lord and His Lover

The Lord:
The Lord says to His people, "I have always loved you."
(*Malachi 1: 2*).

The Lover:
It is time for You to act, O Lord; for Your law is being broken.
(*Psalm 119: 126*).
My zeal wears me out, for my enemies ignore Your precepts.
(*Psalm 119: 139*).

The Lord:
Israel, I will make you my wife; I will be true and faithful;
I will show you constant love and mercy and make you Mine forever.
I will keep My promise and make you mine, and you will acknowledge Me as the Lord.
At that time I will answer the prayers of My people Israel.
I will make the rain fall on the earth, and the earth will produce grain and grapes and olives.
I will establish My people in the land and make them prosper.

I will show love to those who were called "Unloved," and to those who were called "Not-My-People" I will say, "You are My people," and they will answer, "You are our God." *(Hosea 2: 19-23)*.

The Lover:
O God, do not keep silent; be not quiet, O God, be not still.
See how Your enemies are astir, how Your foes rare their heads.
With cunning they conspire against Your people; they plot against those You cherish.
"Come," they say, "let us destroy them as a nation, that the name of Israel be remembered no more."
With one mind they plot together; they form an alliance against You...
(Psalm 83: 1-5).

The Lord:
I, the Sovereign Lord, solemnly promise that the surrounding nations will be humiliated.
But on the mountains of Israel the trees will again grow leaves and bear fruit for you, My people Israel. You are going to come home soon. I am on your side, and I will make sure that your land is plowed again and crops planted on it. I will make sure your population grow. You will live in cities and rebuild every-thing that was left in ruins. I will make people and cattle increase in number. There will be more of you than even before, and you will have many children. I will let you live, and I will make you more prosperous than ever. Then you will know that I am the Lord. I will bring you, My people back to live again in the land. It will be your own land, and it will never again let your children starve. *(Ezekiel 36: 7-12)*.

The Lover:
How awesome is the Lord Most High, the great King over all the earth!
He subdued nations under us, people under our feet. He chose our in-heritance for us, the pride of Jacob, whom He loved...
For God is King over all the earth; sing to Him a psalm of praise.
God reigns over the nations; God is seated on His holy throne.
(Psalm 47: 2-4; 6-8).

The Lord:
...I will use you to show the nations that I am holy.
I will take you from every nation and country and bring you back
to your own land.   (Ezekiel 36: 23 (d)-24).

Everyone will talk about how this land, which was once a wilderness, has become like the Garden of Eden, and how the cities
which were torn down, looted, and left in ruins, are now inhabited and fortified. Then the neighbouring nations that have survived will know that I, the Lord, rebuild ruined cities and replant
waste fields. I, the Lord, have promised that I would do this – and
I will.   *(Ezekiel 36: 35-36)*.

The Lover:
Great is the Lord, and most worthy of praise, in the city of our God, His
holy mountain. It is beautiful in its loftiness, the joy of the whole earth.
Like the utmost heights of Zaphon is Mount Zion, the city of the Great
King.   (Psalm 48: 1-2).

The Lord:
And you, Jerusalem, where God, like a shepherd from His
lookout tower, watches over His people, will once again be the
capital of the kingdom that was yours.   *(Micah 4: 8)*.

The Lover:
Rulers persecute me without cause, but my heart trembles at Your
word. I rejoice in Your promise like one who finds great spoil.
                                              (Psalm 119: 161-162).

The Lord:
Many nations have gathered to attack you. They say, "Jerusalem
must be destroyed! We will see this city in ruins!"
But these nations do not know what is in the Lord's mind. They
do not realise that they have been gathered together to be punished in the same way that grain is brought in to be threshed.
The Lord says, "People of Jerusalem, go and punish your enemies! I will make you strong as a bull with iron horns and bronze

hoofs. You will crush many nations, and the wealth they got by violence you will present to Me, the Lord of the whole world."

(Micah 4: 11-13).

The Lover:

For this is our God forever and ever; and He will be our guide even to the end.

(Psalm 48: 14).

The Finale

And the Lord will take possession of Judah as His inheritance in the Holy Land, and will again choose Jerusalem.

"Be silent, all flesh, before the Lord, for He is aroused from His holy habitation!"

(Zechariah 2: 12-13)

Appendix II

God affirms Israel as His People: Despite Attempts to Delegitimize Israel!

- I am God and always will be. No one can escape from My power, no one can change what I do. (*Isa 43: 13*).
- The Lord says, "Listen to Me, Israel, the people I have called! I am God, the First and the Last, the only God!" (*Isa 48: 12*).
- He said to me, "Israel, you are My servant; because of you, people will praise Me." (*Isa 49: 3*).
- I will give up whole nations to save your life, because you are precious to Me and because I love you and give you honour. Do not be afraid – I am with you! (*Isa 43: 4, 5 (a)*).
- The Lord says, "Listen now, Israel, My servant, My chosen people, the descendants of Jacob.
  I am the Lord who created you, from the time you were born. I have helped you. Do not be afraid; you are My servant, My chosen people whom I love. (*Isa 44: 1-2*).
- The Lord says, "Israel, remember this, remember that you are My servant. I created you to be My servant, and I will never forget you. (*Isa 44: 21*).
- I, the Lord, will rescue all the descendants of Jacob, and they will give Me praise. (*Isa 45: 25*).

- The Lord will use His holy power; He will save His people, and all the world will see it. (*Isa 52: 10*).
- Israel you are like a young wife, deserted by her husband and deeply distressed. But the Lord calls you back to Him and says: For one brief moment I left you; with deep love I will take you back. I turned away angry for only a moment, but I will show you My love forever. So says the Lord who saves you. (*Isa 54: 6-8*).

(Source: *Good News Bible Translation*. Note: All pronouns pertaining to God begin with uppercase letters this was done to be consistent with the style in the *Prophecy Study Bible*).

Appendix III

The Interview List

NAME	DESIGNATION	ORGANI-SATION	LOCA-TION
MK and Minister Isaac Herzog	Minister for Social Affairs and Services	Ministry for Social Affairs and Services	Jerusalem Israel
MK Benjamin "Benny" Begin	Cabinet Minister	The Knesset	Jerusalem Israel
MK Prof. Arieh Eldad	Member of the Knesset	The Knesset	Jerusalem Israel
MK Danny Danon	Member of the Knesset and Deputy Speaker (Member of the Defence & Foreign Affairs Committees)	The Knesset	Jerusalem Israel

Mayor Nir Barkat	Mayor of Jerusalem	Office of the Mayor Jerusalem	Jerusalem Israel
Mr. Moshe Benzioni	Political Adviser to the Mayor of Jerusalem	Office of the Mayor of Jerusalem	Jerusalem Israel
Prof. Robert Aumann Noble Winner in Economics in 2005	Professor Emeritus of Mathematics & Economics and Member of the Center for the Study of Rationality	Center of Rationality Hebrew University Jerusalem	Givat Ram Jerusalem Israel
Dr. Mordechai Kedar	Research Associate	Bar Ilan University	Ramat Gan, Israel
US Department of State	——	US Department of State	Washington DC
Congressman Doug Lamborn	US Representative	Congress Cannon House Office Building House of Representatives	Washington DC
Maj.-General Robert Mood	Chief of Staff and Head of Mission	The United Nations Truce Supervision Organisation (UNTSO)	Jerusalem Israel
H.E Al-Allaf	Ambassador and Permanent Representative of Jordan	The Permanent Mission of the Kingdom of Jordan to the United Nations	New York

H.E. Paul Badji	Ambassador and Permanent Representative of Senegal	The Permanent Mission of the Republic of Senegal to the United Nations	New York
H.E Daniel Carmon	Ambassador and Deputy Permanent Representative of Israel	The Permanent Mission of Israel to the United Nations	New York
H.E Dr Riyad H. Mansour	Ambassador of the Observer Mission of Palestine	The Observer Mission of Palestine to the United Nations	New York
H.E Omar Jelban	Chargé d'affaires	Embassy of Libya	London
H.E Amr Ramadan	Deputy Ambassador	Embassy of Egypt	Washington DC
Ms. Meltem Buyukkara	Counsellor	Embassy of Turkey	London
Mr. Phillip Holzapfed	Representative	Embassy of Germany	Washington DC
Mrs. Sarah Stern	Founder & President	Endowment for Middle East Truth (EMET)	Washington DC
Ms. Zahava Goldman	Senior Legislative Assistant to Congressman Henry A. Waxman	Congress Rayburn Building House of Representatives	Washington DC
Mr. Gershom Gale	Editor: The Jerusalem Post Christian Edition	The Jerusalem Post	Jerusalem Israel

Mr. Jan Willen van der Hoeven	Director	The International Christian Zionist Center (ICZC)	Jerusalem Israel
Ray & Sharon Sanders	Founders & Directors	Christian Friends of Israel (CFI)	Jerusalem Israel
Mr. Malcolm Hedding	Executive Director	The Christian Embassy (CE)	Jerusalem Israel
Rev. Dr. Petra Heldt	Executive Secretary	The Ecumenical Theological Research Fraternity (ETRF)	Jerusalem Israel
Mr. Aryeh Routtenberg	Author, Historian and Senior Guide	Field School of Kibbutz Kfar Etzion	Gush Etzion Israel
Ms. Oriya Dasberg	Public Relations Tourist Officer	Public Relations Tourist Association	Gush Etzion Israel
Mr. David Wilder	Spokesman	The Jewish Hebron Group	Hebron Israel
Yossi & Hanna Nussbaum	Artist	Note: Hanna was a young child who was sent away with others before Gush Etzion fell to the Jordanian Army. Her father Shlomo Rozen died at age 29 along with other defenders of Gush Etzion	Gush Etzion Israel
Ms. Miriam Trachtman	Social Worker	Department of Social Work, Ministry for Social Affairs	Sderot Israel
Mr. Yulia Kutishev	Veteran Fireman	Sderot Fire Department	Sderot Israel

Mr. Walid S Abu Alhalaweh	Public Relations Officer	The Hebron Rehabilitation Committee	Palestin-Hebron Israel
Mrs. Ruhi Avital	Former Council Member	Council of Ofra	Ofra Israel

Note: Fr. Humam Khzouz, Chancellery and General Administrator, Latin Patriarch of Jerusalem, invited me to attend a Press Conference at the Notre Dame Hotel in Jerusalem on Wednesday 20 May 2009 following the visit of Pope Benedict XVI, to Israel. This invitation was in response to my letter of request to interview His Beatitude Fouad Twal, Latin Patriarch of Jerusalem. The Press Conference was sponsored by the Latin Patriarch in Jerusalem. The five members of the panel were as follows:

i) His Beatitude Fouad Twal, Latin Patriarch of Jerusalem – Leader of the panel
ii) Most Reverend Raphael Minessian; Armenian Catholic Patriarchal Exarch of Jerusalem and Amman
iii) Archbishop Antonio Franco, Apostolic Delegate in Jerusalem and Nuncio in Israel
iv) Bishop Kamal Bathish, Emeritus Auxiliary Bishop – (retired)
v) Fr. Peter Felet, Secretary of the Bishops Conference.

Appendix IV

Dateline of Hebron's History

The overwhelming perception among Gentiles, whether they are Americans, Arabs, Europeans, Asians, Africans or even folks from the Caribbean and Latin America, is that Jews belong elsewhere, anywhere, once it's not in their ancestral homeland, in Palestine. Therefore, for the curious and also for the records: the State of Israel is located in its ancestral homeland, the same contested territory called Palestine. This land has belonged to Jews for centuries. The area was fully Jewish and controlled by Jewish kings such names that are familiar to us include: King Saul, King David, King Solomon and many, many others. Likewise, for those who claim to love Jesus but hate the Jews, your religion is in vain. Jesus also lived in this same territory!

Consequently, *the Dateline of Hebron's History* is presented for careful consideration. See when Abraham arrived, where he buried Sarah his wife and where Caleb possessed following his re-entry into Canaan, along with Joshua. The two were among the 12 spies, only these two: Joshua and Caleb were kept alive of the 12, after they gave a good report when they were sent by Moses to spy out the land of Canaan. Caleb was given Hebron.

See also how the Arabs have attacked Jews and slaughtered many in 1929 and at other times. The Arabs have sought to deny the Jews their rich heritage and rights to the area. The Arabs have been waging intifadas in the economic, diplomatic and military streams for a long time against Israel. This conflict will only continue as long as *the global elites* stand in denial of the fundamentals. The era of Abraham and the other ancestors of the Israelites have left no doubt as to their presence in: symbols and traditions. However, most importantly, their deeds are captured in the Torah and the Bible.

Finally, see in the records how often the Jews were expelled from Hebron in Israel. Remember their expulsions all across Europe from century to century? Accordingly, as the world leaders consistently call Jewish towns and cities "settlements," their call for "withdrawals" from "settlements" are calls for future expulsions or banishments of Jews from their homes, once again! Such is the kind of peace the international community offers Israel!

Dateline of Hebron's History

DATE	EVENT
1735 BCE	Abraham comes to Canaan and settles in Hebron.
1675 BCE	Abraham purchases the cave.
1250 BCE	Joshua leads Tribes of Israel. Caleb occupies Hebron.
1007 BCE	David is anointed king at Hebron.
587 BCE1	1st Temple destroyed, Edomites settle in Hebron area.
445 BCE	Jews return to Zion.
164 BCE	Hasmonean Revolt. Judah Macabee conquers Hebron.
30 BCE	Construction of enormous edifice over Machpela Cave.

70 CE	2ndTemple, Jerusalem, Hebron destroyed.
132 CE	Bar Kochba Revolt. Hebron in center of revolt area.
330 CE	Byzantine Conquest. Church built over Ma'ara.
4th – 6th Century	Jews continue to pray at Ma'ara and Elonei Mamre.
638 CE	Islamic Conquest Mosque built in the Ma'ara. Jews still pray in Ma'ara Synagogue.
10th Century	Arabs build "Yusufia" attached to Ma'ara.
1100	Crusader Conquest, Hebron Jews banished. Church built in Ma'ara.
1171	Visit by Benjamin Metudelah.
1166	Rambam visits Hebron and prays at Ma'ara.
1260	Mamaluk Conquest.
1267	Jews banned from Ma'ara. Ramban visits Hebron "to acquire a burial site".
1489	R' Ovadiah of Bartenura sojourns in Hebron.
1517	Ottoman Conquest, Anti-Jewish riots.
1540	R' Malkiel Ashkenazi buys land and builds the Jewish Quarter and the Avraham Avinu Synagogue.
1583	Mystics from Safed, including the "Reishit Chochmah", R' Eliyahu Di Vidas move to Hebron.
1630	Decrees against Hebron's Jews "The Purim Window Miracle".

1753	The "Chidah", R' Chaim Yosef David Azulai goes to Europe as fund raiser on behalf of Hebron's Jews.
1811	R' Chaim HaMizri buys the lands of Tel Hebron on behalf of Hebron's Jews.
1819	Fourth Lubavitcher Rebbe calls on his followers to settle Hebron. Many do so.
1834	Earthquake Ibrahim Pasha Conquest. Attacks on Jews.
1856	R' Eliyahu Mani arrives from Baghdad and settles in Hebron.
1871	Yisrael Avraham Romano builds Beit Romano, Istanbuli Synagogue.
1881	The " Charif", R' Chaim Rachamim Yosef Franco, Chief Rabbinic Justice of Hebron.
1893	Ground floor completed of the "Chessed LeAvraham" Health Clinic.
1901	R' Chizkiya Medini, the "S'dei Chemed" moves to Hebron and is appointed city rabbi.
1909	Yosef Avraham Shalom adds a floor on to the "Chessed LeAvraham" Clinic.
1912	The Lubavitcher Rebbe, Shalom Ber Schneerson buys Beit Romano and founds Yeshivat "Torat Emet".
1914	WW I. Community Weakened and impoverished.
1917	British Conquest.
1925	Community recovers Slobodka Yeshiva ("Knesset Yisrael") arrives.
1929	1929 Riots. Hebron Massacre. Jews banished, community destroyed.

1931	Part of community returns.
1935	Gerrer Rebbe visits Hebron, prays on 11th step.
1936	Hebron Jews banished by British.
1948	State of Israel, Hebron conquered by Jordan. Jewish Quarter and Cemetery destroyed. Avraham Avinu Synagogue becomes trasheap and animal pen.
1967	Hebron Liberated, R' Shlomo Goren waves Israeli Flag at Ma'ara.
1968	Hebron settlers return. Pesach Seder at Park Hotel. After five weeks they are moved to the Civil Administration Bldg, there they set up a community yeshiva and factories.
Oct. 1969	Grenade thrown at Jews by the Ma'ara. Dozens wounded Vice Premier Yigal Alon announces a Jewish city will soon be built near Hebron.
Sept. 1971	Residents move into Kiryat Arba.
1975	Prof. Ben-Zion Tavger begins to uncover remains of Avraham Avinu Synagogue.
April 1979	Women and children enter Beit Hadassah.
Jan. 1980	Residents move into Ramat Mamre.
May 1980	Six Jews Murdered at Beit Hadassah. Govt. decides to renew Hebron community.
1981	Dedication of renewed Avraham Avinu Synagogue.
Aug. 1984	Tel Hebron settled. New "Admot Yishai" (or "Tel Rumeida") neighborhood.

1986	Families move into renewed Beit Hadassah.
1989	New homes dedicated in the Jewish Quarter.
Sept. 1990	Residents move into "Givat Ha'avot" neighborhood.
1994	Hamas plans major terror attack in Hebron. Purim incident at Ma'ara.
1995	Floors added to Beit Schneerson. Nachum Hoss and Yehuda Partush murdered at edge of Hebron.
Jan. 1997	Israeli Gov't Abandons most of Hebron to P.A. Jews left surrounded by enemies, open to attack from hills.
Sept. 1998	R' Shlomo Raanan Zt'l murdered in Admot Yishai.
1999	"Beit Nachum Veyehuda" built in Avraham Avinu Neighborhood. Excavations uncover Tel Hebron treasures.
2000	"Beit Hashisha" built. 2001 "Oslo War". Arab terror rampant. Hebron Jews under constant fire. Shalhevet Pass shot from Abu Sneineh Hills.
2002	Israeli Defense Forces retake hills surrounding Hebron, finally ending daily shooting attacks, following the murder of five year old Danielle Shefi at Adura community.
2005	Beit Menachem built and dedicated at Admot Ishai (Tel Rumeida) neighbourhood.

2007	Hebron community concludes purchase of Beit HaShalom. Jewish families populate 4000 sq meter building on road between Hebron and Kiryat Arba.
2008	Defense Minister Ehud Barak orders expulsion of Jews from Beit HaShalom after having lived there for twenty months.
2010	Jewish community receives official statistics: 500,000 visit Ma'arat HaMachpela in 2009. Less than half that number visits the Moslem side of the holy site.

With blessings from Hebron,
David Wilder

Also see: http://www.hebron.com/english/article.php?id=176

Reprinted with permission, courtesy of David Wilder

Appendix V

The History of Eretz-Israel – the Land of Israel

Year/Period	Experience/ Invader	Other Information
66-70	The Jewish war against the Romans	The 2nd fall of Jerusalem and the destruction of the 2nd Temple.
603	Persians	611 arrived at Antioch 613 Damascus 614 Eretz-Israel
634-1099	Arab Period	632 the death of Muhammad.
1071	Seljuk and Fatimid Invasion	1098 The Seljuk General Atsiz captures Jerusalem.
1099-1291	Crusader Period	1209-39; 1243-44 Christians occupied Jerusalem, the Christians did not initially

		allow the Jews access to the city (Jerusalem). 1236 a special agreement permitting them to visit the Holy City was arranged; it included a special permit for Jewish dyers to settle in Jerusalem...
1291-1516	Mamluk Period	The return of Muslim rule for two-and-a-half centuries.
1517-1917	Ottoman Period	1517-1574 The Golden Period of Ottoman Rule. 1512-20 Selim I 1516 Selim I defeated the Egyptians. 1520-66 Jerusalem rebellion during the reign of Selim I's son – Suleiman the Magnificent. 1548 The Constitution of the province of Damascus which included Eretz-Israel was established. 1526-1554 Jewish families living in Jerusalem increased from 200 to 338 Jews in Safed numbered approximately 10,000

		1576 Turkish decree ordered the expulsion of 500 to 1,000 wealthy Jewish families of Safed,forcing them to move to Cyprus 1625 a greedy Bedouin Sheikh, Muhammad ibn Farukh tyrannised the Jewish population through the imposition of heavy taxes. Gaza was a thriving Jewish community. It was also an asylum for Jewish refugees. Jerusalem was the centre of most of the scholars of Eretz-Israel and even attracted some of the great scholars from countries of the East In the 17th century the Jewish population succeeded in consolidating its position in Jerusalem and in the entire section of the country 1832-40 Egypt ruled Syria and Eretz-Israel 1838 the Egyptian Government permitted Britain to open a regular Consulate in Jerusalem. 1820 most of the Jews lived in the four holy

		cities: Jerusalem, Safed, Tiberius and Hebron. They laboured under a heavy yoke of taxes imposed by the Turkish officials. "The extortions oppressions were so numerous that it was said that the Jews had to pay for the very air they breathed."
1917-1948	British Mandate Period	1939-1945 Britain gives very little support to rescuing the Jews fleeing the Holocaust in Europe 1946 Britain divides Palestine enabling the creation of Jordan 1947 Arabs rejects the UN Partition Plan of Palestine for Jews and Arabs in the remainder of the territory. 1948 Britain leaves Eretz-Israel as its Mandate expires.
1948 to 2010	The State of Israel	1948 the Declaration of Independence of the State of Israel. 1948-49 War of Independence. Jordan seizes parts of Jerusalem, Judea and Samaria. Egypt captures Gaza.

		1949 Israel becomes a UN Member State. retakes Judea and Samaria as well as Gaza 1973 the War of Atonement, the Yom Kippur War. 2006 and 2008 Israel wars with terrorists: Hezbollah and Hamas proxies of Iran and Syria. 2005 the Road Map Initiative. Israel is being asked to divide the ap- proximately 23 percent territory in her posses- sion-so that there can be the creation of a Palestinian State. 2010 Israel is harassed by her neighbours, faces terror attacks and flotilla skirmishes. Israel has to always defend her ac- tions. Israel enjoys very little international sup- port. Source: Encyclopaedia Judaica Vol. 9 Is-Jer. Jerusalem: Keter Publishing House, Israel, 1971.

Source: Encyclopaedia Judaica Vol. 9 Is-Jer. Jerusalem: Keter Publishing House, Israel, 1971.

Appendix VI
Map of Ancient Israel

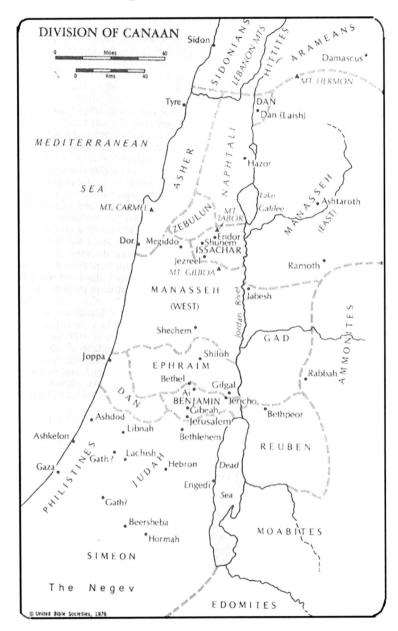

DIVISION OF CANAAN

Sidon

SIDONIANS

LEBANON MTS.

HITTITES

ARAMEANS

Damascus

MT. HERMON

Tyre

DAN
Dan (Laish)

MEDITERRANEAN

ASHER

NAPHTALI

Hazor

SEA

MT. CARMEL

Lake
Galilee

MANASSEH
(EAST)

Ashtaroth

ZEBULUN

MT.
TABOR

Dor   Megiddo   Endor
Shunem
ISSACHAR

Jezreel

MT. GILBOA

Ramoth

MANASSEH
(WEST)

Jordan River

Jabesh

Shechem

GAD

AMMONITES

Joppa

Shiloh

EPHRAIM

Bethel

Gilgal

DAN

Ai

BENJAMIN   Jericho

Rabbah

Gibeah

Ashdod

Jerusalem

Bethpeor

Libnah

Bethlehem

Ashkelon

PHILISTINES

Gath?   Lachish

REUBEN

Gaza

JUDAH

Hebron

Dead

Engedi

Sea

Gath?

Beersheba

MOABITES

Hormah

SIMEON

The   Negev

© United Bible Societies, 1976

EDOMITES

Good News Bible. Good News Translation New York: American Bible Society.

241

Appendix VII
Map of Israel (Current)

© 2006 Copyright Carta, Jerusalem

Courtesy of Carta, Jerusalem

http://www.mfa.gov.il/MFA/Facts+About+Israel/Israel+in+Maps/
Israel+within+Boundaries+and+Ceasefire+Lines+-+200.htm

Endnotes

Chapter 1

[1] John C. Hagee, General Editor, *Prophecy Study Bible* (NKJV) (Nashville: Thomas Nelson, 1997), Genesis 6: 5-7.

[2] Ibid., Genesis 9: 8,11-13.

[3] Ibid., Genesis 12: 1-2.

[4] Ibid., Genesis 25: 6.

[5] Ibid., Genesis 26:3-4.

[6] Good News Bible, Good News Translation (New York: American Bible Society), Romans 9: 7-13.

[7] John C. Hagee, General Editor, *Prophecy Study Bible* (NKJV), (Nashville: Thomas Nelson, 1997), Genesis 32:26-28.

[8] Ibid., Deuteronomy 7:6, 9.

[9] Ibid., Jeremiah 29: 10, 14.

[10] Ibid., Ezra 1: 1-4.

[11] Paul Mendes-Flohr and Jehuda Reinharz, eds., The Jew in the Modern World, A Documentary History, Second Edition (New York: Oxford University Press, 1995), 304.

[12] Ibid., 306.

[13] Ibid., 307.

[14] John P. Mc Ternan, As America – Has Done to – Israel, The Result: Massive National Disasters (Pennsylvania: Whitaker House, 2008), 71.

[15] Ibid., 72.

[16]David Brog, <u>Standing with Israel</u>, Why Christians Support The Jewish State (Florida: Front Line, 2006), 2.

[17]Ibid., 3.

[18]Ibid., 21 & 22.

[19]Moshe Aumann, <u>Conflict & Connection</u>, The Jewish-Christian-Israel Triangle (Jerusalem: Gefen Publishing House, 2003), 3.

[20]Ibid., 138.

Chapter 2

[1]Proclamation of Independence, The Declaration of the Establishment of the State of Israel, Provisional Government of Israel, <u>Official Gazette</u> Number 1; Tel Aviv, 14.5.1948, 1, http://www.knesset.gov.il/doc/eng/megilat_eng.htm

[2]Ibid., 1.

[3]Aryeh Routtenberg, <u>The Etzion Bloc in the Hills of Judea</u> (Jerusalem), 2.

[4]Ibid., 9.

[5]Ibid., 13.

[6]John C. Hagee, General Editor, *Prophecy Study Bible (NKJV)* (Nashville: Thomas Nelson, 1997), Deuteronomy 31: 3, 7-8.

[7]Ibid., Joshua 1: 1, 4-5.

[8]Ibid., Joshua 9: 1-2.

[9]Ibid., Joshua 11: 16, 19-20, 23.

[10]Benjamin Netanyahu, <u>A Durable Peace</u>, Israel And Its Place Among The Nations (New York: Warner Books, 1999), xv.

[11]Ibid., xvi.

[12]Ibid., xvi.

[13]Moshe Aumann, <u>Jerusalem</u>, Israel Today No. 37 (Jerusalem: Israel Digest, 1968), 43.

[14]Ibid., 43.

[15]Ibid., 43.

[16]Howard Grief, <u>The Legal Foundation and Borders of Israel under International Law</u>, A Treatise on Jewish Sovereignty over the Land of Israel (Jerusalem: Mazo Publishers, 2008), 18.

[17]Ibid., 19.

[18]Ibid., 150.

[19]UN General Assembly Resolution 181, <u>Partition Plan</u>, 29 November, 1947, http://www.mfa.gov.il/MFA/Peace+Process/ Guide+to+the+Peace+Process/UN+General+Assembly+Reso lution+181.htm

[20]David Brog, <u>Standing with Israel</u>, Why Christians Support The Jewish State (Florida: Front Line, 2006), 123.

[21]MFA Newsletter, Ministry of Foreign Affairs, Israel, "Address by PM Netanyahu to the Christians United For Israel Jerusalem Summit," 8 March, 2010, 2.

[22]John C. Hagee, General Editor, *Prophecy Study Bible (NKJV)* (Nashville: Thomas Nelson, 1997), Deuteronomy 30: 5.

[23]Ibid., Ezekiel 34: 13.

Chapter 3

[1]MFA Newsletter, Ministry of Foreign Affairs, Israel, PM Netanyahu addresses AIPAC conference in Washington, "Jerusalem is not a settlement," It is our capital, www.mofa.gov.il, 22 March, 2010, 1.

[2]John C. Hagee, General Editor, *Prophecy Study Bible (NKJV)* (Nashville: Thomas Nelson, 1997), Psalm 122: 3 & 4.

[3]Ibid., Psalm 125: 2.

[4]MFA Newsletter, Ministry of Foreign Affairs, Israel, PM Netanyahu addresses AIPAC conference in Washington, "Jerusalem is not a settlement," It is our capital, www.mofa.gov.il, 22 March, 2010, 3.

[5]Ibid., 3.

[6]Ibid., 3.

[7]"Quartet urges Israeli settlement freeze," Mideast peacemakers 'condemn' East Jerusalem building plan, <u>Msnbc.com news serv-ices,</u> Friday March 19, 2010.

[8]Ibid., 2.

[9]"Obama's Turn Against Israel," The US makes a diplomatic crisis out of a blunder, Editorial, The <u>Wall Street Journal,</u> http://online.wsj.com/article.....oveLEFTTop, March 15, 2010, 1.

[10]Ibid., 1.

[11]Ibid., 2.

[12]Ibid., 3.

[13]Israel Eldad & Arieh Eldad, The Challenge of Jerusalem, Betwixt Thicket and Altar (Israel: Alex Klevitsky, 1998), 11.
[14]John C. Hagee, General Editor, Prophecy Study Bible (NKJV) (Nashville: Thomas Nelson, 1997), Ezekiel 14: 13.
[15]Israel Eldad & Arieh Eldad, The Challenge of Jerusalem, Betwixt Thicket and Altar (Israel: Alex Klevitsky, 1998), 11.
[16]Ibid., 12.
[17]Encyclopedia Judaica, Volume 9 IS-JER, Encyclopedia Judaica Jerusalem (Jerusalem: Keter Publishing House Ltd., 1971), 238.
[18]John C. Hagee, General Editor, Prophecy Study Bible (NKJV) (Nashville: Thomas Nelson, 1997), Jeremiah 5: 18-19.
[19]Good News Bible, Good News Translation (New York: American Bible Society), Exodus 34: 14.
[20]John C. Hagee, General Editor, Prophecy Study Bible (NKJV) (Nashville: Thomas Nelson, 1997), Jeremiah 5: 24.
[21]Ibid., Jeremiah 32: 2 & 6.
[22]Ibid., Jeremiah 32: 10-15.
[23]Ibid., Jeremiah 32: 36.
[24]Ibid., Jeremiah 32: 37-38.
[25]Good News Bible, Good News Translation (New York: American Bible Society), Isaiah 45: 12-13.
[26]Ibid., Ezra 4: 1, 4 & 5.
[27]Ibid., Ezra 6: 6 (c), 12.
[28]Israel Eldad & Arieh Eldad, The Challenge of Jerusalem, Betwixt Thicket and Altar (Israel: Alex Klevitsky, 1998), 34 &
[29]Moshe Aumann, Jerusalem, Israel Today No. 37 (Jerusalem: Israel Digest, 1968), 53.
[30]Moshe Aumann, The Palestinian Labyrinth – a way out (Jerusalem: Israel Academic Committee, 1985), 17.
[31]John C. Hagee, General Editor, Prophecy Study Bible (NKJV) (Nashville: Thomas Nelson, 1997), Psalm 83: 2-4.
[32]Ibid., Jeremiah 2; 37.
[33]Ibid., Jeremiah 32: 41, 44.
[34]Good News Bible, Good News Translation (New York: American Bible Society), Psalms 105: 10-11.

Chapter 4

[1] Benjamin Netanyahu, <u>A Durable Peace</u>, Israel And Its Place Among The Nations (New York: Warner Books, 1999), xii.

[2] MFA Newsletter, Ministry of Foreign Affairs, Israel, "Deputy Foreign Minister Ayalon addresses the Council of Europe," Jerusalem: MFA, 26 Jan, 2010, 1.

[3] John C. Hagee, General Editor, *Prophecy Study Bible (NKJV)* (Nashville: Thomas Nelson, 1997), Isaiah 66: 7-10, 16.

[4] Ibid., Ezekiel 36: 22-24, 34.

[5] Richard N. Hass and Martin Indyk, "Can Washington Midwife Middle East peace?" Beyond Iraq, <u>Foreign Affairs</u> (January / February 2009), 45.

[6] Ibid., 47.

[7] Ibid., 57.

[8] Walter Russell Mead, "Change They Can Believe In," To Make Israel Safe, Give Palestinian their Due: Can Washington Midwife Middle East Peace? <u>Foreign Affairs</u>, (January / February 2009), 59.

[9] Ibid., 67.

[10] Joan Peters, <u>From Time Immemorial</u>, The Origins Of The Arab-Jewish Conflict Over Palestine (New York: Harper & Row, 1984), 80.

[11] Ibid., 80.

[12] Ibid., 4.

[13] Ibid., 4.

[14] Ibid., 5.

[15] Howard Grief, <u>The Legal Foundation and Borders of Israel under International Law</u>, A Treatise on Jewish Sovereignty over the Land of Israel (Jerusalem: Mazo Publishers, 2008), 519.

[16] Ibid., 519.

[17] Ibid., 459.

[18] David Brog, <u>Standing with Israel</u>, Why Christians Support The Jewish State (Florida: Front Line, 2006), 107 & 108.

[19] Ibid., 108 &109.

[20] Ibid., 110.

[21] Ibid, 110.

[22] Howard Grief, <u>The Legal Foundation and Borders of Israel under International Law</u>, A Treatise on Jewish Sovereignty over the Land of Israel (Jerusalem: Mazo Publishers, 2008), 74.

[23]Ibid., 74.

[24]British White Paper of 1939, http://www.hagshama.org.il/en/ resources/view.asp?id=135

[25]Benjamin Netanyahu, A Durable Peace, Israel And Its Place Among The Nations (New York: Warner Books, 1999), 3.

[26]Ibid, 4

[27]Ibid., 4 & 5.

[28]Ibid., 5.

[29]Bill Jones and Dennis Kavanagh, British Politics Today, Seventh Edition (Manchester: Manchester University Press, 2003), 2.

[30]John C. Hagee, General Editor, Prophecy Study Bible (NKJV) (Nashville: Thomas Nelson, 1997), Exodus 29: 45.

[31]Ibid., Isaiah 55: 8 & 9.

Chapter 5

[1]John C. Hagee, General Editor, Prophecy Study Bible (NKJV) (Nashville: Thomas Nelson, 1997), Esther 1: 1 & 3: 1.

[2]Ibid., Esther 3: 5-6

[3]Ibid., Esther 3: 8-9.

[4]Ibid., Esther 7: 3-4.

[5]Ibid., Esther 7: 9 -10.

[6]MFA Newsletter, Ministry of Foreign Affairs, Israel, "Address by Prime Minister Benjamin Netanyahu to the United Nations General Assembly General Debate – 64th Session," New York: United Nations, 24 September 2009, 2.

[7]Ibid., 3.

[8]MFA Newsletter, Ministry of Foreign Affairs, Israel, "Address by PM Netanyahu to the Christian United For Israel Jerusalem Summit," 8 March, 2010, 1.

[9]Ibid., 1.

[10]MFA Newsletter, Ministry of Foreign Affairs, Israel, "Iran: Excerpt from PM Netanyahu's address to the Jewish Agency Board of Governors," 22 February, 2010, 2.

[11]Ibid., 2.

[12]John C. Hagee, General Editor, Prophecy Study Bible (NKJV) (Nashville: Thomas Nelson, 1997), Zechariah 9: 16.

[13]Ibid, Zechariah 2: 8.

[14]<u>Good News Bible</u>, Good News Translation (New York: American Bible Society), Zechariah 2: 9.

[15]Moshe Aumann, <u>The Palestinian Labyrinth – a way out</u> (Jerusalem: Israel Academic Committee, 1985), 33.

[16]Ibid.,35.

[17]"Prime Minister Benjamin Netanyahu's foreign policy speech at Bar IIan University," Full text, <u>Haaretz</u>, Sunday 14 June, 2009, http://www.haaretz.com, 1.

[18]Ibid., 2.

[19]Ibid., 5.

[20]Moshe Aumann, <u>Land Ownership in Palestine 1880-1948</u> (Jerusalem: Israel Academic Committee on the Middle East), 22.

[21]John C. Hagee, General Editor, *<u>Prophecy Study Bible</u> (NKJV)* (Nashville: Thomas Nelson, 1997), Amos 9: 14-15.

[22]Ibid., Hosea 14: 9.

[23]Moshe Aumann, <u>Land Ownership in Palestine 1880-1948</u> (Jerusalem: Israel Academic Committee on the Middle East), 23.

[24]Nicole Jansezian, "With Obama at helm, Iranian Threat Looms large, How will Obama change the Middle East?" Times of Change, <u>Israel Today</u>, Magazine, December 2008, www.israel-today.co.il, 3.

[25]Ibid., 3.

[26]Jack W. Hayford, Litt. D., General Editor, <u>Spirit Filled Life Bible</u> (NKJV), (Nashville: Thomas Nelson, Inc., 1991), Proverbs 16:2.

[27]"Netanyahu vows to work with Obama for peace," <u>Haaretz.com</u>, by News Agencies, 22 February, 2009, www.haaretz.com/hasen/spages/1066078.html, 1.

[28]Ibid., 1.

[29]Ibid., 1.

[30]David Parson, "Poised over The Panic Button," New Players in Old Game, <u>The Jerusalem Post, Christian Edition,</u> in Partnership with the International Christian Embassy (Jerusalem, June 2009, www.jpost.com/ce), 4.

[31]Ibid., 5.

[32]Jan Willen van der Hoeven, "What Will History Record?" Director, International Christian Zionist Center, (Thursday 28 May, 2009), 2.

[33]Ibid., 2.

[34]Ibid., 2.

[35]"Obama's Mideast plan calls for demilitarised Palestinian State," The Jerusalem Post, JPost .Com Staff, Mideast, Jpost.com, 20 May, 2009, http://www.jpost.com/servlet/Satellite?cid=1242212419666&pagename=JPost%2FJPArticle%2FShowFull, 1.

[36]"Full Text of Obama's Cairo Speech," The Jerusalem Post, Mideast.Jpost.com, (4 June, 2009), http://www.jpost.com/servlet/Satellite?apage=1&cid=1244034998314&pagename=JPost%2FJPArticle%2FShowFull, 1.

[37]Ibid., 1.

[38]Ibid., 5.

[39]Herb Keinon, "Analysis: Is Obama looking for a fight over 'natural growth'?" The Jerusalem Post. International, Jpost.com, 28 May, 2009, http://www.jpost.com/servlet/Satellite?cid=1243346492983&pagename=JPost%2FJPArticle%2FShowFull, 1.

[40]Ibid., 2.

[41]Esther Levens, "Congress Sends a Resounding Message of Pro-Israel Support," Press Release- Contact @ elevens@israelunity-coalition.org, (Friday 16 April, 2010), 1

[42]Ibid., 1.

Chapter 6

[1]Good News Bible, Good News Translation (New York: American Bible Society), Genesis 1: 1-2.

[2]Ibid., Romans 1: 18-23.

[3]John C. Hagee, General Editor, Prophecy Study Bible (NKJV) (Nashville: Thomas Nelson, 1997), Genesis 15:13-14, 16.

[4]Good News Bible, Good News Translation (New York: American Bible Society), Exodus 23: 22 (b)-33.

[5]Ibid., Jeremiah 1: 17-19.

[6]John C. Hagee, General Editor, Prophecy Study Bible (NKJV) (Nashville: Thomas Nelson, 1997), 1 Kings 16: 25-26.

[7]Ibid., 1 Kings 16: 30.

[8]Ibid., 1 Kings 16: 31.

⁹Ibid., 1 Kings 18: 20-21.

¹⁰Ibid., Jeremiah 51: 15-16, 19 (d).

¹¹Ibid., Isaiah 43: 10-13.

¹²Ibid., Isaiah 44: 6, 8 (b).

¹³Good News Bible, Good News Translation (New York: American Bible Society), Exodus 24: 9-11.

¹⁴John C. Hagee, General Editor, *Prophecy Study Bible* (NKJV) (Nashville: Thomas Nelson, 1997), Psalm 18: 6-10, 16-17.

¹⁵Good News Bible, Good News Translation (New York: American Bible Society), Daniel 6: 25-27.

¹⁶MFA Newsletter, Ministry of Foreign Affairs, Israel, PM Netanyahu addresses AIPAC conference in Washington, "Jerusalem is not a settlement," It is our capital. www.mofa.gov.il, 22 March, 2010, 1.

¹⁷Good News Bible, Good News Translation (New York: American Bible Society), Hosea 14: 7-8.

Chapter 7

¹John C. Hagee, General Editor, *Prophecy Study Bible* (NKJV) (Nashville: Thomas Nelson, 1997), Nehemiah 1: 3.

²Ibid., Nehemiah 1: 19-20.

³Ibid., Nehemiah 4: 1.

⁴Ibid., Nehemiah 4: 7-8.

⁵Ibid., Nehemiah 4: 9.

⁶Ibid., Nehemiah 6: 1-2.

⁷Ibid., Nehemiah 6: 3.

⁸Ibid., Numbers 10:9.

⁹Ibid., 2 Samuel 21: 15-22.

¹⁰Good News Bible, Good News Translation (New York: American Bible Society), 2 Kings 6: 8-12.

¹¹Ibid., 1 Chronicles 16: 8-18.

¹² "PA Officials: Abbas expects US pressure to push out Netanyahu," The Jerusalem Post, MiddleEast.Jpost.com, Jpost.Com.Staff http://www.jpost.com/servlet/Satellite?cid=1243346501041&pagename=JPost%2FJPArticle%2FShowFull, 29 May, 2009, 1.

¹³Ibid., 1.

[14]Bat Ye'or, "Islam and Dhimmitude," Where Civilisations Collide, trans. Miriam Kochan and David Littman (Madison: Fairleigh Dickinson University Press, UK, 2002), 41.
[15]Ibid., 40.
[16]Good News Bible, Good News Translation (New York: American Bible Society), Isaiah 45: 22- 25.
[17]Ibid., Isaiah 49: 8.
[18]Ibid., Isaiah 49:16.

Chapter 8
[1]Charter of the United Nations and Statute of the International Court of Justice, Article 1: 5.
[2]Good News Bible, Good News Translation (New York: American Bible Society), Numbers 15: 41.
[3]John C. Hagee, General Editor, Prophecy Study Bible (NKJV) (Nashville: Thomas Nelson, 1997), Genesis 35: 12.
[4]Ibid, Genesis 48: 3-4.
[5]Good News Bible, Good News Translation (New York: American Bible Society), Obadiah: 15-18.
[6]Ibid., Joel 3: 1-3.
[7]Ibid., Joel 3: 17.
[8]Ezekiel 37: 1-5, 10-14, 21-22.
[9]MFA Newsletter, Ministry of Foreign Affairs, Israel, "Speech by PM Netanyahu to the President's Conference," 20 October 2009, 4.
[10]Ibid., 5.
[11]Ibid., 5.
[12]"Theodore Roosevelt Acceptance Speech," The Nobel Peace Prize 1906, Acceptance by Herbert H.D Peirce, American Envoy, 1906, http://nobelprize.org/nobel_prizes/peace/laureates/1906/roosevelt-acceptance.html, 2.
[13]Moshe Aumann, The Palestinian Labyrinth – a way out (Jerusalem: Israel Academic Committee, 1985), 26.
[14]"Abbas: Violence will break out unless core issues resolved," Jerusalem Post, Online Edition, JPost.com Staff and AP, The Jerusalem Post, 30 October, 2007, http://www.jpost.com/servlet/Satellite?cid=1192380691772&pagena,1.

[15]Itamar Marcus and Barabra Crook, "Mahmoud Abbas: I do not accept the Jewish State, call it what you will," Palestinian Media Watch Bulletin, (Jerusalem: PMW Bulletin, 28 April, 2009, www.pmw.org.il), 1.

[16]MFA Newsletter, Minister of Foreign Affairs, Israel, "Deputy FM Ayalon calls on Fatah and Palestinian Authority to stop 'Culture of Hate,' " (Communicated by the Bureau of Deputy Foreign Minister Ayalon, 1 February, 2010), 1.

[17]Ibid., 1.

[18]Good News Bible, Good News Translation (New York: American Bible Society), Numbers 16: 11.

[19]United Nations General Assembly, Report of the Human Rights Council, Report of the Independent International Fact-Finding Mission, Sixty-fourth Session, Agenda item 64, /64/490, 29 October 2009, 13.

[20]Ibid., 13.

[21]Ibid., 17.

[22]Ibid., 17.

[23]Ibid., 18.

[24]MFA Newsletter, Ministry of Foreign Affairs, Israel, "Israel's Analysis and Comments on the GAZA Fact Finding Mission REPORT," (Communicated by the Foreign Ministry Spokesperson, 15 September 2009), 1.

[25]Ibid., 1.

[26]United Nations General Assembly, Report of the Human Rights Council, Report of the Independent International Fact-Finding Mission, Sixty-fourth Session, Agenda item 64, /64/490, 29 October 2009, 26.

[27]MFA Newsletter, Ministry of Foreign Affairs, Israel, "Israel's Analysis and Comments on the GAZA Fact Finding Mission REPORT," (Communicated by the Foreign Ministry Spokesperson, 15 September 2009), 2.

[28]United Nations General Assembly, Report of the Human Rights Council, Report of the Independent International Fact-Finding Mission, Sixty-fourth Session, Agenda item 64, /64/490, 29 October 2009, 32.

[29]MFA Newsletter, Ministry of Foreign Affairs, Israel, "Israel's Analysis and Comments on the GAZA Fact Finding Mission

REPORT," (Communicated by the Foreign Ministry Spokesperson, 15 September 2009), 2.

[30]United Nations General Assembly, Report of the Human Rights Council, <u>Report of the Independent International Fact-Finding Mission</u>, Sixty-fourth Session, Agenda item 64, /64/490, 29 October 2009, 423.

[31]Ibid., 424.

[32]MFA Newsletter, Ministry of Foreign Affairs, Israel, "Statement by Israel Ambassador Leshno Yaar to the UN Human Rights Council," Text, 12th Regular Session United Nations Human Rights Council, Agenda Item 7, 29 September 2009, 3.

[33]"Hamas and the Terrorist Threat from the Gaza Strip," The Main Findings of the Goldstone Report Versus the Factual Findings, <u>Intelligence and Terrorism Information Center</u>, Israel, http://www.terrorisminfo.org.il/malam_multimedia/English/eng_n/pdf/, March 2010, II.

[34]<u>Good News Bible,</u> Good News Translation (New York: American Bible Society), Isaiah 45: 17.

[35]"Hamas and the Terrorist Threat from the Gaza Strip," The Main Findings of the Goldstone Report Versus the Factual Findings, <u>Intelligence and Terrorism Information Center</u>, Israel, March 2010, http://www.terrorisminfo.org.il/malam_multi-media/English/eng_n/pdf/, VIII.

[36]Ibid., 16.

[37]Ibid., 34.

[38]MFA Newsletter, Ministry of Foreign Affairs, Israel, "Danny Ayalon pens historic op-ed in largest pan-Arab daily newspaper," (Communicated by Bureau of the Deputy Foreign Minister, 15 December 2009), 1.

[39]Ibid., 3.

Chapter 9

[1]<u>Good News Bible</u>, Good News Translation (New York: American Bible Society), Jeremiah 29: 11.

[2]Ibid., Numbers 22: 5 (b)-6, 12.

[3]Ibid., Numbers 24: 2-11.

[4]Ibid., Numbers 33: 51-55.

[5]John C. Hagee, General Editor, *Prophecy Study Bible (NKJV)* (Nashville: Thomas Nelson, 1997), Ezekiel 34: 11-13.

[6]Ibid., Jeremiah 31: 10.

[7]<u>Good News Bible</u>, Good News Translation (New York: American Bible Society), Jeremiah 30: 3 & 17.

[8]John C. Hagee, General Editor, *Prophecy Study Bible (NKJV)* (Nashville: Thomas Nelson, 1997), Exodus 6: 6-7.

[9]Ibid., Isaiah 49: 25 (b)-26.

[10]Howard Grief, <u>The Legal Foundation and Borders of Israel under International Law</u>, A Treatise on Jewish Sovereignty over the Land of Israel (Jerusalem: Mazo Publishers, 2008), 470.

[11]Joan Peters, <u>From Time Immemorial</u>, The Origins of The Arab-Jewish Conflict Over Palestine (New York: Harper & Row, 1984), 14.

[12]Howard Grief, <u>The Legal Foundation and Borders of Israel under International Law</u>, A Treatise on Jewish Sovereignty over the Land of Israel (Jerusalem: Mazo Publishers, 2008), 482.

[13]John C. Hagee, General Editor, *Prophecy Study Bible (NKJV)* (Nashville: Thomas Nelson, 1997), Jeremiah 23: 7-8.

[14]<u>Good News Bible</u>, Good News Translation (New York: American Bible Society), Isaiah 45: 20-22.

[15]John C. Hagee, General Editor, *Prophecy Study Bible (NKJV)* (Nashville: Thomas Nelson, 1997), Isaiah 14: 26-27.

Chapter 10

[1]<u>Good News Bible</u>, Good News Translation (New York: American Bible Society), Numbers 33: 3-4.

[2]Ibid., Zechariah 8: 1-3, 6 (b).

[3]Ibid., Deuteronomy 32: 39-43.

[4]Ibid, Deuteronomy 33: 29.

Chapter 11

[1]Good News Bible, Good News Translation (New York: American Bible Society) Joshua 2: 1-3; 8-13.

[2]Ibid., Joshua 4: 24.

[3]Ibid., Joshua 6:20 (b)-22; 2425.

[4]Moshe Aumann, Conflict & Connection, The Jewish-Christian-Israel Triangle (Jerusalem: Gefen Publishing House, 2003), 184.

[5]Ibid., 185.

[6]Petra Heldt and Malcolm Lowe, "Theological Significance of the Rebirth of the State of Israel," Different Christian Attitudes, in Immanuel, People, Land and State of Israel, Jewish and Christian Perspective (Jerusalem: Jewish National and University Library, 1987-88), 133.

[7]Malcolm Hedding, "Armageddon now?" The Jerusalem Post Christian Edition, Preparing for the worst, (Jerusalem: The Jerusalem Post, February 2010, www.jpost.com/ce), 41.

[8]Ibid., 41.

[9]Shlomo Mordechai, "The Star of David and the Cross," Israel Today, Pope Benedict XVI, The Church and Israel (Jerusalem: 1 Shmuel HaNagid St, June 2009, www.israeltoday.co.il), 3.

[10]Malcolm Hedding, "The Church's tragic legacy," The Jerusalem Post Christian Edition, New players in an Old Game (Jerusalem: The Jerusalem Post, June 2009, www.jpost.com/ce), 41.

[11]Good News Bible, Good News Translation (New York: American Bible Society) Joshua 12: 7.

Chapter 12

[1]Good News Bible, Good News Translation (New York: American Bible Society) Zechariah 9: 14-16.

[2]Chaim Herzog, The War of Atonement, The Inside Story of the Yom Kippur War, with New Introduction by Brigadier General Michael Herzog (London: Greenhill Books, 2003), xi.

[3]Ibid., xiii.

[4]John C. Hagee, General Editor, *Prophecy Study Bible* (NKJV) (Nashville: Thomas Nelson, 1997), Jeremiah 51: 20.

[5]Ibid., Jeremiah 31: 35-36.

[6]Ibid., Job 38: 2-3.

[7]Ibid., Job 3-5.
[8]Ibid., Exodus 14: 3-4.

Chapter 13
[1]Dore Gold, <u>Hatred's Kingdom</u>, How Saudi Arabia Supports the New Global Terrorism (Washington DC: Regnery Publishing, INC., 2003), 9.
[2]Ibid., 10.
[3]Muammar al-Qadhafi, <u>The White Book: ISRATINE</u>, A proposal by the President of Libya, 26.
[4]Ibid., 47.
[5]John C. Hagee, General Editor, *Prophecy Study Bible (NKJV)* (Nashville: Thomas Nelson, 1997), Obadiah 1: 15.
[6]Ibid., Zechariah 1: 14-17
[7]<u>Good News Bible</u>, Good News Translation (New York: American Bible Society), Revelation 22: 3 (b) & 4.
[8]Ibid., Revelation 21: 26-27.

Epilogue
[1]John C. Hagee, General Editor, *Prophecy Study Bible (NKJV)* (Nashville: Thomas Nelson, 1997), Psalm 18: 25-26.

Bibliography

Biblical Texts:

Jack W. Hayford, Litt. D. General Editor. <u>Spirit Filled Life Bible</u>. NKJV. Nashville: Thomas Nelson, Inc., 1991.

John C. Hagee. General Editor. *Prophecy Study Bible*. *NKJV*. Nashville: Thomas Nelson, 1997.

<u>Good News Bible</u>. Good News Translation New York: American Bible Society.

<u>New Covenant</u> Prophecy Edition with Psalms. International Bible Society. Colorado Springs: USA (c) 2008.

Books, Pamphlets and Articles:

al-Qadhafi, Muammar. <u>The White Book: ISRATINE</u>. A proposal by the President of Libya.

Aumann, Moshe. <u>Conflict & Connection</u>. The Jewish-Christian-Israel Triangle. Jerusalem: Gefen Publishing House, 2003.

Aumann, Moshe. <u>Jerusalem</u>, Israel Today No. 37. Jerusalem: Israel Digest, 1968.

Aumann, Moshe. <u>The Palestinian Labyrinth – a way out</u>. Jerusalem: Israel Academic Committee, 1985.

Aumann, Moshe. <u>Land Ownership in Palestine 1880-1948</u>. Jerusalem: Israel Academic Committee on the Middle East.

Binmore, Ken. <u>Game Theory</u>. A very short Introduction. Oxford: Oxford University Press, 2007.

Brog, David. <u>Standing with Israel</u>. Why Christians Support The Jewish State. Florida: Front Line, 2006.

Chomsky, Noam. <u>The Fateful Triangle</u>. The United States, Israel And The Palestinians. "A rigorous myth-shattering account." London: Pluto Press, 1983.

Covarrubias, Jack and Tom Lansford. Editors. <u>Strategic Interests in the Middle East.</u> Opposition and Support for US Foreign Policy. VT Ashgate Publishing Company.

Eldad, Israel and Arieh Eldad. <u>The Challenge of Jerusalem.</u> Betwixt Thicket and Altar. Israel: Alex Klevitsky, 1998.

Esposito, John L. <u>UNHOLY WAR</u>. Terror in the Name of Islam. New York: Oxford University Press, 2002.

Gardner, David. <u>Last Chance</u>. The Middle East in the Balance. London: I. B. Tauris & Co Ltd, 2009.

Gelvin, James L. <u>The Israeli-Palestinian Conflict.</u> One Hundred Years of War. New Edition. New York: Cambridge University Press, 2007.

Gill, Moshe. <u>A History of Palestine, 634-1099.</u> Translated from Hebrew by Ethel Broido. New York: Cambridge University Press, 1992.

Grief, Howard. <u>The Legal Foundation and Borders of Israel under International Law</u>. A Treatise on Jewish Sovereignty over the Land of Israel. Jerusalem: Mazo Publishers, 2008.

Gold, Dore. <u>Hatred's Kingdom</u>. How Saudi Arabia Supports the New Global Terrorism. Washington DC: Regnery Publishing, INC., 2003.

Hartley, Cathy, ed. <u>A Survey of Arab-Israeli Relations</u>. 2nd Edition. London: Europa Publications Limited, 2004.

Hass, Richard N., and Martin Indyk. "Can Washington Midwife Middle East Peace?" Beyond Iraq. <u>Foreign Affairs</u>. January / February 2009.

Hedding, Malcolm. "Armageddon now?" The Jerusalem Post Christian Edition. Preparing for the worst. Jerusalem: The Jerusalem Post & The Christian Embassy, Jerusalem. February 2010, www.jpost.com/ce.

Hedding, Malcolm. "The Church's tragic legacy." The Jerusalem Post Christian Edition. New players in an Old Game. Jerusalem: The Jerusalem Post & The Christian Embassy, Jerusalem. June 2009, www.jpost.com/ce.

Heldt, Petra and Malcolm Lowe. "Theological Significance of the Rebirth of the State of Israel." Different Christian Attitudes. In Immanuel. People, Land and State of Israel. Jewish and Christian Perspective. Jerusalem: Jewish National and University Library, 1987-88.

Herzog, Chaim. The War of Atonement. The Inside Story of the Yom Kippur War. With New Introduction by Brigadier General Michael Herzog. London: Greenhill Books, 2003.

Herzog, Chaim. The Arab-Israeli Wars. War and Peace in the Middle East. Updated by Shlomo Gazit. Introduction by Isaac Herzog and Michael Herzog. London: Greenhill Books, 2005.

Hudson, Michael C. Arab Politics. The Search for Legitimacy. New Haven: Yale University Press, 1977.

Jansezian, Nicole. "With Obama at helm, Iranian Threat Looms Large. How will Obama change the Middle East?" Times of Change. Israel Today Magazine. December 2008, www.israel-today.co.il.

Jeffries, J.M.N. The Balfour Declaration. Published on the occasion of the 50th Anniversary of the Balfour Declaration. Beriut: The Institute for Palestinian Studies, 1967.

Jones, Bill and Dennis Kavanagh. Politics Today. British Politics Today. Seventh Edition. Manchester: University of Manchester, 2003.

Keinon, Herb. "Analysis: Is Obama looking for a fight over 'natural growth'? The Jerusalem Post. International. Jpost.com, 28 May, 2009, http://www.jpost.com/servlet/Satellite?cid=1243346492983&pagename=JPost%2FJPArticle%2FShowFull.

Levens, Esther. "Congress Sends a Resounding Message of Pro-Israel Support." Press Release- Contact @ elevens@israelunity-coalition.org. Friday 16 April, 2010.

Mansfield, Peter. The Arabs. Third Edition. London: Penguin Books, 1992.

Marcus, Itamar and Barabra Crook. "Mahmoud Abbas: I do not accept the Jewish State, call it what you will." Palestinian Media Watch Bulletin. Jerusalem: PMW Bulletin. 28 April, 2009, www.pmw.org.il.

Mc Ternan, John P. As America – Has Done to – Israel. The Result: Massive National Disasters. Pennsylvania: Whitaker House, 2008.

Mead, Walter Russell. "Change They Can Believe In." To Make Israel Safe. Give Palestinian their Due: Can Washington Midwife Middle East Peace? Foreign Affairs. January / February 2009.

Mendes-Flohr, Paul and Jehuda Reinharz, eds., The Jew in the Modern World. A Documentary History. Second Edition. New York: Oxford University Press, 1995.

Mestyn, Trevor, ed, etal. The Cambridge Encyclopedia of The Middle East And North Africa. Cambridge: Cambridge University Press, 1988.

Mordechai, Shlomo. "The Star of David and the Cross." Israel Today. Pope Benedict XVI. The Church and Israel. Jerusalem: 1 Shmuel HaNagid St, June 2009, www.israeltoday.co.il.

Netanyahu, Benjamin. A Durable Peace. Israel And Its Place Among The Nations. New York: Warner Books, 1999.

Parson, David. "Poised over The Panic Button." New Players in Old Game. The Jerusalem Post Christian Edition. In Partnership with the International Christian Embassy Jerusalem June 2009, www.jpost.com/ce.

Peters, Joan. From Time Immemorial. The Origins Of The Arab-Jewish Conflict Over Palestine. New York: Harper & Row, 1984.

Reich, Bernard, ed, etal. An Historical Encyclopedia of the Arab-Israeli Conflict. Connecticut: Greenwood Press, 1996.

Routtenberg, Aryeh. <u>The Etzion Bloc in the Hills of Judea</u>. Jerusalem.

Stookey, Robert W. <u>America and the Arab States: An Uneasy Encounter</u>. Center for Middle East Studies. The University of Texas at Austin. New York: John Wiley & Sons Inc., 1975.

van der Hoeven, Jan Willem. <u>Babylon or Jerusalem</u>. Shippensburg: Destiny Image, 1993.

van der Hoeven, Jan Willen. "What Will History Record?" Director: International Christian Zionist Center. Thursday 28 May, 2009.

van der Hoeven, Jan Willem. "Islam not Territories," The Main Reason for the Present Middle East Conflict! 12/03/2001.

Wallace, Rebecca M.M. <u>International Law</u>. Fifth Edition. London: Sweet & Maxwell, 2005.

Ye'or, Bat. "<u>Islam and Dhimmitude</u>." Where Civilisations Collide. Translated by Miriam Kochan and David Littman. Madison: Fairleigh Dickinson University Press UK, 2002.

Proclamation of Independence. The Declaration of the Establishment of the State of Israel. Provisional Government of Israel. <u>Official Gazette</u> Number 1; Tel Aviv, 14.5.1948, http://www.knesset.gov.il/doc/eng/megilat_eng.htm.

<u>Charter of the United Nations and Statute of the International Court of Justice</u>. Article 1: 5.

United Nations General Assembly. Report of the Human Rights Council. <u>Report of the Independent International Fact-Finding Mission</u>. Sixty-fourth Session. Agenda item 64, /64/490. 29 October 2009.

UN General Assembly Resolution 181, <u>Partition Plan</u>, 29 November, 1947, http://www.mfa.gov.il/MFA/Peace+Process/Guide+to+the+Peace+Process/UN+General+Assembly+Resolution+181.htm

MFA Newsletter. Ministry of Foreign Affairs, Israel. "Address by PM Netanyahu to the Christians United For Israel Jerusalem Summit." 8 March, 2010.

MFA Newsletter. Ministry of Foreign Affairs, Israel. PM Netanyahu addresses AIPAC conference in Washington. "Jerusalem is not a settlement." It is our capital, www.mofa.gov.il. 22 March, 2010.

"Quartet urges Israeli settlement freeze." Mideast peacemakers 'condemn' East Jerusalem building plan. Msnbc.com news services. Friday March 19, 2010.

"Obama's Turn Against Israel." The US makes a diplomatic crisis out of a blunder. Editorial, The Wall Street Journal. http://online.wsj.com/article.....oveLEFTTop, March 15, 2010.

Encyclopedia Judaica. Volume 9 IS-JER. Encyclopedia Judaica Jerusalem. Jerusalem: Keter Publishing House Ltd., 1971.

British White Paper of 1939, http://www.hagshama.org.il/en/resources/view.asp?id=135

MFA Newsletter. Ministry of Foreign Affairs, Israel. "Address by Prime Minister Benjamin Netanyahu to the United Nations General Assembly General Debate – 64th Session," New York: United Nations. 24 September 2009.

MFA Newsletter. Ministry of Foreign Affairs, Israel. "Address by PM Netanyahu to the Christian United For Israel Jerusalem Summit." 8 March, 2010.

MFA Newsletter. Ministry of Foreign Affairs, Israel. "Iran: Excerpt from PM Netanyahu's address to the Jewish Agency Board of Governors." 22 February, 2010.

"Prime Minister Benjamin Netanyahu's foreign policy speech at Bar IIan University." Full text. Haaretz. Sunday 14 June, 2009, http://www.haaretz.com.

"Netanyahu vows to work with Obama for peace." Haaretz.com, By News Agencies. 22 February, 2009, www.haaretz.com/hasen/spages/1066078.html.

"Obama's Mideast plan calls for demilitarised Palestinian State." The Jerusalem Post. JPost .Com Staff, Mideast, Jpost.com. 20 May, 2009, http://www.jpost.com/servlet/Satellite?cid=12422 12419666&pagename=JPost%2FJPArticle%2FShowFull.

"Full Text of Obama's Cairo Speech." The Jerusalem Post. Mideast.Jpost.com. 4 June, 2009, http://www.jpost.com/servlet/Satellite?apage=1&cid=1244034998314&pagename=JPost%2FJPArticle%2FShowFull.

MFA Newsletter. Ministry of Foreign Affairs, Israel. PM Netanyahu addresses AIPAC conference in Washington. "Jerusalem is not a settlement." It is our capital. www.mofa.gov.il. 22 March, 2010.

"PA Officials: Abbas expects US pressure to push out Netanyahu." The Jerusalem Post, MiddleEast.Jpost.com. Jpost.Com.Staff http://www.jpost.com/servlet/Satellite?cid=1243346501041&pagename=JPost%2FJPArticle%2FShowFull. 29 May, 2009.

MFA Newsletter, Ministry of Foreign Affairs, Israel. "Speech by PM Netanyahu to the President's Conference." 20 October 2009.

"Theodore Roosevelt Acceptance Speech." The Nobel Peace Prize 1906. Acceptance by Herbert H.D Peirce. American Envoy. 1906, http://nobelprize.org/nobel_prizes/peace/laureates/1906/roosevelt-acceptance.html.

"Abbas: Violence will break out unless core issues resolved." Jerusalem Post, Online Edition. JPost.com Staff and AP. The Jerusalem Post. 30 October, 2007, http://www.jpost.com/servlet/Satellite?cid=1192380691772&pagena.

MFA Newsletter. Ministry of Foreign Affairs, Israel. "Deputy Foreign Minister Ayalon addresses the Council of Europe." Jerusalem: MFA, 26 Jan, 2010.

MFA Newsletter. Minister of Foreign Affairs, Israel. "Deputy FM Ayalon calls on Fatah and Palestinian Authority to stop 'Culture of Hate.' " Communicated by the Bureau of Deputy Foreign Minister Ayalon. 1 February, 2010.

MFA Newsletter. Ministry of Foreign Affairs, Israel. "Danny Ayalon pens historic op-ed in largest pan-Arab daily newspaper." Communicated by Bureau of the Deputy Foreign Minister. 15 December 2009.

MFA Newsletter. Ministry of Foreign Affairs, Israel. "Israel's Analysis and Comments on the GAZA Fact Finding Mission

REPORT." Communicated by the Foreign Ministry Spokesperson. 15 September 2009.

MFA Newsletter. Ministry of Foreign Affairs, Israel. "Statement by Israel Ambassador Leshno Yaar to the UN Human Rights Council." Text, 12th Regular Session United Nations Human Rights Council. Agenda Item 7, 29 September 2009.

"Hamas and the Terrorist Threat from the Gaza Strip." The Main Findings of the Goldstone Report Versus the Factual Findings. Intelligence and Terrorism Information Center. Israel. http://www.terrorisminfo.org.il/malam_multimedia/English/eng _n/pdf/. March 2010.